Nozick's Libertarian Project

Bloomsbury Studies in Political Philosophy

Bloomsbury Studies in Political Philosophy presents cutting-edge scholarship in the field of political philosophy. Making available the latest high-quality research from an international range of scholars working on key topics and controversies in political philosophy and political science, this series is an important and stimulating resource for students and academics working in the area.

Also available from Bloomsbury:
The Concept of Justice – Thomas Patrick Burke
Perfecting Justice in Rawls, Habermas and Honneth – Miriam Bankovsky
Rawls, Dewey, and Constructivism – Eric Thomas Weber

Forthcoming:
The Limits of Reason in Hobbes's Commonwealth – Michael P. Krom
Morality, Leadership and Public Policy – Eric Thomas Weber
Ricoeur, Rawls and Capability Justice – Molly Harikat Mann

Nozick's Libertarian Project

An Elaboration and Defense

Mark D. Friedman

B L O O M S B U R Y
LONDON · NEW DELHI · NEW YORK · SYDNEY

Bloomsbury Academic
An imprint of Bloomsbury Publishing Plc

50 Bedford Square	175 Fifth Avenue
London	New York
WC1B 3DP	NY 10010
UK	USA

www.bloomsbury.com

First published by Continuum International Publishing Group 2011
Paperback edition first published 2012

© Mark D. Friedman, 2011

British Library Cataloguing-in-Publication Data
A catalogue record for this book is available from the British Library.

ISBN: HB: 978-1-4411-7093-4
PB: 978-1-4411-0297-3

Library of Congress Cataloging-in-Publication Data
Friedman, Mark D.
Nozick's libertarian project : an elaboration and defence / Mark D. Friedman.
p. cm.
Includes bibliographical references (p.).
ISBN 978-1-4411-7093-4
1. Libertarianism. 2. Nozick, Robert. Anarchy, state, and Utopia. I. Title.
JC585.F762 2011
320.51'2–dc22
2010034379

Typeset by Newgen Imaging Systems Pvt Ltd, Chennai, India

To Judah, *may he grow up in a freer and better world.*

For a nation to love liberty, it is enough that she understand it; for her to be free, it is enough that she wishes it.
　　　Marquis de Lafayette, Address to the National Assembly, Paris [1789][1]

A people that loves freedom will in the end be free.
　　　Simon Bolivar, Letter from Jamaica [1815][2]

Every nation has the government it deserves.
　　　Joseph de Maistre, Letter to X [1811]

Contents

Preface

I first read *Anarchy, State, and Utopia* in 1979 as part of a law school seminar. At that time I was not persuaded by its arguments nor moved by the philosophy it espouses. However, over the following many years my healthy skepticism regarding the efficacy of governmental social programs gave way to serious doubts about their *legitimacy*. This unease led me to reread *ASU* early in this century, and I found myself attracted then by the clarity of Nozick's moral vision and his commitment to the dignity of persons.

Inspired by Nozick's views, I resolved to delve into the literature of political theory to determine for myself whether his arguments could stand up to the withering criticism they have provoked from the notoriously liberal academic establishment. I discovered that while *ASU*'s central arguments are debated in college and university classrooms around the country, and have been analyzed in countless books and journal articles, he has few defenders, even among those who hold positions that are generally thought to be libertarian. Academic disciples of Ayn Rand are scarce, and in any case fiercely loyal to her "Objectivist" philosophy. Similarly, Nozick's acceptance of the legitimacy of state authority for purposes of national defense and law enforcement irreconcilably estranges him from those rare scholars, the "anarcho-capitalists," who regard the state as intrinsically evil.

While there are a number of high-profile economists who defend unfettered capitalism, they do so on pragmatic grounds, that is pointing to the productivity of free markets and the failure of governmental programs to achieve their stated objectives. While Nozick embraces most of their conclusions, his reasoning is completely different. The state's social engineering projects are to be condemned, he claims, not for their inefficiency but on account of their immorality. Thus, he and *laissez-faire* economists are mere fellow travelers.

Nozick never returned to the ring to defend his libertarian theories prior to his untimely death in 2002, preferring to devote his energy to resolving other challenging philosophical problems. He thus remains a sort of prophet without honor in his own country. His views are well known, widely discussed, respected for their originality and the sophistication with which they are articulated (if nothing else), but generally dismissed as implausible.

Against this background it occurred to me to investigate whether the natural rights/minimal state project that Nozick fought for is still viable, and having convinced myself that it is, I resolved to do what I could to answer the criticisms leveled against it. What you are now reading is the result of this effort.

I wish to express my heartfelt gratitude to a number of people in connection with this work. First and foremost, I wish to thank my wife Aracelly for her extraordinary patience and unwavering support. I also wish to express my appreciation to the following individuals for their helpful comments on various parts of this volume and/or for sharing their insights on relevant topics: Kasper Lippert-Rasmussen, George Klosko, Peter Vallentyne, Richard Arneson, Steve Karavitis, Richard Dagger, Tom Palmer, Edward Feser, David Friedman, Stuart Burns, Brad Hooker, Mario De Caro, Tom Trelogan, and Joe Siegel.

My greatest debt in this regard, however, is to Matt Zwolinski, who generously committed his time to this enterprise, and whose constructive criticism sent me back to the drawing board on numerous occasions in search of arguments he could not so readily demolish. The publication of this study should not suggest that this process reached a satisfactory conclusion, but merely that at a certain point I elected to go to press with the arguments I had, rather than the ones I wish I had.

Introduction: Natural Rights Libertarianism

The inherent vice of capitalism is the unequal sharing of blessings; the inherent virtue of socialism is the equal sharing of miseries.

Winston Churchill[1]

Any political theory that claims to demarcate the appropriate boundary between the authority of the state and the freedom of its citizens must provide convincing answers to an array of fundamental questions. What rights, if any, do people have independently of their recognition by the authorities? Assuming that individuals possess certain liberties simply by virtue of their humanity—known as "natural rights"—what is their moral foundation? What weight do these claims have relative to competing values that might override them in various circumstances? Are some types of rights less stringent than others? What are the practical implications of natural rights on the powers of the state?

It may safely be said that prior to the publication of Robert Nozick's *Anarchy, State, and Utopia* in 1974, the libertarian voice was largely absent from mainstream academic discourse surrounding such issues (all subsequent references to this work will appear parenthetically in the text as "*ASU*," followed by the relevant page number(s)).[2] While Ayn Rand's "Objectivist" philosophy (critiqued in Chapter 1) was and continues to be highly influential in popular culture, she has had few adherents in academia. Similarly, the ideas of Murray Rothbard and other "anarcho-capitalists" (discussed in Chapter 4) have received virtually no scholarly notice outside of the journals of the libertarian movement.

However profound the academic community's previous indifference toward libertarianism, *ASU* simply could not be ignored. Not only was its author a full professor of philosophy at Harvard, but *ASU* won the prestigious National Book Award the year following its publication. It was widely if not warmly reviewed in those forums where weighty ideas are scrutinized and pondered, such as *The New York Review of Books*,[3] *The Yale Law Journal*,[4] and the *Times Literary Supplement.*[5] As acknowledged by a scholar openly hostile to its basic arguments, *ASU* "has achieved the status of a classic [and] ... together with John Rawls's *A Theory of Justice* [1971], it also arguably framed the landscape of academic political philosophy in the last decades of the twentieth century."[6]

Another contemporary philosopher has noted that, *ASU* "now stands unchallenged as the most coherent statement available of the case for a rights-based defense of the minimal libertarian state" (footnote omitted).[7] Indeed, if libertarianism has a credo, it would be the very first two sentences of *ASU:* "Individuals have rights, and there are things no person may do to them (without violating their rights). So strong and far-reaching are these rights that they raise the question of what, if anything, the state and its officials may do."[8] This declaration properly highlights the *moral* dimension of rights: the existence of a right in one person implies that all other people, acting individually or through the state, have a corresponding duty not to interfere with its exercise.

ASU is celebrated in libertarian circles and excoriated outside of them for Nozick's uncompromising rejection of all claims for "social justice," i.e. the view that any distribution of resources that strays too far from strict equality must be condemned. His position is premised on the core idea, referenced above, that the state may not, without violating their moral rights, force individuals to contribute either their labor or their property for the purpose of bringing about some supposedly greater good. The effect of *compelling* persons to do what the majority considers desirable is to shrink what Nozick calls our "moral space." Without the right to be callous, we are deprived of the opportunity to be generous.[9]

In the three and a half decades following *ASU*'s publication scholars have generated a vast body of literature regarding the ideas propounded therein. Unfortunately, from our perspective, Nozick never returned in any substantive way to political philosophy subsequent to *ASU*'s publication.[10] However, as we shall see, in a surprising number of cases he actually anticipated the arguments of his critics, suggesting effective lines of response within the covers of *ASU*.

As will become clear throughout the course of this work, while most of Nozick's arguments have proven durable, others have generally been rejected as unsound. The purpose of this study is to take stock of the natural rights libertarian project in the wake of this scholarship and to advance it as far as we are able in the face of existing objections. We will supplement Nozick's contributions with a variety of worthy ideas from other theorists.

Beyond *Anarchy, State, and Utopia*

It should be noted at this point that although *ASU*'s canonical status seems secure for the foreseeable future, there is something paradoxical about its popularity. While *ASU* has been through over 50 printings since its initial publication and is required reading in political philosophy courses taught at colleges and universities throughout this country and even internationally, Nozick has few followers among the gradually expanding circle of libertarian academics. In fact, I cannot cite a single prominent political theorist who works within the particular rights-based tradition he established.[11]

This curious situation may be due to the rather casual approach Nozick takes to specifying of the ethical foundation of natural rights. As explained in Chapter 1, he justifies libertarian rights by linking them to intuitively appealing ideas regarding the dignity owed human beings simply as functioning members of our species. This special moral status forbids us, acting alone or through the state, from coercing persons in order to achieve some extraneous purpose.

Here, Nozick relies on Kant's notion of persons as "ends in themselves." He expresses this commitment to human dignity in terms of "side constraints," pursuant to which rights are regarded as inviolable. In other words, rights violations are not merely to be minimized, but absolutely forbidden, subject to a possible exception for the avoidance of "catastrophic moral horror" (see *ASU*, 28–35 and 30n). However, Nozick does not develop these attractive notions in a systematic fashion, much less try to deduce the existence of natural rights from some set of indubitable premises. Thus, Thomas Nagel famously charged him with advocating "libertarianism without foundations."[12]

Given the standards generally applied to political theories, Nagel's criticism is somewhat overblown. Nevertheless, it merits a substantive response, which is provided in Chapter 1. There, after tracing the natural rights doctrine back to John Locke's writings and critiquing Rand's theory of rights, I recast Nozick's intuitionist arguments into a formal "proof" of the side constraint view. I do not claim this demonstration to be conclusive in the way of a geometric theorem, but the deductive form makes Nozick's premises explicit and allows us to assess the overall strength of his reasoning.

As suggested by the preceding, the fault line that characteristically divides libertarians and more egalitarian-minded theorists is the stringency to be accorded property or economic rights. However, a rights-based defense is not the only, or even the most popular, justification of unrestricted capitalism. Modern free market economists, such as the late Milton Friedman, have followed classic liberals like Adam Smith and Frederic Bastiat in arguing that government programs are ineffectual or even counterproductive in realizing their goals.

To the extent that economists recommend and politicians enact policies based on expected gains in utility, they are implicitly adopting consequentialist ethics, i.e. as the name implies, the idea that the moral rightness of individual acts or governmental policies is to be evaluated solely on the basis of their outcomes.[13] Although natural rights libertarians generally endorse the prescriptions of *laissez-faire* economists, they do not subscribe to consequentialism. As discussed further in Chapter 1, Nozick-style libertarianism is premised on deontological ethics, which rejects the claim that consequences alone should dictate our moral judgments.

We examine in Chapter 2 Nozick's entitlement theory of justice, according to which all persons are entitled to their holdings so long as they are acquired without wronging others or by indirectly benefiting from such injustices. Nozick claims that under his theory, once it is established that all existing resources are justly held, there is no room for egalitarian arguments to take hold (see *ASU*, 238). In Chapter 3 we consider a variety of criticisms that have been leveled against it.

As Nozick recognizes, the stringency of libertarian rights calls into question what role, if any, is left for the state. In Chapter 4 we analyze whether coercive taxation can be justified even in support of such "core" state responsibilities as national defense and law enforcement. Nozick's justification of the minimal state is generally, and in the opinion of this author, correctly considered a failure. As an alternative, I argue (roughly) that certain activities of the state are essential to the exercise of our moral agency and that therefore coercion in support of such functions stands on a different moral footing than it otherwise would.

Of course, there are seminal libertarian ideas that do not originate with Nozick. In *ASU* and elsewhere Nozick acknowledges his debt to F. A. Hayek, perhaps the most widely respected defender of *laissez-faire* capitalism of the previous generation. Two of his insights have special relevance for our purposes: his understanding of the "rule of law" and the connection he elucidates between economic liberty and freedom generally.

For Hayek, the rule of law is not ultimately reducible to the existence of some set of hallowed constitutional safeguards because the political authorities can always repeal them. If the power of the state is to be constrained it must be through the commitment of the citizenry to a political ideal that will find *expression* in terms of "due process," "equal protection," the "separation of powers," and so on.

Hayek's defense of property rights interconnects with his notion of the rule of law because in his view a society's allegiance to the former generates attitudes that support the latter. Thus, rather than attempting to justify property rights directly on moral grounds, Hayek stresses their instrumental value, as in this famous quotation:

> Economic control is not merely control of a sector of human life which can be separated from the rest; it is the control of the means for all our ends. And whoever has sole control of the means must also determine which ends are to be served.[14]

These ideas come into play at a variety of points in our analysis, but most obviously in Chapter 5. There, by means of case studies of the histories of Britain (and derivatively, the United States), Germany, and Mexico, we illustrate and adduce evidence to support the thesis that the rule of law is possible only in societies where the state does not dominate both the political and economic realms.

Even many critics of libertarianism acknowledge that it is grounded in attractive first principles, i.e. the primacy of rights, the value we accord human autonomy, and a historically justified mistrust of governmental power. However, it is commonly thought that the theory has unacceptable implications; that, for example, it would require society to stand helplessly by and watch widows and children starve to death in the streets if voluntary efforts fail to provide relief. In Chapter 6, we respond not only to this objection, but also to three other "standard" criticisms of rights-based libertarianism.

To briefly summarize what is to follow, this work will defend what I regard as Nozick's central claim: When the state interferes with our autonomy it robs us of a critical portion of our humanity. Accordingly, the use of force or coercion against persons who are not violating or unreasonably threatening to violate the rights of others is wrong, full stop. In short, we will show that, properly understood, libertarianism holds the moral high ground.

Scope and Methodology

Having given a preview of this study's objectives, I wish to briefly describe its limitations and discuss certain methodological issues. As should already be clear, moral claims are at the center of the debate between libertarian and egalitarian theorists. Both schools contend that compelling ethical considerations support their positions and buttress their arguments. Obviously, I will weigh into this debate on the side of the individualist perspective.

For purposes of this effort I am going to ignore the unfortunate fact that the best minds in academic philosophy have been unable to resolve in any convincing way our most basic ethical concerns, such as the objectivity/ subjectivity of moral values, the existence of free will in a deterministic universe, the possibility of moral knowledge and related matters. I will assume, with only brief discussion, the soundness of our conventional, common-sense understanding of morality. That is, words such as "right," "wrong," "good," and "evil" refer to properties that exist independently of our feelings and attitudes about them, even if we are uncertain about the exact nature of these qualities.

Furthermore, I will presuppose, with only a perfunctory attempt at justification, that we can reach valid conclusions about particular cases through our moral intuitions, applied critically in order to identify biases and short-circuit overly emotional responses. And, finally, I will assume that we may choose from various moral theories based on the extent to which they provide rationales that persuasively resolve a wide range of real and imagined cases, as judged by our carefully considered beliefs and opinions.[15]

I see little need to apologize for this approach. If political theorists were to suspend work until definitive answers were found to the fundamental problems of ethics, no progress would be possible in this (or many other) fields for the indefinite future. Therefore, I believe we are justified in proceeding on the basis of what we commonly believe, even if academics are unable to vindicate our ordinary moral consciousness. In any case, this is a difficulty faced by all political philosophers, not just libertarians.

I should also clarify that while this book consists primarily of a series of moral arguments in support of libertarian positions, I will not defend any comprehensive normative theory to the exclusion of all others.[16] Rather, I will limit my brief to establishing that natural rights are built on a sound ethical foundation and will engage more general (and potentially conflicting) moral theories, such as consequentialism, only to the extent that they are inconsistent with the particular principles I wish to advance. I will return to this subject in the next chapter.

Chapter 1

The Ethical Foundation of Natural Rights

Man was first created a single individual to teach the lesson that whoever destroys one life, Scripture ascribes it to him as though he had destroyed a whole world; and whoever saves one life, Scripture ascribes to him as though he had saved a whole world.

The Talmud, Tractate Sanhedrin, Part IV[1]

Libertarianism is all about rights. A great deal of philosophical attention has been devoted to explicating the precise meaning and implications of this concept. We will start our analysis by offering a definition that both reflects how we commonly talk about rights and is neutral between competing theories regarding their content: a "right" is a justified moral claim for action or forbearance on the part of other persons. This description excludes contractual rights and those conferred by law, as our particular interest lies in those *moral* rights, if any, that we enjoy entirely as a consequence of our status as human beings, i.e. "natural rights."

The commonsense notion of rights just described embodies the idea of "correlativity," which is to say that the possession of a right by one person implies a corresponding *duty* on the part of someone else to act or not act in certain ways.[2] As discussed more fully below, libertarians generally recognize only the existence of "negative rights" or rights of noninterference. As John Hospers expresses it, these rights are respected "when one is not coerced by other human beings, and can make one's own decisions and act on them."[3]

In sharp contrast, positive (or welfare) rights may be understood as any right that would, in Hospers' words, require "not only noninterference, but also some positive action on the part of others." Accordingly, "If one person has a positive right to receive assistance in some endeavor, others are duty bound to render the assistance, no matter how it may interfere with their plans for their own lives."[4] Subject to the potential exceptions discussed in

Chapter 6, libertarians generally deny the existence of positive rights, and moreover hold that should they exist, the state may not legitimately enforce them.

Before proceeding further, it is necessary to pause very briefly to locate libertarian theory within the realm of normative ethics, i.e. (roughly) the search for principles of morality that will enable us to classify actions as right or wrong. Natural rights libertarianism's traditional philosophical opponent has been consequentialism; very briefly, the doctrine that "choices—acts and/or intentions—are to be morally assessed solely by the states of affairs they bring about."[5] The most familiar version of consequentialism is the classical utilitarianism of Jeremy Bentham and John Stuart Mill, i.e. the view that moral agents should act to promote the greatest balance of happiness (or pleasure) for all persons affected by their decisions.

Libertarians hold that rights generally trump consequentialist calculations, and this tenet places their doctrine squarely in the camp of what philosophers term "deontological" ethics.[6] Kant, the most influential deontological philosopher, insists that we must evaluate the morality of an action "not in the purpose to be attained by it but in the maxim in accordance with which it is decided upon."[7] One scholar describes the logic behind Kant's idea as follows:

> When we do something because it is our moral duty…we are motivated by the thought that, insofar as we are rational beings, we must act only as this fundamental law of (practical) reason prescribes, a law that would prescribe how any rational being in our circumstances should act.[8]

Thus, for Kant and other deontologists, "what makes a choice right is its conformity with a moral norm,"[9] and not its expected or actual outcome.

While all natural rights libertarians are deontologists, it is far from the case that all deontologists are libertarians. There is no reason, in principle, why egalitarian political theories may not be constructed along deontological lines. For example, John Rawls's liberal masterpiece, *A Theory of Justice*, is deontological according to most of the criteria applied by moral philosophers in that, among other things, he holds that the right does not consist in maximizing the good, he places considerations of justice at the heart of his theory and his is an imperatival ethical theory.[10]

We should note here that libertarians are not committed to banishing consequentialist reasoning from the normative landscape. Not all moral choices implicate individual rights, and in such cases utilitarian (or other consequentialist) calculations may be perfectly appropriate (as will be seen in Chapter 6). However, libertarians must be prepared, in the usual case, to uphold the primacy of rights even when doing so will, so far as we can tell, produce adverse outcomes.[11] Accordingly, rather than launching a full-scale attack on consequentialism generally, I will limit myself to defending the validity of natural rights principles when they seemingly conflict with this doctrine's prescriptions.

The remainder of this chapter will be devoted to explicating and defending the libertarian view of natural rights. I begin with Locke's seminal account, which while insufficiently grounded for modern tastes, remains highly influential in its justification of private property. We will then examine Ayn Rand's famous "Objectivist" solution to the problem of supplying an ethical foundation for rights claims, and explain why academic philosophers have almost uniformly rejected her approach. As a preferable alternative to the Randian model, I present Nozick's arguments for "side constraints" in the form of a deductive proof.

Natural Rights

The late-seventeenth-century English philosopher, John Locke, is commonly credited with articulating the first systematic analysis of natural rights in his famous *Two Treatises of Government*.[12] His investigation occurs within the framework of an imagined pre-political world, a "state of nature," in which individuals operate outside of the matrix of legally enforced norms that constrain their behavior in civilized society. However, Locke's primordial world is a political but not a moral anarchy, since it "has a Law of Nature to govern it, which obliges every one: Reason, which is that Law, teaches all Mankind, who will but consult it, that being all equal and independent, no one ought to harm another in his Life, Health or Possessions."[13] Therefore, if an individual or group threatens to aggress against a person's property (broadly construed), the innocent party is entitled by the law of nature to defend himself and punish the offender.[14]

For Locke, natural law not only authorizes but favors the creation of private property:

God, who hath given the World to Men in common, hath also given them reason to make use of it to the best advantage of Life and convenience. The Earth, and all that is therein was given to Men for the Support and Comfort of their being. And though all the Fruits it naturally produces, and Beasts it feeds, belong to Mankind in common...there must of necessity be a means *to appropriate* them some way or other before they can be of any use.[15]

Locke's justification of individual acquisition starts with the seemingly self-evident proposition that "every Man has a Property in his own Person."[16]

From this premise he reasons that self-ownership extends to the work of a person's hands, i.e. we are entitled to retain the fruits of our labor, including the "privatization" of land by enclosing and working it.[17] According to Locke, such claims do not violate the legitimate rights of others because due to the efficiency of private property, "he who appropriates land to himself by his labor does not lessen but increases the common stock of mankind."[18] In Chapter 3 we address in detail various challenges that have been raised against the justice of the Lockean model of initial ownership.

Locke anticipated that individuals living in a state of nature would, pursuant to a tacit "social contract," ultimately adopt some formal method of governance for the purpose of safeguarding their lives and possessions:

> [T]he end of the law is... to preserve and enlarge Freedom. For in all the states of created beings capable of laws, where there is no law there is no Freedom. *For liberty is to be free from restraint and violence from others;* which cannot be where there is no law: and it is not, as we are told, a liberty for every man to do what he lists [likes]. (For who could be free when every other man's humour might domineer over him?) *But a liberty to dispose, and order as he lists, his person, actions, possessions, and his whole property,* within the Allowance of those laws under which he is, and therein not be the subject of the *arbitrary* Will of another, but freely follow his own. (Emphasis added)[19]

Thus, Locke conceives of natural liberty primarily as the right to be free from the predations of others.[20]

Accordingly, the legitimate role of the state is to enable people to "pursue happiness" without fear of aggression. If a ruler betrays the consent of the governed and makes himself a tyrant, the populace is, according to Locke, justified in "appealing to Heaven," i.e. invoking its natural rights and revolting against him.[21]

As noted above, Locke claimed to derive natural rights from the dictates of natural law, a doctrine that remained influential during his era. Mark Murphy has summarized the "paradigmatic" natural law doctrine as consisting of two theses: "that from the God's-eye point of view, it [natural law] is law through its place in the scheme of divine providence, and from the human's-eye point of view, it constitutes a set of naturally binding and knowable precepts of practical reason."[22]

Locke equivocated between the idea that natural law can be deduced by human reason and that it had to be accepted simply as the Creator's will, and did not appear to recognize the doctrinal problems produced by this ambiguity. Accordingly, as Nozick concludes, he failed to "provide anything remotely resembling a satisfactory explanation of the status and basis of the law of nature in his *Second Treatise*" (*ASU*, 9).[23] Therefore, modern libertarian philosophers have felt compelled to offer a more systematic and coherent justification for natural rights than is found in Locke.

Nevertheless, it is apparent that Locke's basic conception has an undeniable intuitive force. It seems clear that most of us believe that we would be morally justified (if not obligated) to resist a murderous, tyrannical regime, even one elected through an unquestionably democratic process. But on what non-theological basis can we rightly oppose our duly elected government or disobey its laws? Of course, one possible response is that, as Locke claims, all persons have natural rights that entitle them to rebel against tyranny. We will now examine whether it is possible to establish a philosophical justification for this belief.

The Randian theory of natural rights

Rand formulated what is perhaps still the leading account of libertarian rights, at least in the popular mind.[24] She named her philosophy Objectivism, reflecting her conviction that both knowledge and values are objective. As we shall see, Rand's approach flies directly in the face of David Hume's famous and highly influential observation in Book III of his *Treatise of Human Nature* [1740], that, as paraphrased by a modern philosopher, "no set of statements of fact by themselves entails any statement of value."[25] Hume's claim is commonly known as the "is-ought gap" (or "Hume's law").[26] Rand sought to overcome this metaphysical divide by grounding moral values (and rights) in what she regards as certain objective features of *homo sapiens*.

What follows is not intended as an exhaustive study or evaluation of Rand's ethical theory. There is simply not the space for that here, particularly in light of the fact that her defenders have elaborated and developed her basic ideas in a number of different directions.[27] Nevertheless, I hope that my discussion will at least serve to clarify why Rand has so few academic followers and why an alternative approach is worth considering.

Randian ethics starts with the premise that all living things are primarily driven by self-preservation, and that each species pursues this directive in its own peculiar way: "that which is required for [an organism's] survival is determined by its *nature*, by the kind of entity it is."[28] Furthermore, according to Rand, "An organism's life is its standard of value: that which furthers its life is the *good*, that which threatens it is the *evil*."[29] Therefore, it is nonsense to talk of values without reference to the nature of the being that holds them: "The fact that a living entity *is*, determines what it *ought* to do. So much for the issue of the relation between '*is*' and '*ought*.'"[30]

Rand asserts that alone among all (known) life forms, Man is not born with an "automatic code of survival," i.e. he is not endowed with instinctive behavior patterns that will preserve his life. Rather, she says, "Man's particular distinction from all other living species is the fact that *his* consciousness is *volitional*."[31] By this, Rand means that human beings can only "survive" (as the particular type of organism we are) by actively employing our reason to discover those values appropriate to our nature. She does not deny that an individual may physically survive by various forms of parasitical behavior or aggression, but only at the cost of self-destruction, i.e. by "turn[ing] himself into a subhuman creature."[32]

Accordingly, in stark contrast to conventional morality, for Rand our moral duties are not to others, but rather consist of our obligation to "earn the right to hold oneself as one's own highest value by achieving one's own moral perfection."[33] This obligation implies that "the achievement of his own happiness is man's highest moral purpose," where "happiness" is understood as "the successful state of life."[34] Thus, her moral philosophy is a form of ethical egoism (discussed in more detail below), where the pursuit of our self-interest is defined in terms of the realization of our natural virtues.[35]

John Hospers has summarized Rand's central thesis this way:

Since reason is man's basic means of survival, the life appropriate to man is the life appropriate to man as a rational being. Reason is the faculty that identifies and integrates the material provided by man's senses. According to this system of ethics, *rationality* is man's foremost virtue and the source of all his other virtues. Accordingly, evasion, the refusal to think, the suspension of his consciousness, is man's basic vice. Since man must produce the things his life requires, productive work is a cardinal virtue of this ethical code. Since the achievement of values involves an effort and a struggle, man must consider himself a worthy beneficiary, must consider his life worth preserving—hence another cardinal virtue of this code: *pride*.[36]

Rand supposes that her conception of negative rights flows directly from her underlying ethical theory. For her, rights "are the concept that provides a logical transition from the principles guiding an individual's actions to the principles guiding his relationship with others."[37] Man's obligation to pursue his rational self-interest imposes a duty of non-aggression on the part of others, but no positive duty of beneficence: "the right to life means that a man has the right to support his life by his own work...it does not mean that others must provide him with the necessities of life."[38] The primary challenge facing Rand's defenders is to show (i) that her ethical theory is sound and (ii) that it can credibly support a libertarian theory of rights.

A variety of obvious questions may be raised regarding any ethical system that incorporates the natural law conception of Man's objective characteristics or purpose. First, different observers may reasonably disagree on what feature(s) constitute our species' essential nature, and there appears no clear way to arbitrate this dispute.[39] Instead of "rationality," one could, it seems, just as easily posit our capacity for empathy or mutual cooperation as humankind's characteristic attribute or, if one is cynical, our capacity for wanton destruction and aggression.

Second, the origin of each individual's obligation to pursue his or her natural purpose is unclear. We can fairly ask, why is it *wrong* to act "unnaturally" or "irrationally"? A person who fails to promote her own flourishing or acts contrary to her biological purpose may be guilty of some form of cosmic betrayal, but it is not evident that one can tease an "ought" out of putative facts of this sort. As Murphy expresses this objection, "the paradigmatic natural law view is unable to show that the natural law is intrinsically morally authoritative: the precepts of the natural law can be rules that all of us human beings are *obligated* to obey, that it would be *wrong* for us to disobey, and that we would be *guilty* for flouting only if these precepts are imposed upon us by an authoritative being—perhaps a being like God."[40]

If this is correct, then the basis for our obligation to respect rights is obscure. Remember, we started with the understanding of rights as justified *moral* claims against other persons, who are under a corresponding duty to honor them. Under Randian ethics, persons assert the right to act in accordance with their inherent nature. But, if they have no moral *duty* to act "rationally," then their desire to do so is purely subjective. Why (in the absence of conventional moral standards) are others obligated not to interfere? Moreover, even if individuals *are* under a duty to act rationally, it is *still* unclear how this would, under a natural law conception, establish an obligation on the part of others to let them, especially if the desires of rational agents happen to conflict, as discussed below.[41]

In addition to problems raised by Objectivism's natural law foundations, all versions of "ethical egoism" are subject to certain standard criticisms that have caused it to have few academic adherents outside of the libertarian movement.[42] Ethical egoism is, most broadly, the view that that "it is necessary and sufficient for an action to be morally right that it maximize one's self interest."[43] As you will recall, Rand holds that the individual's interests lie in the pursuit of his or her own happiness, understood as living a certain type of life.

Perhaps the most obvious objection is that this account of morality is markedly counterintuitive in that it apparently must deny that we are *obligated* to sacrifice our own trivial interests in order to satisfy the acute needs of others. For example, I happen upon a man drowning in a swimming pool and can save him simply by tossing him a nearby life preserver. While it is perfectly reasonable for a libertarian to reject state *enforcement* of such ethical duties, it is very different, and much less plausible, to deny that such obligations *exist.*

Rand, in discussing rescue cases of this sort, opines that:

> The proper method of judging when or whether one should help another person is by reference to one's own rational self-interest and one's own hierarchy of values: the time, money or effort one gives or the risk one takes should be proportionate to the value of the person in relation to one's own happiness.[44]

The conflict between Rand's admonition and our everyday moral instincts should be apparent. Under conventional ethical standards our duty to rescue the drowning stranger, when we can do so at no risk to ourselves, exists quite independently of our rational self-interest and personal values. Our ordinary moral consciousness demands that we save this individual because persons are intrinsically valuable.

Of course, if our rational self-interest happens to generally coincide with our ethical obligations as usually understood, this objection would vanish. However, I can discern no connection between the characteristically human virtues identified by Rand—rationality, productiveness, self-esteem—and the internalization of norms that would compel me to recognize the acute need of others as a consideration that should influence my actions. As far as I can see, only the pull of conventional moral values will have this effect.

A closely related problem is that ethical egoism appears to sanction what would be regarded as plainly immoral conduct by ordinary standards. This is brought to the fore by imagining cases where interests conflict. Whereas conventional morality demands that we pursue our individual objectives without violating the equal rights of others, it does not appear that ethical egoism imposes a comparable constraint.

Suppose that two egoists are competing for the same lucrative and desirable employment position. Since both would benefit from having this job and since both are entitled (under this theory) to pursue their selfish interests, why should they not, if they can get away with it, adopt blatantly unethical means to secure this opening?

Rand and her defenders have attempted to escape this difficulty by building respect for the rights of others into the very concept of "rationality," so that to be a "rational" person is to not aggress against others.[45] However, this move simply compounds the arbitrary selection of rationality as our defining characteristic with an artificial definition of this term.[46] In other words, "rationality" is, outside of Randian ethics, generally understood simply as the capacity to reach sound conclusions, judgments, or inferences. There appears to be no obvious link between this ability and any particular set of values, such as non-aggression. One could, with equal justification, superimpose on "rationality" the trait of deviousness or duplicity.

In short, ethical egoism appears to lack certain features that we expect in a credible system of morality. As Kai Nielsen puts it:

> We have moral standards to impartially adjudicate the conflicting interests of individuals and groups; but if each individual's own rational self-interest is taken as the standard, in reality we have no standard by which to adjudicate these conflicting interests. The very *raison d'être* of morality has been frustrated. Thus self-interest, no matter how enlightened, cannot be our standard of *moral* appraisal. "Ethical egoism" cannot possibly be an ethical or moral doctrine.[47]

Not only does Rand's ethical system not ground an obligation for persons to act in accordance with their nature, but the duties derived from what supposedly are our essential characteristics depart radically from our ordinary moral standards and her theory is therefore implausible. Finally, it fails to explain why, even ignoring the other objections, individuals have a duty to respect the rights of others. Given the conceptual difficulties posed by the Objectivist account of rights, it behooves libertarians to search for an alternative justification.

Nozick's account of rights

Nozick, in *ASU,* adopts a completely different strategy for grounding natural rights.[48] Rather than attempting to derive libertarian rights in a top-down fashion from an overarching normative theory, he offers what is essentially a *political* doctrine, i.e. a theory regarding the limits of legitimate state authority, supported by an intuitionist, Kantian-based argument for "side constraints." In what his critics regard as a gross understatement, Nozick acknowledges in his Preface that, "This book does not contain a precise theory of the moral basis of individual rights" (*ASU,* xiv).

In place of such a full-blown theory, Nozick attempts to show that only the libertarian conception of rights as side constraints against aggression is compatible with our pre-theoretical beliefs regarding the moral status of persons. He introduces the idea of side constraints in the course of considering the extent to which the fundamental interests of individuals may justly be sacrificed for the "greater good" (see *ASU,* 28–30). At one extreme would be the view that the rights of particular individuals have no special moral significance and must always yield if they stand in the way of achieving a greater benefit for others. A second, intermediate position is that while individual rights should generally be respected, they may be overridden when required to minimize the total number of rights violations.

This idea would commit us to a form of consequentialist ethics, where the good to be promoted is the absence of rights violations. But an inherent feature of consequentialism is that it endorses the subordination of the interests of any particular individual or group if this would promote the good overall. Accordingly, on this view, we would be permitted to violate one innocent person's right of free expression if this would (somehow) prevent a larger number of similar violations.

Nozick rejects this idea in favor of side constraints, meaning that respect for individual rights should not be a mere goal, but that we must regard their violation as not even an option. Here, he appeals to Kant's notion of humans as "ends in themselves," quoting Kant's second formulation of the Categorical Imperative: "Act in such a way that you always treat humanity, whether in your own person or in the person of any other, never simply as a means, but always at the same time as an end" (*ASU,* 32).[49] An appropriate commitment to human dignity implies, says Nozick, that "individuals are inviolable;" that is, violations of their rights are unconditionally prohibited (see *ASU,* 28–35).

Another way to express this Kantian principle is to invoke, as Nozick does, the "separateness of persons" (see *ASU,* 32–3). When we speak of individuals having to make sacrifices for the greater or common good, we are, says Nozick, perverting the language by pretending that everyone gains from whatever objective is being promoted. In reality:

> There are only individual people, different individual people, with their own individual lives. Using one of these people for the benefit of others, uses him and benefits the others. Nothing more. What happens is that something is done to him for the sake of others. Talk of an overall social good covers this up. (*ASU*, 33)

In fact, our strong intuitive commitment to side constraints indicates to Nozick a potential argument for libertarian rights. First, he says, anyone *denying* the existence of such constraints faces one of three implausible alternatives: (i) reject *all* side constraints, (ii) produce a competing explanation of why we intuitively embrace side constraints rather than the "minimization of rights violations" view or (iii) accept the root idea regarding the separateness of persons, and yet attempt to show that sacrificing some individuals for others is compatible with it (see *ASU*, 33–4).

Based on his conclusion that none of these options is viable, Nozick conceives a way to derive libertarian rights:

> Thus we have a promising sketch of an argument from moral form to moral content: the form of the argument includes F (moral side constraints); the best explanation of morality's being F is p (a strong statement of the distinctness of individuals); and from p follows a particular moral content, namely, the libertarian constraint [prohibiting aggression against another]. (Footnote omitted) (*ASU*, 34)

In other words, we can only explain our instinctive embrace of side constraints by reference to some underlying moral view that entails libertarian rights. I will analyze Nozick's reasoning in some detail, but before doing so I must pause to describe the form of argument being offered. He is relying here on an "argument from the best explanation" (sometimes called an "inference to the best explanation"). In simplest terms, this argument moves, per Gilbert Harman, "from the fact that a certain hypothesis would explain the evidence, to the truth of that hypothesis."[50]

An argument from the best explanation is an accepted form of inductive logic, one that we make frequent use of in everyday life and in science. Harman provides the example of a detective's methodology in solving a

crime: after examining the evidence and ruling out all other possible sus-
pects, the sleuth concludes, "The butler did it."[51] In other words, he can
infer this suspect's guilt from the fact that this explanation best fits the
relevant evidence. Similarly, Harman states that, "When a scientist infers
the existence of atoms and subatomic particles, he is inferring the truth
of the explanation for various data which he wishes to account for."[52] We
should bear in mind, however, that this form of argument at best produces
a probabilistic conclusion, since we cannot exclude the possibility that an
even *better* explanation will emerge.

Having outlined the structure of Nozick's argument, we must pause to
clarify what he has in mind when he proffers "a strong statement of the
distinctness of individuals" as the best explanation for our commitment
to side constraints. There is, it seems to me, an obvious gap in his reasoning because the notion of the "separateness" of persons does not by itself
account for why we should prefer the side constraint view to the goal of
minimizing rights violations. However, I believe there is a logical interpretation of Nozick's argument that resolves this puzzle.

To see this we must focus on his answer to the following question: "in
virtue of precisely what characteristics of persons are there moral constraints on how they may treat each other or be treated?" (*ASU*, 48). Here
again, his response is distinctly Kantian, positing that individuals have a
special standing because in addition to having the three attributes commonly cited by theorists—rationality (the capacity to use abstract concepts),
free will, and moral agency (the capability of guiding one's behavior by
moral principles)—humans are an organism with the "ability to regulate
and guide its life in accordance with some overall conception it chooses
to accept" (*ASU*, 49).[53] We will refer to this set of features as "rational
agency."

Given the central role Nozick accords this characteristic in rationalizing
our commitment to side constraints, I believe that hypothesis "p" in his argument (the separateness of persons) explains why "[t]here is no justified sacrifice of some of us for others" only because he builds the feature of rational
agency into his notion of "separateness."[54] Therefore, as seen below, I have
construed Nozick's hypothesis regarding the "distinctness of individuals" to
implicitly mean individuals in their capacity as rational agents. To briefly
outline his argument, which I will flesh out below: we accept the existence
of side constraints; the best explanation of this commitment is that we are
separate rational agents; rational agents must be treated with appropriate
dignity; appropriate dignity forbids coercion.

You will notice that Nozick's approach bears a superficial resemblance to Rand's argument in that it incorporates the concept of a distinctive human attribute(s). However, Nozick does not claim that this feature is an objective virtue that grounds a comprehensive ethical theory. Rather, he relies on our common sense morality for the idea that persons enjoy a special moral status and then seeks to explain this intuition.

Nozick's more modest ambition permits libertarian rights to peacefully coexist with positive moral duties to others. As shown below, a Nozickian libertarian can consistently hold that we have obligations to assist our needy fellow humans *and* that it is nevertheless morally impermissible to coerce persons to satisfy such duties. Nozick expressly ducks the question of whether this prohibition on compulsion may be overridden in order to prevent catastrophic outcomes (see *ASU*, 30n). We will take up this issue in Chapter 6, but in the meantime the reader should keep in mind this possible qualification to the absolute nature of rights.

Nozick's derivation of libertarian rights has been harshly criticized, particularly by philosophers of a more egalitarian bent, as unsupported either by formal argument or by appeal to compelling moral intuitions.[55] Thomas Nagel observes that Nozick's arguments against state enforced income redistribution proceed from the "unargued premise" that "individuals have certain inviolable rights which may not be intentionally transgressed by other individuals or the state for any purpose."[56]

However, this criticism is, in my judgment, unfair. As described above, and as more fully elaborated below, Nozick *does* argue for inviolability by proposing rational agency as the best explanation for our strong, widely held intuitions regarding side constraints. Nagel would certainly be demanding too much if he expects Nozick to demonstrate the inviolability of rights without employing at least one premise that cannot be established deductively. Because, as discussed further below, all formal arguments (that do not wish to grapple with Hume's law) ultimately rest on assumptions that are themselves incapable of proof, such a demonstration is impossible.

Nagel and other critics may have missed Nozick's argument because he does not, with great fanfare, present it in a systematic fashion at a single point in his study. I have therefore attempted, for the sake of clarity, to set forth what I take to be Nozick's reasoning in a deductive form, providing supportive argumentation at each step. While I believe that what follows is entirely *consistent* with Nozick's discussion of the ethical foundation of rights in *ASU*, I do not claim that he would *endorse* it. This reluctance is due to the fact that I have, as we have seen, had occasion to interpret his argument in a certain way, and furthermore, I am not confident that he would have presented this "proof" exactly as I have or that he would agree with the additional arguments I have formulated to support it.

Nevertheless, I believe that what follows constitutes the strongest version of any argument for natural rights Nozick might make based on the presuppositions and analysis set forth in *ASU*. Accordingly, while I refer to what follows as "Nozick's argument," nothing important hangs on whether this attribution is justified. Obviously, whatever its paternity, the argument stands (or falls) on its own merits.

A "proof" of natural rights

My reconstruction of Nozick's argument takes the form of five premises and a conclusion. However, I wish to emphasize that by presenting this argument as a deductive proof, I do not mean to suggest that it can have the certainty of a geometric theorem. Philosophy is not a branch of mathematics. These premises are certainly controversial, and cannot be conclusively demonstrated.

Nevertheless, I contend that this argument is persuasive. Moreover, competing political theories are also value-laden, taking (for example) utility or equality as basic, and so must also found these ideals in some fashion. Therefore, the appropriate standard of comparison for Nozick's "proof" is not geometry, but rival political/ethical doctrines.

Set forth immediately below is the outline of this demonstration without elaboration or supporting argumentation. Following this, I defend each premise.

Premise 1. Persons (and potential persons) enjoy a special moral status, meaning that their individual interests are entitled to great moral weight.

Premise 2. The special moral status of persons (and potential persons) renders them morally inviolable, i.e. there are side constraints on how they may be treated.

Premise 3. Persons are rational agents.

Premise 4. Persons are inviolable *because* they are rational agents.

Premise 5. Persons have a right to exercise their rational agency without interference, subject only to the equal rights of other rational agents.

Conclusion: The use of force or coercion against innocent persons (those not engaged in aggression or fraud against other persons) interferes with their rational agency and is therefore morally impermissible.

Argument for Premise 1 [Persons (and potential persons) enjoy a special moral status, meaning that their individual interests are entitled to great moral weight.]

All deductive proofs must start with at least one premise, of which there are only two types, factual or normative. As seen above, Rand starts with the former, and fails to cross the is/ought gap, i.e. her moral principles do not logically follow from her empirical assumptions. Nozick takes the alternative, more conventional approach. The cost of adopting this strategy is that there is (apparently) no knockdown response available to quiet the moral skeptic who simply denies that he has *any* ethical duties to his fellow human beings, and asserts that any beliefs we have to the contrary are simply the product of religious brainwashing or social convention.

However, as explained in the Introduction, this is not a book about meta-ethics. While I believe that there are plausible answers to the moral nihilist, to give this subject a fair treatment would require quite an extended discussion and take us far from the guts of political philosophy. In the notes I offer a brief outline of what I consider to be the most promising strategy for establishing the objectivity of moral values,[57] a strategy I might add that varies somewhat from Nozick's approach in his subsequent book, *Philosophical Explanations*.[58] In any case, since all political doctrines are built on some set of ethical presuppositions, the problem of moral subjectivity presents no special difficulty for libertarians.

Accordingly, there is no "argument" as such for Premise 1. I believe this postulate simply affirms a fundamental moral commitment shared by virtually all persons who have had the opportunity to reflect on it. It is, I claim, the sort of starting point Bertrand Russell, one of the twentieth century's most eminent philosophers, had in mind when he explained the need for bedrock assumptions in the field of ethics:

> Since a proposition can only be proved by means of other propositions, it is obvious that not all propositions can be proved, for proofs can only begin by assuming something… Thus, in the case of ethics, we must ask why such and such actions ought to be performed, and continue our backward inquiry for reasons until we reach the kind of proposition of which proof is impossible, because it is so simple or so obvious that nothing more fundamental can be found from which to deduce it.[59]

However, before proceeding further I wish to clarify one possible ambiguity. By "person" I mean a typical, functioning member of our species. I exclude—for purposes of this argument only—individuals whose cognitive capacity is drastically and permanently impaired, e.g. people with *profound* developmental disabilities, those in a permanent vegetative state and so on. I am not asserting that such individuals do not have a robust set of rights; I am merely noting that this argument is not intended to establish any such claim.

While I exclude those human beings who have been permanently deprived of their reasoning faculties from the definition of "persons," I include within the category of "potential persons" newborns, young children and those adolescents who are not yet adults. Clearly, it is a deeply ingrained feature of our common morality that non-adults are accorded the moral status of persons. While their immaturity justifies various paternalistic interventions that would violate side constraints if applied to adults, we do not apply fundamentally different ethical standards to the treatment of mature and immature human beings. Put most simply, we are just as morally offended by the murder of a two year old, as we are of a 52 year old.

It seems obvious to me that any plausible explanation of this reaction will draw in large part on the fact that infants and children are potential persons, and thus potential rational agents.[60] I exclude fetuses from the definition of "potential persons" not because I doubt that at *some point* in their gestation they should be regarded as such, but because it is not necessary for purposes of this argument to settle this contentious issue.

Argument for Premise 2 [The special moral status of persons (and potential persons) renders them morally inviolable, i.e. there are side constraints on how they may be treated.]

The justification for this proposition is essentially an appeal to our intuitions regarding the implications of our special moral status. Technically, this premise could have been combined with the first, so as to read, "Persons (and potential persons) enjoy a special moral status, meaning that their rights are inviolable," but I separated the two claims in recognition of the need to explain how we get from "special moral status" to "side constraints."

As we have seen, in arguing for side constraints Nozick invokes the Kantian idea of persons as ends-in-themselves, a standing that forbids their use as mere tools to achieve any greater good. One way of understanding this constraint is to contrast it with classical utilitarianism, under which it is permissible to sacrifice the welfare of particular individuals in order to maximize it generally.

So, this doctrine would arguably sanction forced organ transplants, since the welfare gained by a person about to die without a kidney would greatly outweigh the loss of utility experienced by the unwilling donor (who could get along fine with just a single kidney). Of course, libertarians contend that persons have rights against such involuntary transfers notwithstanding the great potential benefit to the recipient. If such rights are absolutely inviolable then no justification could ever be sufficient. Again, we are postponing until Chapter 6 the issue of whether rights must give way in order to prevent moral catastrophes.

The idea that persons' fundamental interests should not generally be subject to utilitarian trade-offs seems firmly entrenched in our ordinary moral consciousness. We can pose the issue of the inviolability of rights quite starkly: suppose that a terrorist organization seizes a group of five innocent hostages and threatens to kill them unless our society executes another innocent person of greater interest to them.

Let us further imagine that because of this organization's past history, information from our intelligence agencies or for other reasons, we have near absolute certainty that the terrorists will take the threatened action against the five hostages if we refuse, but will release them if we comply. And, suppose we have similarly persuasive evidence that making the proposed exchange will not encourage any future hostage-takings. Should we give in?

I believe that the vast majority of both academic philosophers and ordinary people would reject this "devil's bargain." As Frances Kamm and other deontological philosophers have argued,[61] the most convincing explanation for this judgment is our recognition that even if we *save* lives by capitulating in such nightmare scenarios, such a policy is inconsistent with the special status due persons. Philosophers refer to the obligation we feel under certain circumstances to act in ways that do *not* maximize beneficial consequences as a "deontological constraint."

In a recent interview, Kamm explains this deontological logic as follows:

One measure of people's worth is what we judge is permissible to do to them. It is true that the five will be mistreated if I don't harm the one in order to stop their mistreatment. But they will still be the kind of beings who should not be treated in this way. They will still be the kind of beings who are inviolable insofar as it is wrong to harm them in a certain way in order to realize the greater good of minimizing that type of harm. If it were permissible to kill the one to save the others, no one (the one or the five) would have the status of a highly inviolable being.[62]

If we were to make this exchange we would, in Nozick's phrase, be adopting a "utilitarianism of rights," where our goal is merely to minimize the total violation of rights (see *ASU*, 28–9).

Kamm's use of the term "highly inviolable," rather than "absolutely inviolable," reflects the fact that few philosophers are willing to defend the idea that deontological constraints are absolute. That is, that they preclude *all* trade-offs no matter how high the stakes (i.e. better the world should end than we sacrifice one innocent person to save it). However, the argument presented here for libertarian rights does not depend on deontological constraints being unyielding in this way, but merely than they govern our conduct within certain limits. So construed, they are an undeniable aspect of our ordinary moral consciousness. Accordingly, the use of "inviolable" in Premise 2 should be understood in this sense.

Argument for Premise 3 [Persons are rational agents.]

We know that persons are rational agents through introspection and through observation of and interaction with other people, especially those closest to us. Of course, the most philosophically controversial aspect of this claim is the idea of free will. Almost all of us believe that we have free will, understood as the capacity to select (at least in most cases) alternative courses of action ("I didn't *have to* eat desert last night; I *could have* turned down that delicious chocolate cake"). This notion is the linchpin of our ordinary moral consciousness.

Even those academic philosophers who claim that causal determinism makes free will impossible ("hard determinists") and those who uphold free will by giving a much more restricted account of it than we naively hold (e.g. the "compatibilists," who argue that free will is compatible with causal determinism), acknowledge that free will is firmly entrenched in commonsense morality. Hence Peter van Inwagen's observation that "we are certainly condemned to believe in freedom—and, in fact, condemned to believe that we know that we are free."[63] Here again, the difficulty of free will poses no particular problem for libertarians, but equally confronts all political theories, each of which assumes that the audience to which it is directed will be able to heed its recommendations.

Argument for Premise 4. [Persons are inviolable *because* they are rational agents.]

Since even those who regard themselves as animal lovers do not believe that our furry friends are entitled to the *same* moral weight as persons, we may well wonder why this is so. In other words, what is it about people that causes us to regard their unjustified killing as murder, while the killing of a chicken is generally considered a morally permissible means of obtaining food?

Without subscribing to it (or rejecting it), Shelly Kagan labels the strategy of deriving fundamental moral values from our essential characteristics as the "reflection theory," the root idea of which is that:

> [T]he contents of a morality that is appropriate for creatures like us will depend on what creatures like us are like...if we want to know that the contents of morality come to, we can make progress on this question by thinking about which of our features would appropriately play a role in determining the content of morality.[64]

As will be shown below, our rational agency is the *best explanation* for the special status we accord human life.

The different moral weight accorded persons and other animals must be attributable to some common human attribute(s) not possessed by other (known) species. The mastery of calculus, ancient Greek or the possession of a genius-level IQ cannot count, or we would punish the murder of scientists and scholars more severely than manual laborers. In other words, we are searching for the "lowest common denominator" that separates persons from (say) porpoises. Of course, "walks upright on two legs" or similar physical characteristics would qualify, but these clearly seem trivial and contingent.

A wide variety of skills or behaviors, such as language, self-awareness, problem solving, the use of tools, and empathy were once thought to be uniquely human, but as research into animal behavior has advanced it appears more and more the case that these characteristics do not belong exclusively to our species.[65] Since we intuitively believe that there is a *qualitative* difference in the value of a person's life relative to even the most "advanced" animals, we should restrict our search for an attribute or combination of attributes that we alone can be said to possess.

General intelligence is not a serious candidate for the best explanation of our commitment to side constraints because this quality, *by itself*, cannot confer full moral status. This idea originates with Kant, who insists that only "persons," i.e. humans in their capacity as *moral* agents, are entitled to be regarded as ends in themselves. Judith Thomson expresses this point quite elegantly: "the capacity to conform your conduct to moral law is a necessary and sufficient condition for the moral law to apply to you."[66] In other words, the criminally insane, i.e. those who cannot distinguish between right and wrong, even if super-intelligent, do not qualify as Kantian "persons." I do not take her to mean that that are no ethical standards governing our treatment of such people, but only that they are not entitled to the respect due rational agents.

Thus, more or less by the process of elimination, we arrive at the constellation of attributes identified by Nozick, rational agency, as the origin of our special moral standing. However, although I have labeled the value-conferring human attribute cited by Nozick as "rational agency," it seems fairly certain that of the four components that he identifies (rationality, free will, moral agency, and the capacity to guide our lives in accordance with some overall conception we choose to accept), moral agency is the quintessential element.

Initially, note that the first two elements may reasonably be considered simply as necessary conditions for the existence of moral agency. Moreover, in light of the discussion immediately above regarding Kant's understanding of "persons" and Nozick's invocation of the Kantian notion of "respect for persons," his reference to our ability to act pursuant to some "overall conception" likely includes an irreducible moral dimension. In other words, it is plausible to read him here to mean "overall conception *of the good*" that we select.

Before going further, we should clarify that Nozick is careful *not* to claim that human beings are entitled to any special moral weight simply because we are superior to other animals. He notes that such a view would imply that super-beings from another planet would be entitled to sacrifice us for *their* purposes (see *ASU*, 45–7). Accordingly, if it should turn out, contrary to our current understanding, that some animals are rational agents, it would not undermine Nozick's argument for the inviolability of persons, but merely require that such animals be accorded equal respect.

Argument for Premise 5. [Persons have a right to exercise their rational agency without interference, subject only to the equal rights of other rational agents.]

As argued so far, the source of our elevated moral standing lies in our rational agency, and most particularly in our status as moral agents. It seems obvious that the application of force or the threat of force against innocent persons (those not engaged in aggression or fraud) will interfere with the exercise of this capacity. For purposes of establishing an ethical foundation for libertarian rights we would like to conclude, in light of the above, that all other persons are morally required to refrain from such interference.

Nozick expresses this idea as follows:

> If your basic moral characteristic of being a value-seeking individual includes weighting values in free choice...then being responsive to this characteristic and to the originative value you possess will involve respecting your autonomy. Within this domain, it will be impermissible for others to force you away from the bad or less good towards the best; doing so would be anti-responsive to your capacity as a weighter of values. Thereby is a right to personal liberty delineated.[67]

But even granting that it is our rational agency that confers value upon us, *why* are *other persons* required to respect our autonomy? I believe there are two viable ways to respond to this challenge. The first approach simply draws on the powerful intuitive appeal of Kant's injunction to always treat persons as ends-in-themselves, and never merely as a means to some other objective.

If we are to do so, we must first recognize what it is about persons that compels respect and appreciate the nature of what is owed them by virtue of this feature(s). Because the special moral status of rational agents is rooted in their autonomy, appropriate deference requires that they be permitted to live the life they choose, so long as they do not infringe the equal rights of others. Accordingly, the use of force or coercion against persons in order to accomplish some extraneous goal is a morally inappropriate response to the value of autonomy, and is therefore impermissible.

Clearly, this suggestion will not convince the moral nihilist, but it is not intended to. This idea assumes the truth of Premises 1–4, acceptance of which commits us to the belief both that persons are inviolable, and that they are so *because* they are rational agents.

A second response draws on our general commitment to what philosophers call "moral impartiality." There is a widespread (although not universal) agreement among moral philosophers that impartiality, *in some sense*, plays an essential role in moral reasoning.[68] However, there is the usual sharp disagreement as to what that "sense" is, and thus which normative theory best expresses it. For those consequentialists who believe that the focus of our ethical judgments should center on the rightness or wrongness of individual acts (as opposed to general rules of conduct), moral impartiality requires that agents assign identical weight to the good or bad to be experienced by all affected persons.[69]

Among deontologists, impartiality is generally understood as the idea that, in the words of Charles Fried, "the interests, preferences or desires of the agent have no special status or higher priority just because they belong to the agent; that is an agent may not prefer his own interests as such."[70] In other words, an agent must "be morally consistent, in the sense that she will judge her own actions by the same standards she applies to others."[71] The relevance of this concept becomes clear when we note, again, that my construction of Nozick's argument for libertarian rights is directed to those individuals who accept the deontological principle that persons, including themselves, are "inviolable" because they are rational agents.

Accordingly, those whose who subscribe to this view may not, without contravening a basic moral principle, demand respect for their own autonomy while denying equal respect to other persons. This may at first seem like a very weak basis for establishing libertarian rights because many people who accept Premises 1–4 will regard various egalitarian measures condemned by Nozick as consistent with the free exercise of their moral sovereignty. Moral consistency would not, therefore, require them to forswear redistributive taxation or other egalitarian policies since they do not object to being subjected to them.

Nevertheless, such agents will still need to articulate a principled distinction between those redistributive measures they regard as unjust (i.e. outright seizures of property, forced organ donations, confiscatory taxes, etc.) and those that they find inoffensive. However, one implication of Nozick's arguments for his entitlement theory, outlined in the following chapter, is that it is impossible to convincingly draw such lines. Therefore, if Nozick's arguments are as strong as I maintain, then all who assent to Premises 1–4 must either accept egregious interference with their rational agency as morally legitimate, or adopt the libertarian conception of rights.

Against the "respect for rational agency" arguments I have outlined above, it may be objected that appropriate deference requires, in addition to or in place of noninterference, the redistribution of resources so that agents will have adequate means to exercise their autonomy. This argument is addressed in Chapter 6.

Conclusion: The use of force or coercion against innocent persons (those not engaged in aggression or fraud against other persons) interferes with their rational agency and is therefore morally impermissible.

In light of the above, I claim that the Nozickian argument is valid (the conclusion follows from the premises). While each of these premises is controversial, I contend that they are all credible, and therefore we have arrived at a plausible moral foundation for libertarian rights. We should note that Nozick does not expressly apply his argument to state action. In other words, he takes his argument to show "that moral side constraints limit how *people* may behave to each other" (emphasis added) (*ASU*, 51). We leave until Chapter 4 the question of whether a state, even a minimal one, has any greater moral authority to disregard side constraints than do individuals.

The Self-ownership Thesis

Before concluding this chapter, we must correct an error that has frequently crept into discussions of Nozick's derivation of rights. I refer here to the unfortunate tendency of commentators to interpret his argument as based on self-ownership.[72] To cite one of numerous examples, Jonathan Wolff in his book *Robert Nozick: Property, Justice and the Minimal State* writes, "Nozick is distinctive in the emphasis he puts on self-ownership."[73] As you will recall from our discussion earlier in this chapter, this concept is Locke's starting point in his defense of private property.

While, as discussed in the following chapter, self-ownership plays a role in Nozick's account of how property may be justly acquired in a state of nature, he does not attempt to derive natural rights from this idea. Such an argument would ground the inviolability of persons in their ownership of their bodies and their labor, and would assimilate rights violations to (as appropriate) trespass or the nonconsensual confiscation or destruction of property.[74] But Nozick does *not* make this argument; in fact, he uses the term "self-ownership" in *ASU* only once.

He does so not in Part I of *ASU*, where he derives natural rights, but in Part II, in which he attacks the morality of redistributive taxation. In the course of this discussion Nozick asserts that such taxes "involve a shift from the classical liberals' notion of self-ownership to a notion of (partial) property rights in *other* people" (*ASU*, 172). This is the extent of his overt reliance on "self-ownership" in *ASU*.

Nozick's single, offhand reference to self-ownership contrasts sharply with his far more elaborate discussion of Kantian principles in developing the notion of side constraints, including the invocation of Kant's second formulation of the Categorical Imperative. Moreover, in his discussion of animal rights Nozick expressly suggests "utilitarianism for animals, Kantianism for people" (*ASU*, 39) as the appropriate formula before finally rejecting utilitarianism as too lax a standard (*ASU*, 42).

Most importantly, since Nozick was seeking the strongest rationale for libertarian rights, he has good reasons for not relying primarily on self-ownership.

First, I believe that the idea of self-ownership does not provide a convincing, stand-alone basis for side constraints. We can see this by asking in what sense humans are self-owners while all other animal species are not. These beings "own" themselves in the sense of controlling their bodily movements and functions. Yet we generally believe that side constraints do not apply to animals, so some other factor must be at work. As argued above, it is rational agency that forces us to take seriously the notion of human self-ownership, while largely ignoring the self-ownership of other animals.[75]

Similarly, as far as I can tell, we cannot derive the inviolability of rights from self-ownership. Recall the scenario discussed above regarding the impermissibility of killing one innocent person to save five others. While the special status of moral agents renders them immune from the sort of consequentialist trade-off contemplated in this example, I see no comparable implication from self-ownership. After all, the five hostages in our scenario are *also* self-owners. Therefore, I do not see how principles of self-ownership would exclude the sort of consequentialist trade-offs condemned by Nozick as a mere "utilitarianism of rights."

Nothing above is intended to suggest that Nozick would deny the *fact* of self-ownership. As described in the following chapter, he follows the path blazed by Locke in defending the morality of "full capitalist property rights," and self-ownership is the first step in this argument. However, Nozick simply assumes, as I believe he is entitled to do, that we own ourselves. Not only does it seem impossible to construct a convincing account of how other people could legitimately come to own us, at least absent our consent, but it seems to me that "self-ownership" is self-evidently true.

On this view, the "self" simply *is* that part of "us" that constitutes our identity, which by its very nature is ours alone. If another person were to own you in the same way that things are owned, you would no longer have a "self" but would be an extension of your owner's self, i.e. his alter-ego. Accordingly, when Nozick objects to redistributive taxation as equivalent to some people taking an ownership interest in others, he is simply using a metaphor to dramatize the moral force of side constraints.

The point of this section is not terminological. By, in my judgment, misconstruing Nozick as relying on the self-ownership thesis as the foundation of rights, commentators shift the focus of the ideological debate to competing interpretations of self-ownership. Egalitarians reject "formal" self-ownership in favor of "substantial" self-ownership, by which they mean possession of sufficient assets to live "meaningful" lives.[76] This interpretation, they claim, justifies the redistribution of holdings. But (as seen in Chapter 6) if we understand Nozick's fundamental concern to be the coercion of rational agents, the egalitarian impulse has a much harder time taking hold.

Chapter 2

The Entitlement Theory

You shall not commit a perversion of justice; you shall not favor the poor and you shall not honor the great; with righteousness shall you judge your fellow.

Leviticus, 19:15[1]

There is always inequity in life. Some men are killed in a war and some men are wounded, and some men never leave the country... Life is unfair.

John Fitzgerald Kennedy [1962]

Citizens' lawful private property is inviolable. The State, in accordance with law, protects the rights of citizens to private property and to its inheritance.

Constitution of the People's Republic of China,
Chapter 1, Article 13 [2004 Amendment][2]

In the previous chapter we reviewed Nozick's account of the foundation of libertarian rights, and found it to be plausible and firmly rooted in our commonsense moral judgments. One implication of this argument is that innocent persons may not be coerced, including for purposes of redistributing resources. However, this discussion did not address how libertarian rights to property may justly arise and (assuming they can) whether they must yield when confronted by claims of "social justice." It is to these questions that we now turn.

One of Nozick's great contributions to political philosophy is his formulation of the entitlement theory of justice (hereinafter Entitlement Theory). This model of justice instantiates Nozick's conception of libertarian rights developed in Chapter 1, particularly the idea that persons may not be used solely as a means of achieving some greater good. The originality of the Entitlement Theory lies in its refusal to engage in a fruitless search for a principle that will produce the "ideal" distribution of wealth, instead looking exclusively to the circumstances under which property is acquired and transferred (see *ASU*, 149–51).

Indeed, Nozick introduces the Entitlement Theory by expressly contrasting it with the notion of distributive justice, the very name of which implies that there is some pool of "found" assets that must be fairly parceled out. However, not only is this assumption false, but, he says, it is not obvious a priori why property holdings should any more be subject to reallocation than "the distribution of mates in a society in which persons choose whom they shall marry" (*ASU*, 150).

In this chapter we will first outline the substance of Nozick's theory and then review the relatively few, but powerful, arguments he advances on its behalf. We will then consider certain of the common objections that have been raised against these specific arguments. We will leave to the following chapter my response to the more fundamental criticisms that have been leveled against the Entitlement Theory.

Three Principles of Justice

Nozick's thesis is elegant in its simplicity:

1. A person who acquires a holding in accordance with the principle of justice in acquisition is entitled to that holding.
2. A person who acquires a holding in accordance with the principle of justice in transfer, from someone entitled to the holding, is entitled to the holding.
3. No one is entitled to a holding except by (repeated) application of 1 and 2 (*ASU*, 151).

A set of holdings is just "if everyone is entitled to the holdings they possess under the distribution" (ibid.). Nozick acknowledges that his theory is incomplete in one important respect: a principle of rectification is required to address the effect of past injustices that may have shaped current holdings (see *ASU*, 152).

As will become clear below, it is not essential to Nozick's overall enterprise that he fill in all the details of the three constituent principles of the Entitlement Theory, but it will suffice if he can establish a presumption in its favor. Nozick's general strategy is two-fold: (i) demonstrate that his schema is the only one consistent with the notion of side constraints, defended in Chapter 1, and (ii) demolish all competing theories, leaving his as the "last man standing."

Just acquisition

Before turning to Nozick's critique of all egalitarian theories of political justice,[3] we will consider what he has to say regarding the three principles of the Entitlement Theory. Nozick draws on certain features of Locke's state of nature analysis in constructing his first principle, "justice in acquisition." As you will recall from Chapter 1, in Locke's view the natural right of self-preservation encompasses the acquisition of external resources, subject only to the just claims of others. Accordingly, in order to defend the morality of individual ownership, he felt compelled to show that property held in common could be "privatized" without violating this constraint.

Initially, it is important to understand that while (as reviewed in Chapter 1) Locke held that "God gave the World to Men in Common," in the same breath he avers that "it cannot be supposed he meant it should always remain common and uncultivated. He gave it to the Industrious and Rational (and *Labour* was to be *his Title* to it;) not to the Fancy or the Covetousness of the Quarrelsom and Contentious."[4] Thus, he views resources held "in common" as not "owned" in the conventional sense at all, but available for appropriation. As explained below, the failure of the common users to *develop* the resource precludes them from asserting a just claim of Lockean ownership.

Locke starts with self-ownership as his first principle, such that "every Man has a *Property* in his own *Person*. This no Body has any Right to but himself."[5] From the premise, he moves to the conclusion that the fruits of a person's labor are also his:

> Whatsoever then he removes out of the State that Nature hath provided, and left it in, he hath mixed his *Labour* with, and joined to it something that is his own, and thereby makes it his *Property*. It being by him removed from the common state Nature placed it in, it hath by this *labour* something annexed to it, that excludes the common right of other Men. For this *Labour* being the unquestionable Property of the Labourer, no Man but he can have a right to what is once joined to, at least where there is enough, and as good left in common for others.[6]

Starting with the simplest case, the consumption of wild fruits and berries, Locke holds that the labor expended to gather them is sufficient to confer individual ownership, subject to the condition that a person cannot justly claim more than "one can make use of to any advantage of life before it spoils."[7] If the consent of others were required, "Man had starved, notwithstanding the Plenty God had given him."[8] However, a more complex account is required with respect to "capital" resources, such as land, minerals, timber, and so forth.

Locke does not develop his concept of "labor mixing" in any depth, so Nozick (sympathetically) interprets him as conditioning the just appropriation of nature's capital goods on *improving* them in some significant way; for instance, by fencing and cultivating raw land. As Nozick puts it, "Perhaps the idea...is that laboring on something improves it and makes it more valuable; and anyone is entitled to own a thing whose value he has created" (*ASU*, 175).[9] However, this process takes place subject to an important proviso; since others are also entitled to self-preservation, the reduction to individual ownership must leave, in Locke's words, "enough and as good left in common for others" (the "Lockean proviso").

Accordingly, Nozick notes, an appropriation would be deemed unjust if it worsens the situation of others by, for example, placing all of the water in the desert in one party's hands. In Nozick's adaptation of Locke's model the proviso continues to cast a "historical shadow" over resource acquisition, such that if all the other water holes in the desert later dry up, the owner of the sole "productive" one cannot charge what he will or deny water to others (see *ASU*, 180).

As Nozick recognizes, the repercussions of the reduction of natural resources to private property will extend far into the future. Therefore, with respect to the generations that arrive on the scene after original appropriation is no longer possible, the Lockean proviso is, in its naïve form, incomplete at best. This is because the requirement that others not be made worse off invites the question, "worse as compared to what?" (see *ASU*, 175–8). If this proviso requires that second or third generation claimants have the *identical* opportunities available to the original acquirers, the "enough and as good left for others" test cannot be satisfied. Clearly at some point all the available land and natural resources will be claimed and nothing left over for others to appropriate in the first instance.

As Nozick observes, if we adopt this restrictive perspective, the acquisition of the last unclaimed plot of land was illegitimate, as all other individuals are cut off from initial appropriation, i.e. they are made worse off. If the ultimate acquisition of previously unclaimed property is set aside as immoral, then the penultimate appropriation was as well, because it prevented the final claimant from making her acquisition, thus making her worse off, and so on back down the chain of appropriations.

It would be a serious error, however, to jump from the fact that at some point the *original* acquisition of external resources must come to an end, to the conclusion that the *institution* of private property is morally suspect. The obvious answer to the question "worse off as compared to what," is the situation that would prevail if the reduction of property to individual ownership were not permitted, i.e. if external resources remained subject to some form of common ownership or collective control (see *ASU*, 177).[10] If the Lockean proviso is understood this way, we have good cause to believe that subsequent generations were, far from being damaged by original appropriation, actually benefited by it.

First, as David Schmidtz has argued, if we are concerned about the welfare of future generations, we should focus on the relationship between individual ownership and the continued *existence* of natural resources. In the absence of appropriation, natural resources may be destroyed altogether by the well-known phenomenon that economists have labeled "the tragedy of the commons." This description reflects the fact that the collective use of an otherwise renewable natural resource will tend to destroy the asset over time because individual members of the community have no incentive to limit their use.[11] In other words, consumers of such resources find themselves in a sort of "prisoner's dilemma," where the optimal strategy is to use as much of the resource as possible before others exhaust it.

This phenomenon explains the dramatic depletion of the oceans' fish stocks: if this asset were privately owned, it would be managed in such a manner as to maintain its long-term economic value (as are privately owned forests, since companies like Weyerhaeuser expect to be in the timber business a *long* time). As Schmidtz writes, "what we must preserve for future generations is the opportunity to use resources, not opportunities to originally appropriate them."[12] If we accept that the critical responsibility of initial claimants is to conserve natural resources, then, as Schmidtz observes, privatization may not only be permissible, it may be morally required.[13]

Furthermore, once the initial appropriation process for any natural resource is reasonably far along, what inevitably develops is a well-organized *market* for that asset, including land. Thus, all existing residential real estate in this country is now owned, yet millions of homes are on the market at any moment. Accordingly, it is difficult to see how the current generation of homeowners was prejudiced by being deprived of its opportunity to clear their property of trees, build their log cabin, plant their crops and so on. Indeed, it simply does not follow from the fact that all of a particular resource has been appropriated that others are denied its use and enjoyment, or an opportunity for welfare equal or superior to that available to the original acquirers.[14]

Thus, in justifying private ownership Nozick follows Locke in stressing its economic advantages:

> [Private property] increases the social product by putting the means of production in the hands of those who can use them most efficiently (profitably); experimentation is encouraged, because with separate persons controlling resources, there is no one person or small group whom someone with a new idea must convince to try out; private property enables people to decide on the pattern and types of risks they wish to bear, leading to specialized types of risk bearing; private property protects future persons by leading some to hold back resources from current consumption for future markets. (*ASU*, 177)[15]

Accordingly, he concludes, because capitalism is a superior economic model to all of its competitors, "the free operation of a market system will not actually run afoul of the Lockean proviso" (*ASU*, 182). There are complications arising from this interpretation of the welfare baseline, which are addressed in Chapter 6.

Based on the above reasoning, in a state of nature, persons can, subject to the Lockean proviso, justly acquire raw materials by improving them: land by homesteading, minerals by mining and smelting, timber by harvesting and milling, and so on. Even after the initial round of appropriation is closed, subsequent generations are free to use property (that otherwise might have been destroyed) by means of rent or purchase. The economic vitality and ever-improving standard of living in capitalist societies shows that their members were not made worse off by being denied the opportunity for original appropriation.

We must stop at this point and stress the importance of the "development" (or "improvement") condition suggested by Nozick as an essential part of Lockean appropriation. The requirement that an appropriator invest her time, energy and/or capital in improving a natural asset, rather than merely claiming it (by, for instance, simply placing a fence around it) is an integral part of our willingness to regard Lockean appropriation as conferring a libertarian property right. You will recall that in Chapter 1 we defined a "right" as a justified moral claim. This understanding clearly limits what may qualify as a right.

For example, it is absurd to speak of a "right" to vandalize the property of others for our own amusement because this would sanction the violation of the moral rights of other persons on a wholesale basis. Of course, we may be able to imagine extreme or unusual *cases* where we would conclude that a generally enforceable right might permissibly be overridden, but this fact does not undermine the idea that we cannot have a broad right to engage in unethical conduct.

Accordingly, in outlining the conditions that will support a right to privatize property, Nozick (following Locke) is at pains to construe this right in a way that does not contravene the just claims of contemporary non-appropriators or those persons coming on the scene when original acquisition is no longer possible. Out of such concerns is born the Lockean proviso. Without the improvement condition, it might seem that the structure of property ownership rests on the entirely arbitrary fact of who got there first.

The development requirement is a key element in our judgment regarding the justice of original acquisition because it introduces the element of *desert*. While the opportunity to originally appropriate may depend on luck, the fact that the acquirer must make a substantial *investment* of her time and energy to secure her prize (a commitment avoided by the timid or lazy) aligns the Lockean model with our ordinary moral intuitions. If privatization harms no one else *and* the acquirer increases the value of the claimed resource through her own labor, then I believe we are morally compelled to recognize her full right to this property. What more could we reasonably ask of her?

Anticipating the attacks that will come from those denying that initial ownership can justly arise in the way he has described, Nozick poses the following challenge:

> Those believing in collective property, for example those believing that a group of persons living in an area jointly own the territory, or its mineral resources, also must provide a theory of how such property rights arise; they must show why the persons living there have rights to determine what is done with the land and resources there that persons living elsewhere don't have (with regard to the same land and resources). (*ASU*, 178)

We will have reason to return to this point when we review in the next chapter various objections to the Entitlement Theory.

Justice in transfer, and rectification

The second constitutive element of the Entitlement Theory is the principle of justice in transfer. Nozick has very little to say about the substance of this principle, other than to assert that voluntary exchanges between competent adults will not offend it. As we will discuss below, he is prepared to defend the idea that exchanges of property and/or services characterized by inequalities in the bargaining positions of the parties do not (absent actual fraud or duress) render such transactions unjust.

Nozick's third principle, that only by just acquisition or just transfer can a person obtain morally valid title to property, functions to exclude redistributive transfers. This position is implied by the notion of side constraints developed in Chapter 1. It may be worth noting here, again, that Nozick expressly holds open the possibility that side constraints might be disregarded in order to avoid "moral catastrophes," a subject we explore further in Chapter 6.

Nozick is not substantially more forthcoming with respect to his principle of rectification, and his various remarks on the subject appear to stand in some tension with each other. He notes that since the full ramifications of historical wrongs are difficult to trace, in the absence of a fully worked-out theory of rectification, "past injustices *might* be so great as to make necessary *in the short run* a more extensive state" (my emphasis), and that "one *cannot* use the analysis and theory presented here to condemn any particular scheme of transfer payments, unless it is clear that no considerations of rectification of injustice could apply to justify it" (*ASU*, 231).

On the other hand, Nozick's notion of side constraints would preclude dispossessing persons, in the name of rectification, who did not directly or indirectly benefit from a past injustice. Importantly, he also observes that the widespread occurrence of historical wrongs does not necessarily becloud all current holdings. For example, if on various past occasions *A* stole from *B*, *B* from *C*, *C* from *D*, and so on down to *Z*, but *nevertheless* *A* through *Z* all voluntarily bought Ford automobiles, then the arbitrary nature of the then-existing pattern of holdings "would not place Henry Ford's earnings under a cloud" (*ASU*, 158).[16]

Nozick also quips that regardless of the extent of past injustices, "to introduce socialism as the punishment for our sins would be to go too far" (*ASU*, 231). Finally, since *ASU* was published more than 36 years ago, and since the Great Society programs were conceived as rectification for the evils of slavery and other injustices, perhaps the more-than-minimal state has already reached its sell-by date. An added complication, not discussed by Nozick, is the possibility that programs designed to effect rectification may actually harm the intended beneficiaries.[17]

From our perspective, the essential points regarding Nozick's remarks on the principle of rectification are: (i) it cannot, consistently with his other

principles, justify taking property from persons who did not benefit from
and whose ancestors could not plausibly be accused of benefiting from past
depredations and (ii) that any required restitution would not call into question the *institution* of private property. In other words, once the appropriate
recompense is made, persons would have plenary rights over their property,
including the right to bequeath it, and the Entitlement Theory would sanction the huge inequalities in wealth that would inevitably result.[18] Finally,
although not addressed by Nozick, it seems intuitively obvious that the normative force of any demand for rectification diminishes with the number
of generations intervening between the occurrence of the injustice and the
time the wrong is addressed.[19]

The Entitlement Theory versus Patterned Principles of Justice

As noted above, the Entitlement Theory considers only the circumstances
under which property was originally acquired and transferred in evaluat-
ing the justice of any distribution of holdings. Thus, Nozick refers to it is a
historical principle. In contrast, a theory that evaluates a distribution on the
basis of its structure (who holds how much of what), without regard to how
it arose, is based on *end-results* or *end-state* principles (see *ASU*, 153–5). As a
criterion of distributive justice, utilitarianism is an example of an end state
principle since it looks only at whether the *existing* distribution could be
rearranged to produce greater utility.

Nozick makes one more critical distinction before launching his assault
on competitors to the Entitlement Theory. He refers to any theory of justice "that specifies that a distribution is to vary along with some natural
dimension" as a *patterned* principle (*ASU*, 156); that is, it seeks to enforce
some optimal arrangement of holdings. The allocation of wealth according
to the number of a person's good deeds is an example of a patterned, historical principle, because it would distribute according to past conduct. An
arrangement reflecting the principle that the richest person in society may
not hold "X" times more wealth than the poorest, is a patterned, end-state
principle, since it looks only at current holdings.

All theories of social justice that impose an egalitarian constraint on holdings are patterned. The Entitlement Theory is historical and unpatterned,
as it considers only the circumstances under which holdings arise and is
uninterested in their structure (see *ASU*, 155–7). We now turn to Nozick's
arguments against patterned theories of justice.

The Wilt Chamberlain, "taxation as forced labor" arguments, and inheritance

Nozick's most famous argument against egalitarianism involves the late, great, college and professional basketball player, Wilt Chamberlain (see *ASU*, 160–3). Imagine, he says to his philosophical adversaries, a distribution of resources that satisfies your ideal (perhaps everyone has approximately the same level of wealth). Now, imagine further that someone like Wilt arrives on the scene and offers to play basketball for a particular team in exchange for a $.25 payment per fan per game (to be added to the ticket price, which apparently was *much* lower back then). If his fans are willing to pay this surcharge, over the course of his career Wilt will become very wealthy.

How, Nozick asks, can a distribution considered just at time *T* become unjust at *T* + *1* as a result of a series of *voluntary* exchanges? Do Wilt's fans not have the right to see him play, or is it somehow immoral for Wilt to charge for this privilege? Since both parts of this exchange seem benign, he asserts that an egalitarian pattern can only be maintained by the state through a "continuous [and pernicious] interference with people's lives" (*ASU*, 163), i.e. by prohibiting Wilt from selling his services or by continuously taking from Wilt and redistributing to the ticket-buyers. Thus, in Nozick's memorable phrase, "the socialist society would [in order to preserve its character] have to forbid capitalist acts between consenting adults" (ibid.).

For Nozick, Wilt's claim to his basketball income ultimately rests on the idea of the inviolability of persons, i.e. on the concept of side constraints defended in Chapter 1. The state is using Wilt (and all other individuals subject to redistributive taxation) solely as a means of achieving some greater good. Such manipulation interferes with Wilt's rational agency because it coercively allows others to determine what will be done with the value created by his labor; it makes them figuratively a "part-owner" of Wilt (see *ASU*, 172).

In addition to the Wilt Chamberlain scenario, Nozick argues for capitalist property rights in a second way, i.e. his provocative claim that "taxation of earnings from labor is on a par with forced labor" (*ASU*, 169). Nozick invites us to imagine two people working similar jobs for comparable pay. One prefers to work overtime to earn the additional income required to buy "luxury" goods, while the other foregoes this opportunity in favor of leisure, which he devotes to nature walks and other activities that he can undertake with little or no expense.

Nozick's point is that there is something morally perverse about a system that gives the nature-lover a free pass to enjoy his leisure, while interfering with his colleague's pursuit of material possessions through the imposition of additional taxation. If anything, shouldn't the state be encouraging hard work? If it would be wrong for the state to compel the nature lover to give up some of his free time in order to build housing projects or otherwise advance the cause of what is called social justice, how then, asks Nozick, "can it be legitimate for a tax system to seize some of a man's goods for that purpose?" (*ASU*, 170). Confiscating either a person's time *or* his property violates the side constraint against using individuals purely as a resource for others.

Nozick is not claiming that taxation is the moral *equivalent* of (say) being forced to make bricks without straw in the hot sun under the lash of Pharaoh's taskmasters. Nozick acknowledges that he is unsure whether his claim is the strong one that taxation "is one kind of" forced labor or the weaker one that taxation is so similar to forced labor that "it is plausible and illuminating to view such taxation in the light of forced labor" (*ASU*, 169n). Because I believe it is more defensible, I read Nozick's claim to be closer to the latter idea, i.e. that a non-consensual income tax and forced labor are "on a par" because they are illegitimate for the same reason. We return to this argument later in this chapter.

Nozick has one final point to make against patterned principles of justice, at least insofar as they are invoked against the institution of inheritance.[20] This practice arouses particular hostility in liberal-minded philosophers, because, among other reasons, the recipients have done nothing to deserve the bequest.

However, Nozick argues that our focus should not be on the merits of the beneficiaries, for what is at stake is the right of the holder to bequeath. Few ordinary people would challenge a person's right to dispose of her justly acquired wealth as she wishes during her lifetime, including by gift or by expenditures we would consider self-indulgent, foolish, or wasteful (which brings to mind this old witticism: "I spent most of my money on fast women, fast cars, and booze, the rest...I *wasted*"). If the wealthy have the right to give away or dissipate their wealth, surely, says Nozick, they have the right to pass it on to their children (see *ASU*, 168).

The egalitarian response to the Wilt Chamberlain argument

"Qualified entitlement" arguments

Philosophers sympathetic to egalitarian conceptions of justice have reacted to the Wilt Chamberlain argument with a variety of objections, none of which can, in my opinion, withstand careful scrutiny. While it is obviously impossible to review all such critiques here, two of the most commonly heard are considered below.

One stream of criticism seeks to undermine the force of the Wilt Chamberlain scenario by contesting one of Nozick's key assumptions, i.e. that the imagined distribution in place prior to Wilt's arrival necessarily entails "full capitalist property rights." As Thomas Nagel correctly observes, if persons hold their property under a system of "qualified entitlement," then "what someone holds under such a system will not be *his property* in the unqualified sense of Nozick's system of entitlement. To suppose otherwise is to beg the question."[21] Thus, if his fans do not have absolute title to their property they cannot transfer such rights to Wilt. If all property comes with "strings attached," the state can pull such strings as it sees fit.

Notice first that Nozick sets up the Wilt Chamberlain argument by inviting his philosophical opponent to imagine any "distribution" he considers just, suggesting that, "perhaps everyone has an equal share" (*ASU*, 160). Clearly, Nozick understands "distribution" to mean a pattern of holdings where each party fully owns his share, whatever that happens to be. Therefore, what Nagel proposes is not a distribution as specified by Nozick, but an entirely different theory of property ownership.

Also recognize that for Nagel's system of qualified property ownership to block Nozick's argument, it must be the case, somehow, that Wilt's fans can *never* obtain full capitalist property rights to their resources, even after paying whatever taxes or other obligations are owed. Otherwise, Wilt would demand these "unencumbered" funds in exchange for his services, and Nozick's argument would proceed as intended.

Thus, while Nagel has cleverly found a way to short-circuit the Wilt Chamberlain argument, he does so only by ignoring the challenge (quoted above) posed by Nozick in anticipation of efforts of this sort. That is, those proposing a non-Lockean account of property acquisition, conferring less than complete ownership, must explain how such a system might arise, how these qualified rights came to be held by the state or whatever group enjoys them, the nature of such rights, and so forth. Here, beyond, simply imagining a system of "qualified entitlement" to property, Nagel has nothing to say.

Without an explanation of how a qualified form of property ownership might actually arise in the pre-political world, we are entitled to doubt that it could occur without gross violations of basic rights. At the minimum, we would want to know why talented, hard-working and/or ambitious people would ever agree to such a disadvantageous arrangement and, absent consent, how it could possibly be regarded as just? Not coincidentally, one of the primary criticisms Nozick levels against John Rawls's highly influential

A Theory of Justice is its failure to provide a plausible answer to this very question (see *ASU*, 192–7).

Nagel is right to point out that for purposes of the Wilt Chamberlain argument Nozick simply assumes the existence of unconditional property ownership; however, he does so only after providing an account of how such rights could have justly arisen from a state of nature. Certainly Nagel is entitled to posit an alternative system of property ownership, but if his system is manifestly unjust then it cannot stand as a barrier to Wilt's innocent accumulation of wealth in the manner envisioned in Nozick's argument. Accordingly, I believe that Nagel owes us more than the mere suggestion that people might hold their assets in some qualified manner. In the following chapter we consider more substantial criticisms of the Lockean model of original acquisition, perhaps motivated by the difficulty I have described in Nagel's argument.

The above discussion highlights the continuing relevance of Locke's account of original appropriation, even in light of the fact that our holdings have clearly been shaped by a long and sordid history of unjust wars, aggression, theft, and fraud. The operative question is what baseline assumption regarding the structure of current ownership is most credible in the face of our collective ignorance regarding the full history of much of our property? The Locke/Nozick model shows that it is *possible* to generate capitalist property rights from an entrepreneurial process that does not violate the rights of innocent third parties. In the absence of a plausible competing account of how collective or public ownership of property can justly arise from a state of nature, the first *morally legitimate* property owners must have acquired their resources by the Lockean method (there existing no other means of doing so).[22]

If the original appropriators of external assets obtained capitalist rights to their property, they would then have been in a position to bestow such rights on their descendents or transferees, who could do the same, up until the present day. Even if we somehow rectified all the past injustices that have infected current holdings, we would still end up where we started, i.e. in a world of robust property rights that would preclude the sorts of redistributions favored by egalitarians. This is why the subject of original appropriation remains controversial, as we shall see in the next chapter.

Does Wilt's wealth wrongfully harm others?

In addition to the line of attack developed by Nagel, some liberal-minded philosophers have taken issue with Nozick's assumption that voluntary transfers to Wilt by his fans do not violate the moral rights of other innocent people. Jonathan Wolff voices a fear that if the Wilt Chamberlains of the world are allowed to freely sell their services and exploit their talents and entrepreneurial spirit, a "class of people will emerge who, for example, can raise house prices through speculative buying, and lower wages by forming cartels."[23]

The first point I wish to make is that Wolff's argument is a member of a larger class of claims commonly raised against libertarianism to the effect that it is implausible because it would countenance unacceptable consequences, i.e. people "starving in the streets" rather than taxing the well-off to provide relief. Now, if libertarianism had this implication (or other catastrophic ones) this would certainly reduce its appeal, but for the reasons articulated in Chapter 6 I do not believe that this is so. I will, therefore, defer the discussion of this "macro" issue until then.

With respect to the specific, less horrendous examples raised by Wolff, the threat presented by capitalist greed seems wildly overblown. The short answer to Wolff's concern regarding wage-suppressing cartels is that they cannot long survive in a society governed by rigorous *laissez-faire* principles. In such circumstances, employers outside of the cartel would lure away the conspirators' most productive workers by offering them higher (free market) wages, rendering the cartel members vulnerable to domestic or foreign competitors. While it is true that capitalism does permit the formation of speculative bubbles in a variety of asset classes, including residential real estate, these bubbles invariably burst (as we have just witnessed), thus permitting savers and prudent investors to buy such goods at bargain prices.

There is, however, a larger point that needs to be made in response to Wolff. There are a great many actions that my fellow humans may take that may injure me in some way, but which clearly do not amount to a moral wrong. Imagine that I am a passionate art collector, and have been enthralled by a certain painting for decades. Finally, it comes up for auction at Sotheby's, and I bid more than I can really afford to acquire it. Sadly, a filthy rich parvenu, with no appreciation for this masterpiece as anything other than a vehicle for financial speculation, outbids me. Clearly, my rival has harmed me in some way, but no one could reasonably believe that I have suffered an *injustice*.

Nozick has his own example. He asks us to imagine a situation where 26 men and 26 women each desire to marry (perhaps for ease of exposition Nozick has populated this microcosm with only "straights"):

For each sex, all of that sex agree on the same ranking of the twenty-six members of the opposite sex in terms of desirability as marriage partners: call them A to Z and A' to Z' respectively in decreasing preferential order. A and A' voluntarily choose to get married, each preferring the other to any other partner. B would most prefer to marry A', and B' would most prefer to marry A, but by their choices A and A' have removed these options. When B and B' marry, their choices are not made nonvoluntary merely by the fact that there is something else they each would rather do. (*ASU*, 263)

In short, the fact that when it comes Z's turn to choose, all the more desirable mates are taken, may be unfair in a cosmic sense—perhaps his rivals do not *deserve* their priority in the pecking order—but this does not render the 25 preceding marriages unjust. Regrettably, Z is just out of luck.

It is not clear, then, why the fact that unfettered capitalism may frustrate people's designs or injure them in some way should count against it. In Nozick's terms, voluntary arrangements that affect third parties but do not violate their rights simply "fix the external environment of any given individual and the means that will be available to him" (*ASU*, 238). Of course, we might see things differently if Wolff were able to articulate a moral theory that would convincingly establish a *right* not to be harmed by other people's choices in the circumstances he describes (e.g. real estate speculation) while exonerating choices that we think individuals are entitled to make, i.e. marrying the more desirable mates. But he does not.

As we noted in Chapter 1, Nozick was harshly criticized by liberal-minded philosophers for supposedly advocating "libertarianism without foundations," so it seems only fair to demand of proponents of positive rights (e.g. to purchase a home at a price not inflated by speculators) that they explain the source of such rights and describe their content with some specificity. As discussed briefly below, serious challenges await any such effort.

In addition to the inherent difficulties (seen in Chapter 1) involved in founding any theory of justice, a theory of positive rights faces, I believe, an additional obstacle. One apparent disadvantage of the positive rights conception relative to its negative counterpart is that it must seemingly countenance conflicting claims of right. Most basically, negative rights may be thought of as a universal compact to the effect of "you don't interfere with me or my property and I won't interfere with you or your property." In contrast, positive rights will almost certainly conflict with negative ones, e.g. the right of the needy to welfare will clash with the property rights of the well off.

Moreover, positive rights may themselves be irreconcilable. Imagine a three-person world where A is comparatively well off while B and C are impoverished. *A* has sufficient "excess" resources that, if confiscated, could pull *B* or *C* out of poverty, but not both. If we took more from *A*, he himself would be cast into poverty, and due to the specific nature of *B* and *C*'s needs, any assistance short of the full amount of *A*'s surplus will be useless (perhaps they each desperately need enough cash to purchase a certain machine). Clearly, *B* and *C*'s welfare rights cannot both be satisfied.[24]

Hillel Steiner, one of the first philosophers to explore in depth the problem of conflicting right claims, has written that "the mutual consistency—or compossibility—of all the rights in a proposed set of rights is at least a necessary condition of that set being a possible one."[25] Moreover, the compossibility of a proposed system of rights is "itself a necessary condition of the plausibility of whatever principle of justice generates that set."[26] While Steiner's thesis that any plausible principle of justice must yield a compossible set of rights is certainly controversial, it seems intuitively compelling that, all things being equal, we should at a minimum *prefer* a theory of justice that produces a mutually compatible set of rights over one that does not. It also seems inescapable that a theory of justice built on negative rights will have an easier time satisfying this condition than one emphasizing positive ones.[27]

The liberal response to the "taxation as on a par with forced labor" argument

The reaction of left-leaning philosophers to Nozick's "taxation of income as usefully analogous to forced labor" argument has been no warmer than the reception given his Wilt Chamberlain scenario. Critics have focused on the literal differences between taxation and forced labor, while glossing over the broader implications of the analogy. Thus they have argued that (i) work done subject to a regime of progressive taxation allows the individual to control how much tax he will pay by deciding how much work to perform, which is not true of forced labor and (ii) in contrast to forced labor, the system of progressive taxation permits the worker "a measure of choice as to the nature of the activity at which they work, and who in particular employs them."[28]

It is certainly true that a system of progressive taxation does not compel the taxpayer to work as slave labor in a Stalin-era gulag, but this is not the only form of "forced labor" offensive to our moral principles. By imposing an income tax, the state in effect makes the worker a simple "offer he can't refuse." For example, consider a system that imposes a 33 percent marginal rate on all income above the subsistence level, with the receipts to be used for purposes of social justice.

The state is demanding that for every three hours worked (above that number required to achieve a modest income), it receive the proceeds from one. The worker derives no financial benefit from this labor, so it seems fair to regard it as having been taken from him. If you resist this arrangement, the government will send IRS agents with guns to seize your property. Clearly, there is an element of "force" present in this system. Thus the libertarian argument: labor taken by force equals "forced labor."

As noted above, critics have argued that progressive taxation differs from forced labor in that the worker can control the level of tax "pain" inflicted by the state by working fewer hours. But on this logic, a special tax imposed only on Jews would not be unjust if the victims were permitted to convert to Christianity and thus avoid the tax. Any coercive arrangement that forces individuals to choose between two unjust alternatives, i.e. earning only a subsistence level of income (thus escaping the tax) or submitting to an involuntary taking, is illegitimate (see *ASU*, 169).

The second difference claimed to separate progressive taxation from forced labor is that in the former case the worker gets to decide where and how he will work, while the worst forms of "forced labor" (e.g. manual labor at the point of a gun) deprive him of this freedom. This point is true so far as it goes, but it is insufficient to deflect Nozick's argument.

Remember, he does not claim that redistributive taxation is forced labor, but that it *is on a par with* this practice. Consider the following two cases: a petty scam that cheats a person out of $20 and a sophisticated financial fraud that cheats a person out of $2,000,000, representing his entire life savings. Both actions involve the intentional use of deception to steal a person's property. Nevertheless, even though both schemes are wrong for the same reason, the perpetrators are not equally culpable because the impact on one victim is far more pernicious than on the other.

Similarly, forced labor and compulsory taxation are both objectionable because they involve the imposition of the will of others (acting through the state) on morally sovereign agents. The former may be less evil than the later, but Nozick's argument does not depend on establishing their moral equivalence, only their commonality. While those subject to redistributive taxation remain in control of the logistics of their labor, some of its value is stolen from them and they lose control of how it will be used, which may well be in ways that deeply offend them. Accordingly, Nozick's philosophical adversaries fail to discredit the analogy between taxation and forced labor.

Notice that liberals cannot escape the force of Nozick's argument by altering the form of the tax. A *per capita* tax levied for redistributive purposes would be if anything even worse, perhaps "on a par with" armed robbery, since even the mitigating factors cited above would not apply.

It may be thought that by construing redistributive taxes as constituting a coercive "offer the worker can't refuse," and then condemning this forced choice, I am inadvertently opening the door for parallel attacks on the morality of practices that libertarians would defend, such as "sweatshop" employment and "price gouging" during emergencies. For example, perhaps the employer who takes advantage of an imbalance in the supply and demand for labor in his market by offering bare subsistence wages is compelling a similarly impermissible choice. But there is a simple and decisive rebuttal to this claimed analogy.

As Matt Zwolinski argues, whatever our evaluation of the conduct of the "exploitative" employer or price gouger, there can be no accusation that they are making the workers or purchasers worse off than they would otherwise be.[29] Whatever the background circumstances, the "victimized" workers and consumers must believe that what is offered them is better than their next best alternative, or they would refuse the job or not purchase the goods. In contrast, the person forced to pay taxes for the so-called greater good would benefit if the Tax Man just disappeared. Therefore, the proposed analogy is unpersuasive.

From the libertarian perspective, an interesting implication of Zwolinski's argument is that the use of sweatshop labor and price gouging are not morally objectionable because they lack the necessary element of *coercion*. If the supposed "victims" of the exploitative employer or the price gouger are not made worse off than under the status quo, which they are free to retain, then they are not being involuntarily compelled to do anything.

Inheritance

We are now in a position to consider one of the great *bête noires* of the left: the institution of inheritance. As noted above, Nozick (and libertarians generally) defend this practice on the grounds that a holder, provided he has complied with the principles of justice in acquisition and transfer, can do with his property what he wants, including giving it away or passing it on to his children. Philosophical objections to inheritance typically take the form of arguments (i) that the institution produces a dangerous "concentration of wealth" that harms the less powerful groups in our society,[30] (ii) that the violation of a deceased person's wishes stands on a different moral footing than the violation of a living person's desires[31] or (iii) that it results in arbitrary inequalities in the starting positions of future generations.[32]

The first argument is purely consequentialist, and not convincing even on its own terms. As shown in Chapter 1, the moral force of side constraints outweighs bad outcomes, and here the alleged consequences are vague and speculative. Because heirs have heirs, the number of individuals sharing the initial inheritance tends to expand geometrically with each new generation, thus dispersing their wealth over time.

Moreover, it appears that in the contemporary United States most great fortunes are not dynastic, but created "from scratch," thereby diluting the power of "old money."[33] Even assuming that inheritance concentrates wealth in the hands of a relative few, many of these "trust fund babies" turn out to be "enemies" of their class, e.g. the Kennedy clan, Jay Rockefeller, and countless others. Thus, a "balance of power" is maintained in politics and the marketplace of ideas.

Finally, Hayek has made a persuasive case that the concentration of great wealth in a relatively few hands actually benefits society by allowing these individuals the means to promote the cause of unpopular, "radical" ideas and institutions.[34] Thus, in nineteenth-century America wealthy eccentrics, including Arthur and Lewis Tappan, financed the abolitionist movement and another idle capitalist, Henry Bergh, founded the Society for the Prevention of Cruelty to Animals.

The second argument, i.e. that deceased persons' wishes stand on a different moral footing than those of the living, has been prominently advanced in several places by Hillel Steiner. He accepts that the power to make gifts (of justly acquired property) is "an unimpeachable incident of natural property rights," but seeks to distinguish bequests from gifts. He does so by claiming that an "exchange of correlatives" is a necessary condition for any effective transfer of ownership, either by sale or *inter vivos* donation.

He explains an exchange of correlatives as follows:

> When Red transfers the title of an object O to Blue, he thereby transfers to her (with her agreement) the rights and powers he held against Blue with respect to O. His right that Blue not interfere with his possession of O is replaced by her right that Red not interfere. Correlatively, Blue's duty not to interfere is transferred to Red. Blue is released from a previous restriction on her conduct and Red, as vendor or donor, acquires a corresponding restriction.[35]

While gifts clearly satisfy this condition, bequests, says Steiner, do not. The latter can only take effect at the testator's death and because the deceased cannot, for obvious reasons, exchange his/her rights and duties with the beneficiary in the necessary way, testamentary transfers are ineffective. Since the testator did not validly transfer his/her interest, society is free to redistribute it.[36]

While I endorse the idea that all rights imply a corresponding duty on the part of someone else, the premise that all duties necessarily correlate with rights held by other (living) people is less plausible. This seems quite clear at the intuitive level. Would we really look with equanimity at a son who promises his mother that he will bury her next to her deceased husband, and then dishonors his word in order to save a few bucks on cremation? Thus, even if a deceased testator no longer is in a position to enforce her intent, it does not follow that we have no duty to respect it.

A second response to Steiner's argument, suggested by Peter Jones, is to consider its plain implications.[37] Suppose *A* makes an irrevocable written gift of certain property ("X") to *B*, effective at *A*'s death, and notifies *B* of his good fortune. The irrevocable feature of the gift means that *A* has transferred to *B* certain rights with respect to X (and assumed certain duties), thus satisfying Steiner's "exchange of correlatives" test. Therefore, on Steiner's account, this gift should be effective, even though *A* continues to enjoy the use of his property during his lifetime. Steiner in effect acknowledges this by conceding that an *irrevocable* bequest would for his purposes be the same as an immediate gift (and thus effective).[38]

On the other hand, according to Steiner, if *A* purports to transfer X to *B* by a typical (*revocable*) testamentary bequest, and then dies, his intent should be ignored because *A could have* changed his will (although he did not), and thus there is no binding exchange of correlatives. I suggest that on its face this outcome is arbitrary and counterintuitive because there is no apparent connection between our willingness to respect *A*'s intent and his theoretical ability to revoke his will. Moreover, Steiner's argument is pointless. If irrevocable gifts (and bequests) are morally permissible while testamentary transfers are not (and accordingly are nullified under the law), wealthy people will do the former in place of the latter, and still enjoy the use of their property up until their demise.

The third argument against inheritance, that it represents an unfair, arbitrary advantage for its beneficiaries, brings us back to the distinction between cosmically unfair outcomes and unjust actions that we discussed above with respect to Nozick's marriage lottery. While inheritance may represent an undeserved financial windfall to the testator's offspring, it violates no person's moral rights, and so is not unjust. Accordingly, it is not a proper subject of state action.

Furthermore, while the practice of inheritance may confer an unmerited *financial* advantage on some, inherited wealth is at most only one of countless considerations that may provide an edge in living the good life, however this is precisely understood. In fact, it should surprise no one if "trust fund babies" generally grow up to be *less* happy than your "typical" child. Given that those born to great wealth have no need to *earn* a living, they are often deprived of the self-respect that comes from doing so. This in turn can result in a variety of self-destructive behaviors. I cite the recent generations of the Kennedy clan as "State's Exhibit A" in this case.

In light of the above, none of the standard criticisms of the institution of inheritance have shown it to be unjust.

The Normative Force of the Entitlement Theory

Nozick clearly believes that the Entitlement Theory strikes a decisive blow against egalitarian theories of justice:

> There are particular rights over particular things held by particular persons, and particular rights to reach agreements with others, *if* you and they can acquire the means to reach an agreement...No rights exist in conflict with the substructure of particular rights...The particular rights over things fill the space of rights, leaving no room for general rights to be in a certain material condition. The reverse theory would place only such universally held general "rights to" achieve goals or to be in a certain material condition into its substructure so as to determine all else; to my knowledge no serious attempt has been made to state this "reverse" theory. (*ASU*, 238)

In other words, in the real world we are not dealing with, in Nozick's phrase, "manna from heaven" to which egalitarian principles might usefully be applied (*ASU*, 198). Rather, things exist because people produce them and are held by persons who have acquired them in voluntary transactions. Therefore, these goods are not available for redistribution as they are already spoken for. Is Nozick right, i.e. does his theory "crowd out" competing conceptions of justice?

We must start by reviewing what Nozick thinks he has shown. Critically, he believes that he has established that even if the distribution of natural endowments is random, persons are nevertheless *entitled* to them and to what flows from them. His confidence is based on two different strands of argumentation. First, he appeals to our moral intuitions by means of a counterexample to the claim that we are only morally vested in things we deserve. Thus, while we did nothing to merit the healthy internal organs we were born with, we feel deeply that it nevertheless would be wrong for other persons or the state to compel us to give up a spare kidney, even to save the life of another person (see *ASU*, 206–7).

Nozick clearly thinks this example generalizes. So, he says, if my future wife prefers me to another suitor because of my (undeserved) good looks and intelligence, am I nevertheless not entitled to her love? Should society, in order to correct this putative injustice, subsidize the rejected swain's plastic surgery and (were it practical) intelligence-enhancing classes? (See *ASU*, 237).

Moreover, suppose there are two equally competent dry cleaners in my immediate neighborhood, charging identical prices. For no discernible reason, I use only one of them. Is the owner of this business not entitled to the profits from my patronage, even though he is only "deserving" of half? (See *ASU*, 223).

The general point here, which seems intuitively sound, is that we must distinguish between *injustice*, which is a man-made phenomenon, and the randomness of the cosmos, which may produce results that strike us as unfortunate or unfair. For example, some wicked people live to ripe old age, while many of the righteous are cut down in their prime. And, for no discernable reason, women on average live materially longer than men. Yet, while we may regard such things as arbitrary or regrettable, this reaction is qualitatively different than what we experience upon encountering deliberate cruelty inflicted on one human being by another. Thus, as Hayek observed well in advance of Nozick, "justice, like liberty and coercion is a concept which, for the sake of clarity, ought to be confined to the deliberate treatment of men by other men."[39]

The crucial fact is that those blessed with superior natural endowments did not steal them from the less fortunate. This distribution is simply the product of what Rawls calls a "natural lottery."[40] Since no one is responsible for this distribution it cannot represent an injustice against the less talented. Accordingly, we are compelled to respect the side constraint against coercing innocent persons. While society is obligated to rectify (within certain limits) the evils committed by Man, we have no comparable mandate to take on Mother Nature.[41]

Secondly, Nozick argues that even if justified entitlements must be related to desert in some way, it need not be the case, as he famously expresses it, "that the foundations underlying desert are themselves deserved *all the way down*" (*ASU*, 225). The essence of Nozick's idea is easily captured by an example. Lieutenant Smith may have landed in Normandy on D-Day only because his father secured his admission to West Point by corrupt means, but the fact that Smith didn't deserve his spot in the landing craft doesn't suggest that he was undeserving of the medals he received for heroism during the campaign.

Subject to this clarification, there is good reason to conclude that holdings derived from voluntary transactions are deserved in the morally relevant way. While genetic factors may shape our lives in various ways, we commonly believe that character plays an even more decisive role, and that we are responsible for it. If we do not ordinarily think that people are responsible for their personal qualities, then why do parents commonly advise their children to "make something of yourself" and where did we get the expression a "self-made man"?

Nevertheless, some egalitarians follow Rawls and deny that individuals *are* responsible for their character:

> The assertion that a man deserves the superior character that enables him to make the effort to cultivate his abilities is equally problematic; for his character depends in large part upon fortunate family and social circumstances for which he can claim no credit. The notion of desert seems not to apply to these cases.[12]

However, this move does not appear to be a promising one for egalitarians since, as argued above, it flies in the face of our commonsense understanding of human nature.

Thus, given our commitment to conventional notions of responsibility and desert, proponents of patterned theories of justice face the dilemma described by John Kekes:

> If [egalitarians] acknowledge that people are partly responsible for the property they have, then they must agree with the anti-egalitarian claim that it is morally unacceptable to equalize the property of responsible and irresponsible people. If egalitarians insist that individual responsibility makes no difference in deciding what property people should have, then they are committed to the morally unacceptable policy of depriving good, prudent and law-abiding people of their legally owned property in order to give it to others, even if they are bad, imprudent and criminal.[13]

The logic of Nozick's position now becomes clear. The random distribution of natural endowments is not unjust, and we have no warrant to ameliorate the inevitable results thereof. Moreover, the distribution of holdings under *laissez-faire* capitalism is deserved in the morally relevant sense, even if not "all the way down," and therefore is not suspect even under a more stringent interpretation of the demands of justice.

Thus, there is no short step from the premise that the distribution of natural talents and therefore of wealth is sub-optimal according to some patterned principle of justice to the conclusion that we have a warrant to employ coercion to effect conformity. It is in this way that the Entitlement Theory presents a formidable barrier to the relevance of egalitarian prescriptions. As David Schmitz puts it, "To establish that you have a right to distribute, what we need to show is not that what you want to do with the goods is *fair*. Rather, we need to show that the goods you want to distribute are yours to distribute."[44]

However, we cannot discount out of hand the possibility that liberal-minded philosophers might be able to derive egalitarian principles of justice from even more fundamental or compelling considerations than those relied upon by Nozick. Rawls's *A Theory of Justice* represents such an effort, employing the idea of an imagined, ideal social contract negotiated by suitably impartial persons. Because of its great influence, Nozick devotes a substantial portion of *ASU* to critiquing it. While Nozick makes, in addition to the arguments reviewed above, a number of telling points against *Theory*, it is unnecessary to rehearse them here. It is almost universally recognized among political philosophers that Rawls's project, although brilliant and original, is deeply flawed.[45]

Nozick also considers in *ASU* an argument for equality from Bernard Williams, another prominent philosopher, in his essay "The Idea of Equality."[46] Here, Williams asserts that certain types of activities have "internal goals" that dictate their purpose, e.g. "the proper ground of distribution of medical care is ill health: this is a necessary truth."[47] Since society has the resources to do so, we must pay for indigent medical care because "needs are the ground of the treatment."[48] To refuse, is to create "an irrational state of affairs."[49]

First, Williams' proposition does not appear to be a "necessary truth," since it can be denied without contradiction. It is not contradictory to hold that the proper ground for medical treatment is the ability to pay for it, or the need for it in combination with the ability to pay. If Williams' proposition is not necessarily true, then there is no "irrationality" in refusing to subsidize healthcare for the needy.

Secondly, Nozick points out that if Williams' claim is necessarily true, then it must also be necessarily true "that the only proper criterion for the distribution of barbering services is barbering need" (*ASU*, 234). But why, asks Nozick, can't the barber "cut the hair of only those who pay or tip well?" (Ibid.) Since we do not ordinarily think that society must pay for needy peoples' haircuts, the obvious question is why are medical services different.

Of course, medical care can often save lives while barbering does not, but there is no obvious connection between the importance of a particular activity and the existence or not of an "internal goal" for that practice. Moreover, as Nozick observes, the production of food is an essential activity, but Williams does not claim that farming has "an internal goal that refers to other people in the way that doctoring does" (ibid.). Thus, Nozick concludes,

> When the layers of Williams' arguments are peeled away, what we arrive at is the claim that society (that is, each of us acting together in some organized fashion) should make provision for the important needs of all its members. This claim, of course, has been stated many times before. Despite appearances, Williams presents no argument for it. Like others, Williams looks only to questions of allocation. He ignores the question of where the things or actions to be allocated and distributed come from. (*ASU*, 234–5 [footnote omitted])

It is worth noting that even Nagel, a prominent liberal philosopher, concedes that no effective argument has been put forward for what might be thought of as the most fundamental egalitarian assumption:

> To defend equality as a good in itself, one would have to argue that improvements in the lot of people lower on the scale of well-being take priority over greater improvements to those higher on the scale, even if the latter improvements affected more people. While I am sympathetic to such a view, I do not believe it has ever been successfully defended.[50]

Obviously, the fact that we have not yet encountered a convincing argument for egalitarian principles does not foreclose the possibility of one being formulated in the future. But, at a minimum, it will have to overcome the objections outlined above. In Chapter 6 we consider and reject one such recently developed justification for egalitarian redistribution.

Chapter 3

Critiques of Lockean Appropriation

A people averse to the institution of private property is without the first element of freedom.

Lord Acton, Nationality [1862][1]

As discussed in the previous chapter, the Entitlement Theory rests on the foundational assumption that there exists a just process by which unappropriated natural assets may be converted to private property. If, contrary to the arguments of the previous chapter, Lockean appropriation is pernicious, then the moral legitimacy of full capitalist property rights is thrown into doubt. A number of critics, occupying different positions along the ideological spectrum, have argued that the Lockean model is not persuasive. We turn to these objections below.

Property as a "Bundle of Rights"

One objection to the Lockean account of original acquisition arises out of the idea, developed by Wesley Hohfeld in the second decade of the twentieth century, that we should not regard the ownership of land as consisting of lawful physical possession, but in enjoying an assortment of rights that in their totality confer what we typically think of as "owner-ship."[2] Within the field of American property law, the "bundle of rights" analysis was thought necessary to describe the myriad of different ways that real property may be held.[3] According to this view, simply saying that Smith "owns" Blackacre does not paint a sufficiently accurate picture of his interest in this property if he has sold the mineral and riparian rights, leased the surface rights on a long-term basis, granted easements, and so forth.

Leif Wenar describes Hohfeld's basic insight as follows:

Most common rights, such as the right to free expression or the right to private property, have a complex internal structure. Such rights are ordered arrangements of several basic components—much in the same way that most molecules are ordered arrangements of several chemical elements... These four basic "elements" are the privilege, the claim, the power and the immunity. Each of these Hohfeldian incidents has a distinctive logical form; and each incident can be a right by itself, even when it is not a part of a complex "molecule."[4]

Loren Lomasky and Barbara Fried, among others, have argued that Hohfeld's insight poses a serious problem for the libertarian understanding of rights.[5]

I focus on Lomasky here because Fried's criticism is intended to show that the self-ownership thesis (see Chapter 1) does not generate a satisfying account of individual rights. As indicated above, Nozick relies on rational agency, rather than self-ownership, to ground moral rights, including property rights. Therefore, it seems to me that Fried's critique is applicable principally to the so-called left-libertarians, discussed below. In any case, to the extent that Fried's criticisms apply to the Entitlement Theory, my response would be along the same general lines as discussed below regarding Lomasky.

Turning then to Lomasky's objection to Lockean appropriation, he argues that, "the moral foundations of a theory of property become considerably more tenuous with the specialist's 'bundle of rights' than with an ordinary person's notion of owned things."[6] He continues, while "it is tolerably clear regarding how possession of *things* might be established," it "would seem a gross conceptual confusion to equate material things with bundles of rights."[7] Accordingly, "A theory that might adequately justify property *qua* things cannot be assumed similarly to justify claims to property *qua* bundle of rights."[8]

For the reasons outlined below I believe Lomasky has confused terminology with substantive moral theory. To see this, we must first recognize that Hohfeld's concept of property as "bundle of rights" gave birth merely to a new analytical vocabulary, a way of describing the various interests that may exist with respect to property. Thus, the jurists and attorneys who argued and made law prior to Hohfeld's seminal publication would have had no particular quarrel with the idea that rights in property could be decomposed into finer grained "incidents." It was simply that possession was then considered the defining aspect of ownership.

Hohfeld's taxonomy was useful to lawyers, judges, and academics because it offered a convenient way of describing the increasingly complex and creative divisions of ownership that were then occurring. His conception is neutral with respect to how rights might justly arise and whether particular rights claims are entitled to recognition. Such issues are the gist of moral and political philosophy.

Thus, as Wenar points out, in the Supreme Court's late-nineteenth-century jurisprudence "property" was understood in the traditional way, and the Court held that for the state to be guilty of a "taking" under the Constitution the owner had to be dispossessed of his "thing," his property.[9] However, the "bundle of rights" vocabulary opened the way for litigants to claim that while the state may not have actually confiscated their property, it destroyed one or more of the "sticks" comprising the overall bundle. If the "stick" destroyed by the state has an ascertainable value, then as more recently argued by Richard Epstein and other defenders of property rights, the owner of that "stick" is entitled to just compensation under the Takings Clause.[10]

However, left-leaning legal scholars have rejected this class of claims because it conflicts with their political philosophy. Accordingly, says Wenar, for those who view the legal system as a vehicle for promoting social justice, recognition of the claims of the property right-holder "is wholly dependent on whether the correct theory of justice requires that the act be compensated."[11] Thus, the use of the bundle of rights terminology does not commit the user to any general theory of justice regarding property.

The reason for this, of course, is that this vocabulary is descriptive, not prescriptive. As Arthur Ripstein observes,

> Critics of private property sometimes point to the 'bundle' analysis of property rights introduced by Hohfeld...Its strengths as an analysis of the concept of property remain controversial...Whatever its merits, however, it is of no help in addressing issues of the appropriate normative conception of property.[12]

Accordingly, some academics (including Wenar), have argued that we should abandon Hohfeld's thesis that property consists of a bundle of rights, while retaining his analytical vocabulary.[13]

Returning our focus to Nozick's principle of justice in acquisition, we must remember that he is describing the conditions that when satisfied are sufficient to establish a *moral* claim to property. Lomasky's argument, i.e. property as a bundle of rights, does not directly challenge the ethical foundations of the Lockean model with respect to "things." Rather, he objects to the assumption that appropriating in this manner would entitle one to the entire bundle of rights that we conventionally think of as constituting "ownership."

Frankly, I just fail to see how his argument gains traction. If I, having paid for them, possess a moral right to the six loaves of bread you have just baked, I have an equally compelling claim with respect to the same "half dozen" loaves. Why *wouldn't* we conclude that the same moral judgment that founds a claim to ownership of a thing applies to the cognate assortment of rights, particularly since Lomasky acknowledges that, "The only bundle of rights that can intuitively be *identified* with our ownership of a thing is the bundle that constitutes complete control over that thing" (my emphasis).[14]

The primary difficulty he sees in applying the Lockean account of just appropriation to a "bundle of rights" centers on the alleged problem of explaining how one obtains *less than* the full panoply of rights: "If picking up the acorn confers full rights concerning its disposition, what must one do to acquire the full bundle of rights *minus* the right to bequeath the acorn?"[15] I don't share his puzzlement.

One acquires less than full rights as a result of voluntary arrangements. For example, A wants B to help him clear, fence, and plant Blackacre. Accordingly, A and B agree that in exchange for B's help, B gets all mineral and riparian rights to this land. Provided that B fulfills his part of the bargain, A ends up with less than the full bundle. Lomasky appears to have missed this obvious explanation because he assumes that moral rights generally can only arise by social convention, i.e. that they cannot be justified on other grounds. But, I have attempted to show in Chapter 1 that Nozick is able to do so, and in any event Lomasky's competing account of moral rights as the product of "social determination" is not convincing.[16]

G. A. Cohen's Objections to Nozick's "Justice in Acquisition"

G. A. Cohen has pioneered one of the more influential strategies for undermining the moral legitimacy of full capitalist property rights in natural resources. His critique focuses on the condition, imposed by Locke and Nozick, that the privatization of resources existing in a state of nature does not worsen the condition of others. Cohen correctly notes that the "worse off" requirement is highly sensitive to the baseline used to compare the world in its "pre-owned" and privately owned states.

He then posits certain "public" ownership arrangements that he claims show that Lockean appropriation *does* make others worse off when compared to these baselines, and is thus unjust.[17] If this is so, then the Lockean model must be rejected. This in turn would mean that the Entitlement Theory's requirement of "justice in acquisition" can never be satisfied.

Accordingly, Cohen imagines a two-person world, in which there is a finite quantity of land. *A* and *B* survive by independently gathering agricultural products that grow wild on the unimproved land. Cohen specifies that both parties are equal in their ability to organize labor. In his scenario, *A* conceives of a division of labor that will increase the overall yield from the land, and on this basis appropriates all or most of it. Because of the advantages of this business model, *A* is able to offer *B* a salary (in foodstuffs) that slightly exceeds what he received when the land was unowned commons, while retaining a much greater "profit" for himself.[18]

Why, Cohen asks, should we measure the justice of *A*'s appropriation against the productivity of the land in its unowned state, rather than if *B* had appropriated and then offered *A* the same arrangement?[19] *A*'s appropriation does *not* increase the overall productivity of the common property compared to the situation that would exist if *B* acted first. Yet, says Cohen, it would be allowed to stand if tested under the Lockean model because it does not make *B* "worse off." We shall consider below the circumstance in which *B* is a less skillful organizer than *A*.

Cohen's point is that it seems unjust that *A* would be permitted to privatize under the Lockean paradigm simply because he acted first. Perhaps *B* refrained from privatizing "out of concern for *A*," i.e. he did not want to make him a wage-slave.[20] But, very simply, Cohen's scenario fails to pass muster under the Locke/Nozick model of initial ownership because *A* does not satisfy the development (or improvement) condition emphasized in Chapter 2.

Note first that *A's* putative appropriation differs from the typical procedure envisioned by Locke and Nozick, i.e. he is not claiming ownership of external assets by virtue of his having physically transformed them by means of labor-mixing. Rather, *A* is claiming them as a reward for the development of intellectual property, i.e. his new business model (which can only be implemented with *B*'s cooperation).[21] Accordingly, the key question is what is he thereby entitled to? As specified by Cohen, all *A* did was to suggest a division of labor that was or should have been apparent to both parties. In other words, he failed to *add value* to or *improve* the property in the requisite way, thus failing to satisfy the conditions of Lockean appropriation.

The moral intuition that a person (like *A*) should not be allowed to profit by excluding other people (like *B*) from using an "invention" that is not novel or original is enshrined in our patent law. Under this code, a patent will not issue for a claimed innovation that is *obvious* to one with "ordinary skill" in the relevant art (see *U.S. Code 35*, § 103). Plainly, if *B* were the *superior* organizer, *A* would have an even weaker case for taking the lion's share of the improved harvest under Cohen's scenario.

Having described to his satisfaction one situation (a world owned in common by *A* and *B*, who are equally competent organizers) where Lockean appropriation unfairly makes one party worse off relative to this baseline, Cohen now offers a second example. He claims that Nozick's "justice in acquisition" ignores another "intuitively relevant" view of the state of nature, i.e. that of joint ownership, where all external resources are

> owned by all together, and what each may do with it is subject to collective decision. The appropriate procedure for reaching that decision may be hard to define, but it will certainly not be open to any one of the joint owners to privatize all or part of the asset unilaterally, no matter what compensation he offers to the rest.[22]

If the world in its "virgin" state is jointly owned, then in Cohen's two-person world, *B* has an absolute veto right over any interaction between *A* and external resources. In a jointly owned world with *n* number of persons, there would be *n* number of veto rights over *A*'s appropriation.

Cohen argues that in a two-person, jointly owned world, a *B* who is less talented or energetic than *A* would do better than he would in a world of private property because of the leverage provided by his veto right. This right will enable *B* to negotiate a larger share of the "surplus" created by *A*'s appropriation than if *A* merely has to satisfy the "no worse off" condition. Cohen claims that since an ineffectual *B* will do better in a jointly owned world than he will under a form of ownership that permits the emergence of private property, Lockean appropriation unjustly makes *B* worse off.

However, we must understand that the less talented *B*'s leverage diminishes with each additional person we add to a jointly owned world, as other members of the collective will also have to be placated. Therefore, Cohen's two-person society artificially obscures the relative advantage that private property enjoys over joint ownership in producing societal welfare. In a primitive, collectively owned world of (say) only 10,000 people, neither *A* nor any other person would ever *attempt* to innovate, since the transaction costs and complexities involved in negotiating a satisfactory arrangement with 9,999 other veto-wielding persons would be prohibitive. Therefore, in this world *B* gains nothing by his veto right.

Thus, in a primitive world of 10,000 people governed by Cohen's version of collective ownership, *B* (and everyone else) would be hunting and gathering forever. On the other hand, if individual ownership rights characterize this world, persons would be motivated to innovate and others could copy any successful new technique. Since we live in a world much closer in population to my hypothetical rather than Cohen's, it would appear that mine is the more relevant model with which to evaluate the justice of private property.

There is, in any case, a far more profound problem with the Cohen's construct. As David Conway rightly observes (echoing Locke), such an arrangement would be tyrannical:

> It means that others have a legitimate life or death power over others, who are not posing threats to their own life. Such power over others, I submit, is excessive. No one has the right to forbid another individual to do what is necessary for that individual's survival, provided that what is necessary for that individual's survival falls short of killing someone who is not threatening that individual's survival.[23]

In a world where all human beings have veto rights over any transformation of material resources, a lone mega-suicide bomber would doom the entire human race. Since Cohen offers us no explanation of how such a despotic arrangement could have justly evolved from a state of nature or how it could endure, there is no reason why we should take this model seriously for purposes of testing the fairness of the Lockean model or otherwise.

In fact, Cohen acknowledges that he regards the concept of joint ownership not as a plausible depiction of the world, but as a "polemical" devise to be deployed against Nozick's view "that honouring people's self-ownership requires extending to them a freedom to live their own lives which is incompatible with the equality condition prized by socialists."[24] He acknowledges, that in a jointly owned world: "Self-ownership is not eliminated, but it is rendered useless, rather as it is useless to own a corkscrew, when you are forbidden access to bottles of wine."[25]

However, in his own version of the time-honored childhood defense of "yes, I ate the forbidden cookies, but my brother did too," Cohen asserts that any objection to the "merely formal" nature of self-ownership in a jointly owned world *"would for immediate polemical purposes be laid to rest, if it could be shown that the self-ownership defended by Nozick is itself merely formal."*[26] This argument has been highly influential amongst liberal theorists, so we will pay it appropriate attention.

Note initially that Cohen is incorrectly assuming that Nozick relies on self-ownership as the justification for capitalist property rights when in fact Kantian principles of autonomy are at the core of his argument. As explained in Chapter 1, our rational agency is vindicated when we are free from the coercion of others, whether directed against our person or property. Nevertheless, we will consider whether there is anything in Cohen's argument that might persuade us that respect for rational agency confers a freedom that is merely formal.

To demonstrate the evanescent nature of self-ownership under a regime of private property, Cohen cites the plight of "the most abject proletarian—call him Z—who must either sell his labour power to a capitalist or die" (footnote omitted).[27] According to Cohen, capitalism cripples Z's self-ownership to the same extent that joint-ownership neutralizes Able's [the more productive of the two persons in another of Cohen's jointly owned, veto-wielding worlds]. Thus, says Cohen, Nozick is in a bind since "[e]ither capitalism does not confer consequential self-ownership, since Z's self ownership is not robust enough to qualify as such; or, if it does so qualify, then genuine self-ownership allows the enforcement of equality of condition, since Able's self-ownership is at least as robust as Z's."[28]

If Cohen's point is simply that capitalism cannot *guarantee* a minimum level of welfare for all members of a community, and that this feature dooms it from the moral point of view, then I refer the reader to Chapter 6 where this argument is addressed in the context of more general objections to libertarianism. Therefore, I will consider here whether Cohen's specific comparison of Able and Z is illuminating in any other respect.

Unfortunately, the claimed parallelism rapidly dissolves under scrutiny. In a jointly owned world, coercion is a certainty since our every interaction with the material world is subject to the veto right of each member of the collective. To tweak W. H. Auden's famous line, we must appease one another or die. Thus, the "formality" of Abel's self-ownership (as far as we are concerned, his rational agency) in a jointly owned world is due to the fact that his autonomy is not respected.

In contrast, while Z is free to make whatever use he can of his human capital, this asset is apparently not worth much. Thus, the "formality" of Z's self-ownership (or rational agency) results from the nominal value of his labor and his inability to *force* others to provide for his needs. Howeve⸍ under the dire scenario that Cohen paints, Z is one job offer, gift o⸍ ⸍⸍⸍⸍, break away from having his self-ownership rights fully vindicated (since he would no longer be "abject"). Accordingly, Z's palsied self-ownership is contingent, possibly temporary and idiosyncratic, while the tyranny of joint ownership is necessary, permanent, and universal.[29]

In light of the disanalogies identified above, self-ownership (rational agency) under capitalism and in a jointly owned world are comparable only in the way that, as the cliché goes, an apple is like an orange. Therefore, it is not clear to me what mileage Cohen can get from this argument.

Finally, if capitalism is to be condemned because it *potentially* gives rise to abject Zs, then all other regimes of property ownership must also be evaluated under their "worst case" scenarios. This is because any meaningful moral judgment regarding a system of property ownership is inherently comparative. Otherwise, if full capitalist property rights are found to be unjust, but all competing structures are *worse*, we are forced to the bizarre conclusion that *no* manner of holding property, private or public, is morally legitimate. Therefore, capitalism cannot be condemned for potentially exploiting a few Zs unless Cohen can identify an alternative political/economic system that would produce fewer "abject Zs" without potentially offending rights we consider foundational. In sum, Cohen's attack on the justice of Lockean appropriation is unconvincing.

Left-libertarianism

Cohen's arguments against Lockean appropriation have greatly influenced another group of egalitarians, the "left-libertarians." These philosophers follow Cohen in attempting to show that absolute property rights *cannot* justly arise from a state of nature. If this is the case, then a shadow is cast on the legitimacy of all current holdings.

According to three of its best known proponents (Peter Vallentyne, Hillel Steiner, and Michael Otsuka), left-libertarians embrace "full initial self-ownership for all agents," understood as "roughly the *logically* strongest set of ownership rights over a thing that a person can have compatible with others having such rights over everything else."[30] They accept in principle the self-ownership thesis and a person's entitlement to their talents and the value of their labor, but hold that the external world is originally owned in a manner that does not permit persons to justly establish *unconditional* (capitalist) property rights. As Vallentyne/Steiner/Otsuka have jointly declared:

> Left-libertarianism holds that there is a very significant difference in the
> moral status of agents...and natural resources (resources that have no
> moral standing and which were created by no [non-divine] agent). About
> the former they maintain that full self-ownership is the most appropriate
> reflection of the status (e.g. because it explains/grounds the intuitive
> wrongness of various forms of non-consensual interference with bodily
> integrity), and about the latter they independently maintain that egalitar-
> ian ownership is the most defensible stance.[31]

With respect to the nature of the "egalitarian ownership" referenced
above, the left-libertarians accept that any concept of natural resource ownership that completely forecloses unilateral appropriation, such as Cohen's
jointly owned world, unduly restricts agents' freedom of action and is thus
implausible.[32] They hold that any credible variant will permit individuals to
justly privatize unappropriated resources by "pay[ing] to the members of
society their per capita share of the full competitive value (based on supply
and demand) of the rights that one claims."[33] As discussed more fully below,
Otsuka's derivation of the appropriators' social obligation differs from that
of Vallentyne's and Steiner's.

The left-libertarians hold a variety of differing views regarding the nature
and amount of the payment owed to the social fund. The most modest
proposal would require a relatively small payment representing the rental
that the owner would have had to pay, under competitive conditions, to
use private property during his or her lifetime.[34] At the other extreme, it
is asserted that appropriators owe the fund a payment equal to the above-
referenced rental rate *plus* taxes equal to the benefit they reap from the
appropriation.[35]

It must be understood that left-libertarians hold that even if today's owners
of natural resources have acquired them in apparently benign transactions,
the value of these assets *continues* to be subject to egalitarian redistribution.[36] Thus, Vallentyne/Steiner/Otsuka state that, "the egalitarian principle of justice in acquisition that [left-libertarians] endorse casts a shadow
over the legitimacy of claims of ownership by all subsequent generations."[37]
The general idea seems to be that since no one created the external world,
all humans are entitled to an equal share of the value of natural resources,
regardless of the timing and circumstances of their birth. Therefore, left-
libertarians generally reject the idea that egalitarian redistribution should
take place only within particular communities or states.[38]

Self-ownership under a left-libertarian regime

Our analysis of left-libertarianism will focus primarily on the implications of the claim that the earth was originally owned in some egalitarian fashion (or—per Otsuka—not owned at all, but subject to individual appropriation only upon the satisfaction of a stringent "egalitarian proviso"), since this idea directly threatens the justice of Lockean appropriation. In contrast, Nozickian libertarians do not disagree with left-libertarians regarding the fact of human self-ownership although, as discussed above, they do not attach great moral significance to it. However, two comments regarding the left-libertarian commitment to self-ownership appear to be warranted.

First, the left-libertarians do not argue for self-ownership in any extended way, but adopt it because it best explains, as quoted above, "the intuitive wrongness of various forms of non-consensual interference with bodily integrity." This is not the place for a full debate on this subject but, as outlined in Chapter 1, self-ownership is an inferior explanation for our rights, including those of bodily integrity, when compared to the concept of rational agency. I am aware of no discussion by the left-libertarians of the relative merits of rational agency and self-ownership as explanations of our instinctive commitment to bodily integrity.

Second, the left-libertarian commitment to self-ownership stands in obvious tension with their stance on egalitarian world-ownership. As will be explored in more depth below, they do not offer a specific account of how natural resources came to be owned in an egalitarian fashion, but rely on the truism that no person can claim credit for creating them. Since no one can claim credit, the "default" ownership arrangement should be egalitarian. Of course, this implies that if a person is responsible for creating some asset, then it is hers.

The problem is that, apart from our souls (assuming we have them), we consist of exactly the same material "stuff" as the external world, i.e. atoms, molecules, sub-atomic particles, and so on. While we can claim no credit for creating our bodies, our parents can. The question then naturally arises: why from the left-libertarian perspective do parents not own their children's bodies?[39] If parents own their children the way people own things, then it is difficult to discern the origins of any moral constraints on how they may treat them.

The idea that parents own their children is, I believe, deeply unattractive at the intuitive level. However, even if this unpleasant conclusion can be finessed by the left-libertarians in some way that is not obviously *ad hoc*, it would seem that, given their commitment to the principle of egalitarian world ownership, our bodies should (also) be owned in some collective fashion. If so, this would open the way to precisely the sorts of demands on persons that self-ownership is supposed to foreclose. Nothing said by any of the above-named left-libertarians, so far as I am aware, specifically explains *why* different rules should apply regarding the initial ownership of persons and the external world.[40]

As we have seen, the left-libertarians are drawn to self-ownership as the best explanation of why forced organ transplants, involuntary servitude and similar invasions of our bodily integrity are morally impermissible. Accordingly, they might argue that these intuitions justify the disparate ownership rights that apply to bodies and natural assets. However, it would seem that the question of whether an object can be owned in a particular way is logically *prior* to the question of how we would *like it* to be owned for purposes of preserving consistency with other moral presuppositions.

The left-libertarians make this precise point in arguing that their doctrine has potential conceptual advantages relative to other egalitarian strategies:

> Left-libertarians have a shared normative focus on natural rights of ownership in self and in world...Rawlsian liberal egalitarians, by contrast, share a normative focus on the question of the fair division of the fruits of social cooperation...Left-libertarians regard the question of the conditions under which natural resources may be acquired as prior to the question of the division of the fruits of social cooperation.[41]

Therefore, on their own logic, I do not believe that the left-libertarians are entitled to the assumption that our physical selves are *available* to be owned unconditionally by us.

Left-libertarianism and ownership of the external world

As noted above, the left-libertarians hold that natural resources are subject to some form of "egalitarian ownership" (or egalitarian proviso) that precludes their being reduced to private property without the payment of compensation (in some form) to society at large or to "under-appropriators."[42] Yet, no act of appropriation was required to establish this ownership; apparently, humanity's mere existence is sufficient. I believe there are several problems with this view.

First, as Edward Feser has ably pointed out, there is something markedly counterintuitive about the notion that we come to own things (or establish rights over things) in this way:

> Consider the following: a pebble resting uneasily on the surface of the
> asteroid Eros as it orbits the sun, a cubic foot of molten lava churning a
> mile below the surface of the earth, one of the polar icecaps on Mars...It
> would seem very odd in the extreme to claim that any particular indi-
> vidual owns any of these things. In what sense could Smith, for example,
> who like most of the rest of us has never left the surface of the planet or
> even sent a robotic spacecraft to Eros be said to *own* the pebble resting on
> its surface? But is it less odd to claim that we *all* own the pebble or these
> other things?[43]

Thus, I believe Feser is right to insist that, "the claim that we all own everything is more in need of justification than the claim that no one initially
owns anything."[44]

The closest thing to an account of egalitarian ownership of external
resources that I have encountered is a mere truism of the following sort
offered by Vallentyne: "no human agent created natural resources, and
there is no reason that the lucky person who first claims rights over natural
resources should reap all the benefit that the resource provides."[45] But this
explanation gives rise to at least two conceptual problems. First, notice that
Vallentyne fails to make any argument that would establish that the "lucky
person" should *not* "reap all of the benefit." Thus, we must rely on our
moral intuitions, which I claim are essentially Lockean on this point.

So, we do not create, i.e. we are not responsible for, the existence of our
healthy internal organs, our good looks or our native intelligence, yet we
regard them as *ours*. Moreover, if a small but valuable meteorite happens
to crash into Joe's backyard, I contend that most of us would instinctively
feel that it unconditionally belongs to him. The fact that no other person is
responsible for creating the meteorite is precisely the basis for the intuition
that it belongs to Joe, and not the other way around. In Lockean terms, the
moral foundation for this claim is the same as for wildly growing fruits and
berries, i.e. the simple act of finding them (through luck or otherwise) and
picking them is sufficient to confer rightful ownership.

Second, Vallentyne's account offers no explanation of *how* the world
came to be owned in an egalitarian fashion.[46] This point is, in my judgment,
quite significant. At the most basic level, we *understand* the idea of Lockean
appropriation. Even if we are uncertain about its details or the moral deci-
siveness of this account, it is clear to us intuitively why a person's fencing off
a parcel of land, clearing it, planting it, and so on could confer a just claim

of ownership. As argued above, the notion of desert is an essential part of this equation. On the other hand, I believe that the idea that all Earthlings, upon birth, automatically acquire an egalitarian share of the planet is just *weird*.

Following Feser, I fail to see how the claim that all Earthlings own an egalitarian share of some undiscovered natural resource buried miles under the sea in the middle of the Pacific Ocean differs *in principle* from the claim that we all collectively own resources on some distant asteroid. I submit that in both cases were an entrepreneur to devise a means to successfully commercialize the asset, she has thereby established an unconditional entitlement to the wealth she has created. What did *we* collectively do to deserve any of this value?

Matthew Risse attempts to distinguish what he regards as valid claims for egalitarian ownership of earthly raw materials from what he concedes is the implausible case for egalitarian rights to remote galaxies, by arguing that our planet is a "closed system that all humans need for survival, but this is not true of other parts of the universe."[47] I confess to being uncertain of the point Risse has in mind here. In attempting to distinguish egalitarian world ownership from the unowned cosmos, Risse cannot rely on it being the case that only earthly resources are necessary for our survival, since there is no reason in principle why in the future our lives may not depend entirely on our ability to exploit what are now remote (unowned) resources.

On the other hand, if Risse's point is that earthly resources are part of a "closed system," he fails to explain the moral significance of this distinction, and why this should matter for purposes of assigning ownership. Moreover, as soon as a hypothetical intergalactic entrepreneur arrives at a distant galaxy with the intention of commercializing it, this corner of the "open system" presumably becomes part of the closed system. Yet it seems bizarre that the mere fact of the entrepreneur's arrival on scene changes the ownership status of the remote galaxy from non-egalitarian to egalitarian. Until these apparent logical gaps are filled in, I assert that the same considerations that render distant galaxies available for exploitation should apply to those undiscovered resources much closer to home, including the world in its original state.

In any case, we can note a certain irony. One of the left's recurring indictments of capitalism is that it sanctions large, *undeserved* disparities in wealth, yet any theory of egalitarian, "species ownership"[48] would award the industrious and slothful, the productive and the wasteful, the conservers and despoilers, the same equal undivided share of the planet as their birthright.

This fact may cause some to question whether the left-libertarians' egalitarian intuition is as powerful as they take it to be.

Left-libertarianism and just acquisition

The three left-libertarians whose manifesto we quoted at the beginning of this section differ in their reasons for rejecting the Locke/Nozick theory of just acquisition. As we have just discussed, Vallentyne and Steiner view the external world in its "original state" as owned in some egalitarian fashion, and thus not subject to unconditional appropriation.[49] Since persons in a state of nature could not legitimately acquire unfettered rights to external resources, the current distribution of wealth is fatally corrupted and therefore can be comprehensibly rearranged to conform to a more just pattern.

On the other hand, Otsuka views the world as initially unowned by *anyone*, and therefore available for conversion to private property. Therefore, the appropriators' social obligation arises not from taking a disproportionate share of something that belongs to all, but from an egalitarian proviso that permits unilateral privatization only if the claimants "leave enough so that everyone else can acquire an equally advantageous share of unowned worldly resources" (footnote omitted).[50] Essentially, this condition requires that everyone have an equal opportunity for welfare, which can only be achieved by allocating to those with inferior natural endowments a disproportionate share of the value of external resources.[51]

But, as we shall see, neither account gives us a reason to reject the justice of Lockean appropriation. Staring first with the idea that the world is originally owned in some egalitarian manner; even if true, since the inhabitants did not *do anything* to establish their "ownership" it is difficult to see a justification for excluding appropriators from establishing full, unconditional rights under the Lockean model. If a person invests her labor in improving land, creates value and no other person is *disadvantaged* in the process, then what is moral case against privatization? As is often said in the sports world, "no harm, no foul."

In fact, what Vallentyne does have to say on this subject badly misconstrues, in my opinion, Nozick's position. Thus, he describes Nozick as holding that, "the only payment requirements [for the privatization of natural resources] are those of a quasi-Lockean proviso, which requires roughly that no individual be made worse off (in some appropriate sense) by the appropriation (compared with the situation before appropriation)."[52] No mention is made of the condition that claimants materially improve the resource in some fashion. Since he interprets Nozick in this way, he never confronts the idea that the appropriators must *earn* their full capitalist property rights.

Otsuka repeats this error, and accordingly describes the consequences of Lockean appropriation in near apocalyptic terms:

> Nozick's version of the Lockean proviso is too weak, since it allows a single individual in a state of nature to engage in an enriching acquisition of all the land there is if she compensates all others by hiring them and paying them a wage that ensures they end up no worse off than they would have been if they had continued to live the meager hand-to-mouth existence of hunters and gatherers on non-private land.[53]

Otsuka acknowledges that this argument is a simple restatement of Cohen's two-person world scenario, addressed in the previous section.[54]

As a matter of fairness, Otsuka and the other left-libertarians should interpret Nozick in the light most favorable to his basic principles. Although I believe that Nozick was sufficiently explicit on this point, even if he was not, the improvement condition should be considered. As David Gordon notes, if Otsuka has managed to identify a "loophole" in the Lockean proviso that allows unjust private appropriation, this would call simply for closing the loophole, rather than substituting his radically egalitarian alternative.[55]

Accordingly, Otsuka's case against the Locke/Nozick model of original appropriation is even weaker than Vallentyne and Steiner's. The only affirmative reason he gives us for rejecting it, is that it permits the sort of unfair, debilitating enrichment just described.[56] However, because he has misconstrued Nozick's reasoning on this point he has given us no argument at all for rejecting the justice of full capitalist property rights, except the customary appeal to our egalitarian intuitions.[57] In fact, in the absence of empirical evidence (which he does not adduce), Otsuka cannot exclude the possibility (if not the probability) that the recognition of unconditional property rights will provide greater welfare for the disadvantaged and disabled (the groups he is most concerned to protect) than the enforcement of his egalitarian proviso by a massive state bureaucracy.

Establishing the injustice of Lockean appropriation clearly lies at the heart of the left-libertarian mission, because if unconditional property rights can arise in a morally legitimate fashion, then entitlements thereby are created that are inconsistent with the redistributive schemes favored by them. However, in light of the arguments presented above, the left-libertarians have given us no substantial reason to reject Nozick's principle of "justice in acquisition."

Other objections to left-libertarianism

Another major difficulty with left-libertarianism is that even if we accept the existence of an egalitarian shadow on current holdings, there is, as Risse has observed, a fundamental indeterminacy in this account. As we have seen, Vallentyne and Steiner assert that the world is available for privatization subject to a social payment representing the value of the natural resources appropriated. The issue identified by Risse relates to selecting the point in time at which are we to *value* these resources.[58] Two obvious candidates present themselves: at the time of initial appropriation or today. However, both alternatives are problematic and there appears no principled way to choose between them (we discuss below the application of this argument to Otsuka's "egalitarian proviso").

Since, as Risse argues, constant technological and industrial progress inevitably multiplies what we can *do* with natural resources, and thus their value, the financial significance of such assets at the time we acquired them is quite small relative to what it is today. For example, crude oil had no utility until humanity devised a way to exploit it. Continuous technological innovation will result in "the ratio of value arising from the 'natural' part to that of the 'improved' part of resources continuing to decrease over time."[59] Accordingly, if left-libertarians hold that we should assay natural resources at the time of their appropriation, the portion of society's wealth available for redistribution will shrink to a very thin sliver of the total "pie"—an unattractive outcome for those bent on an ambitious redistributive agenda.

Alternatively, fixing the value of the material world at today's prices will imply that a much greater proportion of society's total wealth is attributable to external resources, and thus subject to redistribution. This answer is, however, also problematic in that it necessarily "grant[s] each member of a new generation a share in the collective achievements of their ancestors."[60] In other words, as we just noted, it was the creativity and inventiveness of earlier generations that produced the value that we would now attribute to natural resources.

It would seem that on left-libertarian principles the creators of intellectual property should have the right to transfer its value to their descendents through gift or bequest, rather than having it taxed away to promote social justice. After all, left-libertarians grant that persons are entitled to the fruits of their labor (though not the value of the natural resources improved by such labor), so as Risse notes, "why do they not obtain a full property right in the 'improved' aspects of the resources they work on?"[61] And, as discussed in Chapter 2, liberals have provided no convincing argument against the justice of intergenerational gifts, nor any persuasive rationale why, if such gifts are permissible, bequests should not be as well.

The heart of the problem Risse has identified is that there appears to be no principled way to value natural assets as "things in themselves." Without human civilization, material resources have nominal value; without worldly resources, there can be no civilization. Any attempt to apportion a specific value to one factor or the other is entirely arbitrary.

Otsuka's version of left-libertarianism does not include the assumption of egalitarian world ownership, and therefore does not require the valuation of the resources "misappropriated" by private property owners. Nevertheless it is still subject to the same basic indeterminacy objection identified above.[62] As Risse notes, the massive redistribution program that would be required to implement the proviso must be carried out against the backdrop of what Otsuka acknowledges to be the "very stringent right to all of the income that one can gain from one's mind and body (including one's labor) either on one's own or through unregulated and untaxed voluntary exchanges with other individuals."[63]

Since we cannot assign a nonarbitrary value to natural resources in their unimproved state (plus our opportunities to improve them), we cannot know that what we take from a person in the name of "equality of condition" does not represent the value generated by that individual's (tax-exempt) labor. Accordingly, his "egalitarian proviso" is incompatible with a "stringent right to income."[64]

The final point I will discuss regarding left-libertarianism is one made by Barbara Fried. Here, I am referring to the fact that left-libertarianism does not provide any novel or interesting justification for egalitarian redistribution. Fried first notes that there is no logical relationship between what she calls the "tax" and "transfer" sides of left-libertarianism, i.e. between the left-libertarian rationale for *what* is owed to the social fund and the logic used in deciding *how* the fund is to be distributed, i.e. to achieve a greater equality of resource holdings, to provide for the most needy, or the handicapped, and so on.[65]

In fact, the logic of the two sides of the ideological equation are in open conflict. As Fried says, "If the state is prohibited from taking more from the talented by virtue of their unequal talents—the premise of left libertarianism—how can it be permitted to give more to the untalented by virtue of their unequal talents?"[66]

Accordingly, the left-libertarian case for redistribution simply rests on the same intuitions regarding the virtues of equality or the greater needs of the worst-off members of society that motivate other patterned principles of justice. Therefore, as Fried observes, this doctrine "is just liberal egalitarianism in drag,"[67] and left-libertarianism adds nothing to the egalitarian claims considered in Chapter 2. In light of the arguments presented here, neither the Vallentyne/Steiner nor the Otsuka version of left-libertarianism provides a plausible reason for rejecting the morality of individual property, and thus no basis for rejecting the Entitlement Theory.

Chapter 4

Justifying the Minimal State

America did not tell the millions of men and women who came from every country in the world and who—with their hands, their intelligence and their heart—built the greatest nation in the world: "Come, and everything will be given to you." She said, "Come, and the only limits to what you'll be able to achieve will be your own courage and your own talent"... Here, both the humblest and most illustrious citizens alike know that nothing is owed to them and that everything has to be earned. That's what constitutes the moral value of America. America did not teach men the idea of freedom; she taught them how to practice it.

> Nicolas Sarkozy, President of France, "Renewing the
> French-American Alliance," Speech to Congress, November 7, 2007[1]

Up until this point, we have focused on the moral force of individual rights vis-à-vis other persons. We have argued that libertarian rights function to define the moral space that persons must enjoy if they are to exercise their rational agency. These rights are vindicated when we are free to live as we please, subject to the equal rights of other rational agents. We have not yet considered whether the state has any greater justification than do private parties for the use of force and coercion in the pursuit of its objectives.

For the reasons described below, libertarians are deeply divided over whether *any* state can be justified, even a minimal one whose role is limited to, in Nozick's words, "protecting all its citizens against violence, theft, fraud, and to the enforcement of contracts and so on" (*ASU*, 26). The "and so on" part of the quoted sentence reflects Nozick's unwillingness to be drawn into the thorny debate regarding the exact dimensions of the libertarian state, a subject I will return to briefly at the end of this chapter.

We will now review Nozick's moral defense of the minimal state, and (sadly) join the chorus of philosophers who find it unsatisfactory. I will then explore the possibility of justifying the minimal state on pragmatic grounds, i.e. as the least bad alternative to anarchy or a more activist state. However, because the persuasiveness of this "least bad alternative" strategy rests on certain controversial empirical assumptions, I then directly defend, based on a "libertarian principle of fairness," the moral legitimacy of the coercive measures required to maintain the minimal state.

Academics, including Nozick, generally follow Max Weber's identification of the irreducible features of the "state" as consisting of the claim to a monopoly of force over some geographic area and the raising of revenue through coercive taxation (see *ASU*, 23–4). Murray Rothbard and other anarcho-capitalists hold that even the minimal state is intrinsically immoral precisely *because* it satisfies both these tests. Thus, Rothbard's blanket assertion that, "the State is an inherently illegitimate institution of organized aggression, of organized and regularized crime against the persons and properties of its subjects."[2]

Of course, as just noted, for a political entity *to be* a state it must claim a monopoly of force. Therefore, Rothbard's argument against the state *cannot* be that "any political entity that claims a monopoly of force is immoral," since this would not be an argument, but a tautology. As I understand his reasoning, it is (roughly) that: (i) any actual or threatened use of force against an innocent person is morally wrong; (ii) all states impermissibly employ force against innocent people by taxing them on a nonconsensual basis and/or by prohibiting the private supply of certain essential services; (iii) therefore, all states violate the moral rights of at least some of their members, and are illegitimate.[3] As seen below, Nozick's defense of the minimal state is an attempt to discredit the second premise of Rothbard's syllogism.

Nozick's Justification of the Minimal State

In the first two sentences of *ASU,* quoted in the Introduction, Nozick proclaims the inviolability of rights, and notes that the moral force of rights calls into question, "what, if anything, the state and its officials may do." In the first part of *ASU* Nozick attempts to answer this question by showing that the minimal state would, given certain reasonable assumptions, arise from a Lockean state of nature without violating the rights of any party. It should be understood that he is not defending the political legitimacy of any existing state, but simply attempting to rebut the anarcho-capitalist claim that *all* states are necessarily pernicious.

His approach has been widely dissected in the literature and philosophers from across the ideological spectrum have found it wanting.[4] Therefore, we will not analyze his extended argument in great detail. However, a limited review will prove useful in illuminating the nature of the controversy between minimal state libertarians and individual anarchists, and will introduce a number of concepts that the disputants traditionally employ in this debate.

Nozick's strategy takes the form of a narrative purporting to demonstrate that the minimal state would naturally, without the conscious design or intention of any party, evolve out of the pre-political world. He terms this an "invisible hand explanation" in honor of Adam Smith's "invisible hand of the marketplace" (see *ASU*, 18).[5]

Nozick cites as an example of such an explanation the emergence of precious metals as a medium of exchange in the primitive world. Market participants would for reasons of self-interest come to value goods that could be readily traded for other desirable things, thereby avoiding the inconvenience and inefficiency of bartering. They would naturally gravitate toward gold and silver as a means of payment by virtue of their having independent uses, durability, divisibility, portability, and so on (see *ASU*, 18). This process would culminate in the universal acceptance of precious metals as "legal tender" without any express agreement or social contract.

Nozick's derivation of the minimal state starts with the commonsense notion that in the pre-political world the demand for security would motivate people to band together into mutual protective associations in order to repel or deter potential aggressors. However, these informal groupings would soon give way to specialized commercial organizations, i.e. "protective agencies" ("PAs") that would sell their services to the public (see *ASU*, 12–13).

For the reasons discussed below, Nozick concludes that this market represents a sort of "natural monopoly," and that over time the competing PAs would merge or confederate into a "dominant protective agency" ("DPA") (see *ASU*, 15–17). The DPA will, in addition to resolving conflicts between its members, punish non-members who aggress against them, using only those legal procedures and punishments that *it* deems reliable and fair. The DPA "will not allow anyone to defend against *them*; that is, it will punish anyone who does so" (*ASU*, 108).

Therefore, the DPA has a unique marketing advantage, since it alone can assure its customers that "Only those procedures *we* deem appropriate will be used on our customers" (*ASU*, 109). As Jonathan Wolff puts it, Nozick is appealing to the idea that, "Other things being equal, people will seek out the largest agency as this will be best able to protect them."[6]

Nozick claims that a DPA may emerge without a single PA achieving a formal monopoly. Even if two competing PAs were to fight to a competitive standstill in a specific territory, they will find it expedient, rather than engage in violent and costly battles, to refer conflicts between their respective members to a neutral forum for resolution:

> Thus, there emerges a system of appeals courts and agreed upon rules about jurisdiction and the conflict of laws. Though different agencies operate, there is one unified federal judicial system of which they are all components. (*ASU*, 16)

Accordingly, says Nozick, this cartel will for all practical purposes function as a DPA.

As a *de facto* monopoly, the DPA has become "the only effective supplier" (*ASU*, 112) of protective services. Its prohibition on enforcement actions against its clients "makes it impossible for the independents credibly to threaten to punish [DPA] clients who violate their rights" (*ASU*, 110). Nozick condones the DPA's imperious policy by invoking the idea of "procedural rights," such that "a person may resist, in self-defense, if others try to apply to him an unreliable or unfair procedure of justice" (*ASU*, 102).

Because the procedures and methods used by independents will seem risky and unreliable to the DPA, it will forbid non-members from enforcing their own rights. Since some of those forbidden from self-defense will not be able to afford the price of membership in the DPA, Nozick holds that the DPA "may have to provide some persons [protective] services for a fee that is less than the price of its services" (*ASU*, 112–13). This "forced membership" is sanctioned by his ill-stared "principle of compensation," discussed below.

This compensatory discount will come out of the pockets of the DPA's existing customers, who must now pay proportionately more. By prohibiting any legal procedure it deems unfair or unreliable, the DPA has claimed a monopoly of force, thus fulfilling the first of Weber's two criteria for the existence of a state. And, by subsidizing the membership of certain unwilling members by charging higher fees to others, it satisfies the second. Therfore, says Nozick, the DPA has evolved innocently into the minimal state.

Criticisms of Nozick's derivation of the minimal state

Unfortunately, virtually every political theorist who has examined Nozick's demonstration regards it (correctly, in my opinion) as a failure.[7] This criticism has taken a number of forms. Perhaps the most obvious objection is that Nozick assumes without sufficient justification that a DPA will inevitably emerge in any geographic area. As noted above, Nozick's claim is based on the idea that "maximal competing protective agencies cannot coexist; the nature of the service brings different agencies not only into competition for customers' patronage, but also into violent conflict with each other" (*ASU*, 17). In other words, the DPA will insist that only its procedures are legitimate and thus drive out all competitors.

However, a number of critics have countered that a DPA might never emerge because (as Nozick himself recognizes) there are strong economic incentives for PAs to resolve conflicts peaceably. As David Friedman argues, "Since warfare is expensive, agencies might include in the contracts they offer customers a provision under which they are not obligated to defend customers against legitimate punishments for their actual crimes."[8] These firms might even be led by their own commercial interests to agree in *advance* to settle disputes through some form of arbitration.[9] As Wolff contends, in such an environment, "small, streamlined agencies which offer 'personal service' may be more effective, if more expensive."[10]

Moreover, it does not seem to follow from the likelihood that competing PAs would refer disputes to neutral third parties for decision that a permanent state-like legal apparatus would emerge. As various commentators have pointed out, if the field is occupied by a number of different PAs, it is more probable that a variety of *ad hoc* trial arrangements, utilizing a variety of different procedures would develop.[11] Similarly, there is no reason why we should anticipate the emergence of a formal appellate court system vested with exclusive jurisdiction over all cases. Instead, appeals might be referred to many different individual arbitrators or panels selected on a case-by-case basis.

Not only is there cause to question Nozick's account of the inevitable emergence of the DPA, but there are also excellent reasons to doubt his claim that it would evolve in a way that is respectful of rights. As referenced above, Nozick relies on the idea that the procedural rights of DPA members justify the prohibition of competing PAs.[12] But, for purposes of his grand strategy the notion of such rights is unhelpful because it rests solely on the subjective judgment of the DPA.

We can highlight this point by imagining that a competing PA simply wishes to use procedures identical to those approved by the DPA. Perhaps it believes it can compete with the DPA by offering highly personalized service for a higher price (or a "bare bones" policy for a very low price). Under such conditions there would seemingly be no legitimate reason for the DPA to refuse to deal cooperatively with this agency by, for instance, referring conflicts to neutral arbitration. Nozick acknowledges that nevertheless,

> there will be a strong tendency for it [the DPA] to deem all other proce-
> dures, or even the 'same' procedures run by others, either unreliable or
> unfair...The dominant protective association will act freely on its own
> understanding of the situation, whereas no one else will be able to do so
> with impunity. (*ASU,* 108)

The fact that Nozick's narrative hinges on the unwillingness of the DPA to expose its customers to the administration of justice by any other party poses, I believe, a serious if not fatal problem. While the DPA's rigid refusal to accept the legitimacy of competing PAs is a necessary step in obtaining its *de facto* monopoly, this procedural "imperialism" seems inconsistent with Nozick's claim that the minimal state can be born innocently. Surely, cli-ents of competing PAs and independents will subjectively fear the methods employed by the DPA, even the "same" ones. Don't these folks have rights equal to those enjoyed by DPA members? And, as Roy Childs argues, "who is to say that the procedures of the dominant protective agency are not among the most unreliable?"[13]

Childs creatively summarizes the difficulty in Nozick's position by means of his own "invisible hand" parable. Suppose, he says, that the minimal state has arisen in the way depicted by Nozick. Now, an entrepreneur comes on the scene who espies a profit-making opportunity; she forms a PA that will attempt to compete with the state apparatus. Careful not to run afoul of the delicate sensibilities of the political authorities, she copies the state's pro-cedures and invites them to sit in on all of her agency's trials, proceedings and so forth. Thus, the state has no apparent excuse for prohibiting her enterprise or refusing to cooperate with it.

Since the upstart firm has only members that join voluntarily, it has no need to offer compensation to individuals *forced* to join, as the DPA is obli-gated to do, yielding it a theoretical competitive advantage. Furthermore, the new venture may be able to exploit advances in technology, an innova-tive business model, more effective management or other factors that would enable it to compete on favorable terms with the bloated state bureaucracy. If so, then Nozick's invisible hand explanation unravels, as we cannot be confident that this new agency (and many others) will not gain market share at the state's expense.

In other words, since Nozick does not show that the market for protec-tive services is a natural monopoly in the strict economic sense, i.e. that "marginal cost is diminishing over a broad range of output levels and minimum average cost can be achieved only by organizing the industry as a monopoly,"[14] the emergence of the minimal state will not happen naturally through the invisible hand of the marketplace. This is why Childs is able to so easily construct a scenario illustrating how it would inevitably devolve.[15]

If the market for protective services is not a natural economic monopoly, then a DPA will only evolve through the intervention of non-market forces. We noted above that the key move here is the DPA's ban on the independent enforcement of justice. Nozick attempts to justify this prohibition by his "principle of compensation," which he develops at length. He intends this principle to apply only in connection with the regulation of certain types of risky behavior, and as described above it would require the DPA to provide discounted membership to those disadvantaged by its prohibition. He illustrates its operation by means of the imaginary case of the epileptic driver (see *ASU*, 78–9, 81–4).

In Nozick's scenario, the epileptic motorist poses a risk to the driving public that is substantially less than the "clear and present danger" presented by a drunk driver (whose conduct may simply be criminalized), but substantially greater than that posed by a "typical" driver. Nozick suggests that society may, without violating libertarian principles, prohibit risky activities of the sort represented by the epileptic driver provided that it compensates appropriately those whose activities are forbidden (see *ASU*, 81). Nozick believes that independents in a state of nature that do not wish to join the DPA are, by analogy, like this epileptic driver.

Critics have identified a variety of deficiencies in Nozick's admittedly not-fully-developed principle of compensation.[16] Most of the objections relate in one way or another to the perceived conflict between Nozick's insistence elsewhere in *ASU* that rights are inviolable and the idea, implicit in the compensation principle, that there exist something akin to "almost rights" that can be taken from you for a price. Nozick himself acknowledges that: "It might be objected that either you have the right to forbid these people's risky activities or you don't" (*ASU*, 83). He dismisses this conclusion as "too short" because, "It may be that you do have a right to forbid an action but only provided you compensate those to whom it is forbidden" (ibid.).

Sadly, it is Nozick that is guilty of too quickly abandoning the more straightforward and defensible understanding of rights. As more than one commentator has noticed, Nozick's view that the DPA has the right to prohibit independent enforcement that it (subjectively) deems risky depends on the plausibility of the idea that that agents do *not* have the inherent right to defend themselves. However, the right of self-defense lies at the very heart of the natural rights theory as articulated by Locke, and in any case is intuitively compelling.

As shown above, Nozick cannot reasonably argue that the independent enforcement of justice presents an inherent risk of aggression to the DPA's membership. Accordingly, contrary to Nozick's claim, the DPA's arrogation of a monopoly on force violates the natural rights of those persons compelled to join. On the other hand, if the DPA were to ban only objectively dangerous methods, Nozick's account would fall through, because competitors could simply mimic the DPA's procedures. Absent a more comprehensive and conclusive economic analysis than Nozick provides, there is no reason to believe that many competing agencies, employing similar or even identical procedures, could not peacefully coexist in the market.

As Nozick recognizes, in all other contexts side constraints preclude nonconsensual invasions of our moral space (what he calls "boundary crossings"), even with compensation. Therefore, his view that the collective fear by the members of the DPA justifies its coercive monopoly is inconsistent with his commitment to natural rights, detailed in Chapter 1. Accordingly, Randy Barnett rightly rejects Nozick's principle of compensation as inconsistent with fundamental libertarian values: "voluntariness is a necessary condition for a morally permissible exchange of values. Compensation is not a sufficient condition for justifying or permitting a rights violation."[17]

Because of the various difficulties discussed above, our judgment is that Nozick's defense of the minimal state is fatally flawed.

Alternative Justifications of the Minimal State

One of the virtues of Nozick's strategy, were it successful, is that it enables him to avoid having to directly answer the question of whether a state is even *necessary*, i.e. whether its essential functions could be provided by one or more private organizations funded by voluntary membership fees. Since, according to Nozick's narrative the state would *inevitably* (and innocently) evolve from a state of nature, this question is rendered moot. Also, on Nozick's account, the DPA-turned-state provides protection against both foreign and domestic predators, thus eliminating the need to consider whether different analyses are necessary to justify taxpayer coercion in these two cases.

We will offer two distinct alternatives to Nozick's justification of the minimal state. The first does not directly challenge the anarchist's claim that the coercion employed even by the minimal state is morally illegitimate. Rather, the argument is based on the idea that a libertarian state is the "least bad" possible outcome relative to anarchy or other more interventionist political arrangements. Second, I will explicitly defend the justice of coercive taxation to fund the military defense of a relatively peaceful and just state against potential aggressors. I will then attempt to extend the *comparatively* uncontroversial analysis described in the preceding sentence to the provision of domestic security.

The state as an inevitable outcome

Some economists that have examined Nozick's "invisible hand" account accept his idea that the protective services industry would eventually consolidate into a single firm or a cartel, but reject his conclusion that this could happen in a way that respects individual rights. Robert Holcombe asserts on the basis of economic and historical analysis that PAs in a state of nature would behave like "little mafias." They would, according to Holcombe, have "every incentive to move from operating as bandits to operating as states" because they would thereby expend fewer resources on unproductive fights with each other, and would be in a better position to raise greater tax revenues from their victims—the rest of society.[18]

He observes that, "Every place in the world is ruled by government."[19] Therefore, in light of this fact and what he regards as the irresistible temptation for organized groups to resort to violence to achieve dominance, he concludes:

> The evidence shows that anarchy, no matter how desirable in theory, does not constitute a realistic alternative in practice, and it suggests that if government ever were to be eliminated anywhere, predators would move in to establish themselves as one by force.[20]

If this is true, the debate regarding the morality of state-enforced coercion is entirely moot. Since a state of some sort is inevitable, there is no real point in debating whether it is intrinsically oppressive, and the only meaningful issue is the nature of the *government* that will manage it.

Therefore, says Holcombe, libertarians should work to establish institutional arrangements—respect for property rights, free markets, constitutional checks and balances, and so forth—that will "prevent the creation of an even more predatory and less libertarian government."[21] A similar concern seems to lie behind Ayn Rand's view that "a society without an organized government would be at the mercy of the first criminal who came along and who would precipitate it into the chaos of gang warfare."[22]

Another economist, Tyler Cowen, concludes that even if you start with the assumption that a state of nature would not be characterized by (as predicted by Holcombe) anarchy in the popular sense (i.e. violent chaos), but instead would evolve into an orderly market for protective services, the final result of this process would not be pretty.[23] He argues that the large number of competing PAs that would exist initially would tend to cooperate so that each agency would be able to assure its customers that it could resolve claims involving all (or almost all) other persons. The formation of a network of cooperating PAs would enable them to discipline, by means of ostracism, those rogue agencies that sought to protect even their guilty members by force.[24]

However, according to Cowen, "the disciplinary actions of the network that put down these outlaws are precisely the actions that could enforce collusion as well."[25] Moreover, says Cowen, because "the forces that usually break down cartels—new entrants and renegade colluders—cannot obtain market share," there is a great danger of abuse and oppression.[26] Thus, he cautions that, "Once the network obtains monopoly power over society's apparatus of adjudication and punishment, it can use this power to achieve monopoly positions elsewhere in the economy."[27] Cowen's pessimistic prognosis regarding the nature of the DPA that would emerge from a state of nature, if accurate, implicitly justifies a role for the minimal state as the "guardian of the guardians."

This idea has been developed by John Hasnas. He notes that even if Cowen's analysis were correct, we would not need the state to *supply* domestic protective services, but only to police those private entities charged with this task. Thus, a democratic government with constitutionally enumerated powers limited to preventing collusion and abuse by PAs would be all the state we would ever need for maintaining law and order.

This entity would still require a monopoly of force sufficient to enforce its regulatory mandate and would fund itself through coercive taxation. Hasnas calls this form of minimal governance the "remedial state," reflecting its role as the guarantor and not direct supplier of essential services.[28] He expressly avoids taking a position in his essay on whether the state has an essential role in defending against foreign aggression.

Defenders of individual anarchy have vigorously contested the bleak assessments of private law enforcement offered by Holcombe and Cowen. As referenced above, against the claim that the PAs will act like "little mafias," they cite the strong economic incentives that would exist for PAs to settle disputes in a rational, nonviolent way.[29] Moreover, they cite literature from game theory that suggests that people's own self-interest would guide them toward cooperation in social situations, particularly if they know that they may have repeated encounters with each other.[30]

Against Cowen's argument that any network of PAs sufficiently cohesive to discipline "outlaw" agencies would be dangerously collusive, Friedman asserts that the threat of tyranny presented by the network of private enforcers is less than that posed by the state itself.[31] Finally, Friedman claims that ordered anarchy of the sort he advocates has existed on a stable basis in a number of societies, including medieval Iceland and the Comanche Indians.[32]

While I believe that Holcombe and Cowen have the better of this argument, their views are predictions based on certain empirical assumptions and extrapolations from historical data and economic theory. Their analyses do not justify state coercion from the moral perspective. If true, their arguments show the state to be only a "necessary evil." Therefore, we are still in need of a *philosophical* defense of the minimal state, i.e. one that shows that it is both useful and not an inherent violator of rights.

A moral justification of the minimal state as provider of national defense

If we are ever fortunate enough to see the day foretold by the prophet Isaiah, when "men shall beat their swords into plowshares" and "the lion shall lie down with the lamb," then we will no longer need the state to protect us from foreign predators. However, until then the strongest moral justification for the state is presented by the need for national defense. In making the case for the state as the necessary supplier of this good, we must distinguish two separate issues: (i) whether we need the state at all for this function and (ii) assuming an affirmative answer to the first question, whether it is legitimate for the state to use coercion to fund this activity.

Murray Rothbard (followed by many other anarcho-capitalists) emphatically denies the first of these two propositions. He claims that all states, regardless of their form of governance present an *equal* danger of external aggression:

> The theoretical reason why focusing on democracy or dictatorship misses the point is that *States—all* States—rule their population and decide whether or not to make war. And *all* States, whether formally a democracy or dictatorship or some other brand of rule, are run by a ruling elite.

Whether or nor these elites, in any particular case, will make war upon another State is a function of a complex interweaving web of causes, including temperament of the rulers, the strength of their enemies, the inducements for war, and public opinion.[33]

Since only states initiate wars, and because there is no reason (so the argument goes) to believe that *ours*, whatever one that happens to be, will engage only (or even primarily) in just wars, there is no legitimate role for the state in providing national defense.[34] Therefore, freedom-loving people, wherever located, should resist the payment of taxes for this (or any other) purpose and actively work to dissolve their state.[35]

In my judgment, Rothbard's argument will persuade only those whose hatred of the state on ideological grounds is so intense that it blinds them to distinctions apparent to all others. Thus, the idea that totalitarian regimes, capable of organizing and conducting such hideous genocidal atrocities as the Holocaust, the systematic rape of East Asia directed by Japan's military junta in WWII, and the self-inflicted Great Famine in the USSR, pose no greater danger to freedom-loving people than states substantially governed by the rule of law, is utterly bizarre.

Even if Rothbard's highly counterintuitive assumption were true, it does not follow that states have no role in national defense. This is so because his argument does not exclude the possibility that a *particular* foreign regime, whatever its form, might be deterred from aggression only by means of large state-directed expenditures on the armed forces.

Thus we find Rothbard, in the context of defending his "revisionist history" of the Cold War, making the following observation about Hitler's surprise attack on the USSR in 1941:

So unprepared was Stalin for the assault, so trusting was he in the rationality of the German-Russian accord for peace in Eastern Europe that he had allowed the Russian army to fall into disrepair. So unwarlike was Stalin, in fact, that Germany was almost able to conquer Russia in the face of enormous odds.[36]

Therefore, regardless of these states' form of governance, Hitler's aggression against the USSR was predictable, and there plainly *was* a role for the Soviet state in providing national defense, a responsibility that Stalin shamefully neglected.

It also seems doubtful as a matter of history that only states initiate aggression. While the term "war" may imply levels of population, military organization and social specialization only present in relatively modern times, the available evidence is that humankind's pre-history, i.e. before the development of states, was hardly peaceful or idyllic. Rather, it seems to have been characterized by widespread violence, pillaging and territorial conquests. Accordingly, it is far from clear that the elimination of states would remove the need for large-scale defense.

This conclusion is buttressed by recent events. Although Rothbard did not live long enough to witness the mega-terrorism of 9/11, the existence of well-organized and financed groups with murderous intent toward the West undercuts his claim that the elimination of states would bring peace. Of course, anarcho-capitalists will reply that Islamic terrorists only hate the governments and not the peoples of the United States and the other nations that have suffered terrorist attacks. But most terrorism has been directed against civilian populations, and the repeated calls by Al-Qaeda spokesmen for the conversion of the West to Islam belies the assertion that dismantling democratic states would leave us to coexist in peace and harmony with these fanatical thugs.

Before proceeding further, I wish to make a brief point about libertarian theory and defense policy. If we recognize liberty as the supreme value, then it seems to follow that it is incumbent upon us to defend it *by any means necessary*, subject only to the equal rights of others. While isolationism has certainly been the dominant libertarian policy prescription,[37] there is nothing, I believe, in the doctrine that compels this view.

Professor Barnett, a prominent libertarian theorist, notes in a discussion of the Iraq War that: "Devising a military defense strategy is a matter of judgment or prudence about which reasonable libertarians may differ greatly."[38] I agree with this statement, and believe that it implies that in particular circumstances an effective defense of our liberty might include alliances of convenience with "unsavory" regimes, the use of foreign aid as a means of influencing other nations to respect our legitimate interests, preemptive strikes against hostile, aggressive countries before they obtain nuclear weapons and interventions against "failed states" that provide safe haven for terrorists. However, the justification for such tactics will depend on a careful analysis of the particular facts and circumstances present in each case, and so philosophers can have little more to say on this subject.

Returning now to the question of whether the state has an irreplaceable role in national defense, I acknowledge that even if we take seriously the threat of foreign aggression or terrorist attack, this would establish only the need for a "state-like entity." Nothing above conclusively demonstrates that this defense could not be supplied by a private entity funded by *voluntary* membership dues or fees, i.e. in Nozick's terms a "super-DPA" dedicated to this purpose. This is an important point, because as George Klosko observes, "if the state is in fact *not* necessary, it becomes difficult if not impossible to establish obligations to support it."[39]

However, given the necessary scope and complexity of strategic defense, and the need to address the problem of free riders (discussed below), I am going to proceed on the assumption that, at the bare minimum, the state enjoys a distinct *advantage* over any private organization in providing national defense. As such, it is reasonable to further assume that there may be real world situations where *only* a state can effectively deter or respond to foreign aggression or mega-terrorism.

Even so, we are still faced with the problem of justifying the use of coercive governmental taxation to finance the military. For purposes of defending such taxation, I will presuppose that the state in question is a relatively just and peaceful one in a world populated by more aggressive ones and/or well-organized, dangerous terrorist organizations dedicated to its destruction. My argument will rest on the claim, defended below, that everyone benefits from the provision of national defense, and by the fact that this function is a classic example of what economists call "public goods."

Economists use this concept to identify those goods with certain characteristics that make it problematic for the private sector to supply them. According to standard economic theory a public good is one that satisfies two technical criteria: it is neither "excludable" (people cannot be prevented from benefiting from it) nor "rival" (one individual's consumption of the good does not diminish any other person's enjoyment of it).[40] Thus, as explained in Greg Mankiw's popular undergraduate economics textbook, "Once the country is defended from foreign aggressors, it is impossible to prevent any single person from enjoying the benefit... [and] when one person enjoys the benefit of national defense, he does not reduce the benefit to anyone else."[41]

Unlike with typical consumer goods, the operation of the free market cannot set the quantity of public goods to be supplied. While the level of consumer demand will determine the number of automobiles produced because at some point it becomes unprofitable to manufacture more, the market cannot set the "proper" level of defense spending because, quite obviously, such a market does not exist. Only the political process can fill this role. If due to free riders a socially desirable public good is seriously undersupplied, we have what economists call "market failure."

So, with respect to national defense the fear is that if it were funded by voluntary contributions many persons would fail to pay their share, hoping to free ride on the backs of others.[42] Of course, it is theoretically possible that the citizens of a relatively just and peaceful society might willingly contribute all the resources necessary to maintain an adequate shield against foreign aggression, but for present purposes this is beside the point. The issue at hand is whether the state would be justified in resorting to coercion in order to correct an undersupply of defense services or to protect responsible citizens from having to pay more than their fair share. To answer in the affirmative, we must find that the recalcitrant citizens of our comparatively benign state owe it a duty that the authorities are entitled to enforce.

Do we have political obligations to the state?

Thus, we collide headlong with what philosophers call "the problem of political obligation." Richard Dagger describes this challenge as the need to explicate how, if at all, citizens come "to have a moral duty to obey the laws of one's country or state."[43] Many theorists deny the existence of any general obligation to do so, asserting that only those few "who have explicitly committed themselves to obey the law, perhaps by swearing allegiance as part of an oath of citizenship, have anything like a general obligation."[44] Before going further, however, we should quickly note that at least some of those philosophers who deny that citizens have a general political obligation acknowledge that there are nevertheless good reasons for them not to disrupt the operations or disobey most of the laws of a reasonably just state.[45]

Although there is certainty nothing like unanimity on this point, the weight of philosophical opinion seems to be that no convincing rationale for political obligation has yet been formulated, even for states that are democratic and substantially governed by the rule of law. This situation is largely the result of A. John Simmons's highly influential 1979 essay, "The Principle of Fair Play." Accordingly, it is to Simmons's arguments that we now turn. We will show that, despite Simmons, a persuasive case can be made for political obligation in the supply of essential public goods.

The title of Simmons's important article refers to the "principle of fair play" (also called the "principle of fairness"), which is thought by many philosophers (including me) to be the most promising basis for deriving political obligation.[46] The primary purpose of his essay is to demonstrate that the principle, which was first articulated (at least in modern times) by H. L. A. Hart,[47] cannot ground a general political obligation.

At its core, the principle of fairness relies on the powerful intuitive pull of the idea that if people join together to accomplish some desirable objective, it is unfair for some members of the group to get the benefits while withholding their contributions. As formulated by Hart, the principle holds that:

> [W]hen a number of persons conduct any joint enterprise according to rules and thus restrict their liberty, those who have submitted to these restrictions when required have a right from similar submission from those who have benefited by their submission.[48]

This principle can potentially establish political obligation, since various activities of the state may be categorized as "joint enterprises" of this sort.

In his essay, Simmons builds on a counterexample presented by Nozick in *ASU* that appears to generally discredit the principle of fair play. Nozick asks his readers to imagine that they belong to a neighborhood association that decides to initiate a system of public entertainment (see *ASU*, 90–5). The association (conveniently consisting of 365 members) assigns to each neighbor one day a year in which he or she will be responsible for providing the entertainment over a public address system. The neighbor in question neither consents to nor rejects this arrangement. Many months elapse during which he tepidly enjoys the entertainment supplied by his neighbors, and then his designated day finally arrives.

Is he morally obligated to take his turn? Despite the fact that he has modestly benefited from the entertainment, Nozick emphatically denies that he is, and this conclusion seems to square with our common moral intuitions. After all, how can a person become obligated to participate in an activity that he did not initiate or actively support, and which provides him with only marginal benefits? Since no obligation has arisen here, the principle of fair play, at least if construed broadly, is shown to be unsound.

Simmons agrees with Nozick's conclusions about this particular case and that it dooms the principle of fairness as articulated by Hart. However, he believes that he can salvage this principle by giving it a "voluntarist" interpretation. He argues that the effectiveness of Nozick's counterexample hinges on the circumstance that the nonparticipating neighbor only passively enjoys what is an "open benefit."[49] As Simmons notes, Nozick has constructed this case in such a way that his protagonist would have to take affirmative steps to *avoid* receiving the benefits, and this is asking too much of him.[50]

Things would be different, says Simmons, if the public address entertainment program was located in a private club and the nonparticipating neighbor was found sneaking in to enjoy the festivities.[51] In this case, the neighbor is morally obligated to take his turn since he actively sought out, i.e. "accepted," the benefits of the joint enterprise. An obvious problem, however, arises with respect to the "acceptance" of public goods such as national defense, since they are both impossible to "seek out" in any way and impossible to avoid (short of leaving the country).

Nevertheless, Simmons holds that either actual consent or willing and knowing acceptance is required to create obligations to fund or otherwise support the supply of public goods. To accept an open benefit "we cannot...regard the benefits as having been forced upon us against our will or think that the benefits are not worth the price we must pay for them."[52] Moreover, to be bound the citizen must regard the benefits received "as flowing from a cooperative scheme," rather than having been (already) purchased by her taxes.[53] The net effect of Simmons's interpretation of "acceptance" is, as he states, that the principle of fairness "at very best...can hope to account for the political obligations of only a very few citizens...[and] it is more likely...that it accounts for no such obligations at all."[54]

However, a number of philosophers have rejected Simmons's claim that psychological acceptance is a necessary condition to the creation of political obligations.[55] Because his position lies closest to the one I will ultimately adopt, I am going to focus on the arguments that George Klosko raises in defense of the principle of fairness. He regards certain public goods, such as national defense, as "indispensable," i.e. "necessary for an acceptable life for all members of the community," and therefore "can be presumed to be beneficial without taking the recipients' views into account."[56] Accordingly, he holds that:

> the existence of *A*'s obligations to scheme *X* are to a large extent independent of particular beliefs that he may have. Though certain of his beliefs may be relevant to the status of his obligations, it is not clear why beliefs about the nature of the cooperative effort required to provide particular benefits fall into this class.[57]

As Klosko formulates it, the principle of fairness operates as follows:

> If [the proponents of the principle] present plausible arguments, then they establish a presumption that recipients have the relevant obligations. They must be able to demonstrate that the three necessary conditions hold, that the benefits are worth their costs and indispensable, and that the benefits and burdens of cooperating with the state are fairly distributed. This presumption is rebuttable.[58]

Based on this understanding, Klosko claims (for example) that if the citizens of country *X* are surrounded by hostile and aggressive neighbors, and if the voters have instituted compulsory military service as the only practical means of ensuring national survival, a typical citizen *A* (assuming he or she is able to do so) is under a strong prima facie obligation to serve.[59]

He concedes that this duty might be overridden in some cases. Thus, if *A* happens to be a sincere conscientious objector, this might (depending on the factual background) affect the nature of his service or even excuse him altogether, but this circumstance would not eliminate the prima facie duty. One consequence of Klosko's approach is that he is able to distinguish Nozick's counterexample of the neighborhood public address system on the grounds that the benefits provided in that case are trivial, i.e. not "indispensable."[60]

In reply to Klosko, Simmons argues in a more recent essay that the principle of fairness cannot impose political obligations even for indispensable public goods.[61] He tries to show this by describing a hypothetical case in which the residents of a rural neighborhood who have traditionally relied on individual wells for their water face a severe drought. Since these wells are now drying up, the neighbors devise a cooperative scheme to solve their problem by means of a trench that will divert water from a distant river to each home.

Simmons asks us to suppose that *A* does not wish to participate in this plan, but prefers to supply his own water by digging a deeper well, that the neighborhood group's trench will traverse the only suitable place on *A*'s property for his intended well, and they refuse to alter its path. Even though *A* will receive water from the cooperative scheme, Simmons claims that "there is something deeply unconvincing about the claim that I *owe* my neighbors reciprocation for essential goods that they, in effect, *force* me to take from them, denying me the option to provide the goods for myself or to do without."[62] In this scenario *A* cannot be justly accused of trying to *take advantage* of his neighbors, and is therefore under no obligation, Simmons says, to participate in the scheme, i.e. pay taxes, take part in the upkeep of the trench, and so on.

Nevertheless, I believe that Klosko's arguments against the "acceptance" condition remain persuasive. Simmons's "individual well" example is simply inapposite, and the reason is obvious. There is no individual "well" that can be dug that will supply the digger with a defense against foreign aggression, nor is there any way to "opt out" of this benefit once it is supplied. For better or worse, we are all in the same boat, and will float or sink together.

Thus, in order to make Simmons's analogy apt, we would have to assume that it is *impossible* for anyone to supply themselves with water through their individual efforts (whether the trench is constructed or not) and *impossible* to deny them the benefits of the trench once built. In these circumstances, we would, I think, feel that all members of the neighborhood are obligated to contribute to this project, even if they claim they don't need or want the benefit, whether sincerely (if irrationally) or in order to free ride.

I believe that Simmons's notion of "acceptance" gains its plausibility from the fact that *ordinarily* we only incur moral obligations through our voluntary commitments. However, this need not be the case. Richard Arneson provides an example of an involuntary obligation, grounded in reciprocity. He asks us to imagine that Smith is involved in a boating accident, is thrown unconscious into the water, and is about to drown. Jones, passing by the scene of the accident, at some risk to himself pulls Smith into his small boat. Unfortunately, Smith's additional weight now causes Jones's boat to leak. If Smith, now alert and fully recovered, helps bail, both men will reach land safely.

However, it turns out that Smith is an excellent endurance swimmer, can swim safely to land, and wouldn't mind the exercise. Is Smith, who never asked for Jones's assistance, not morally obligated to stay and help Jones? Arneson rightly suggests that he is.[63] I contend that a person in the "neighborhood trench construction" case, as I have modified it, who refuses to contribute is committing the same sort of moral wrong as Smith would be (whatever his reasons) if he fails to help Jones in Arneson's example.

The libertarian principle of fairness

If, as I have argued, Klosko is correct and "acceptance" (as understood by Simmons) is not a precondition to the operation of the principle of fairness, we still need to formulate a version of the principle that will generate political obligations that are consistent with the moral claims made in Chapter 1, specifically the key notion of side constraints. For the reasons discussed below, Klosko's version will not suffice.

I believe that Klosko is right, for purposes of defining the scope of political obligations, to distinguish between different categories of public goods. I also believe that what he regards as indispensable ones might *roughly* coincide with the functions of the minimal state. However, I am unconvinced that the logic Klosko uses to justify the principle can be *confined* to goods of this type.

As I understand it, Klosko's argument is *not* that the indispensable nature of a public good is by itself sufficient to justify the coercion of free riders to

fund it. Rather, the importance of the good enables us to presume that everyone actually does want it, with the exception of those (like pacifists) who can
convince us that they are different in this regard from their fellow citizens.

But as a matter of *fact*, i.e. without the need for any presumption, there
may also be discretionary public goods that almost everyone wants—e.g.
cleaner air, less traffic, basic scientific research, and so on. So, why doesn't
the principle also operate in these cases? But, I think that it is obvious (as
Klosko recognizes) that the case for coercion to fund such goods is much
weaker than for indispensable goods such as national defense.

To see this, compare the case for coercive taxation to fund military defense
with another public good, basic scientific research. As argued in Chapter 1,
our special moral status has its origins in our rational agency. This attribute
demands respect in the form of noninterference with our autonomy, i.e.
side constraints against various forms of aggression.

Quite clearly, deterring or preempting foreign attacks and international
terrorism promote rational agency in a way that basic scientific research
does not. While advances in science may improve our standard of living
or extend our life expectancy, they do not materially enhance our ability
to conform our conduct to the moral law, the hallmark of rational agency.
Therefore, the coercion of persons to support national defense is an exception to Nozickian side constraints because it can be justified in terms of the
very value, rational agency, which generates those constraints.

This distinction can be seen in a second way. National defense and basic
science differ with respect to their impact on other members of the community. Contributions in support of basic research are discretionary in a
way that support of national defense is not. Those who free ride on the
funding of the former do not *compel* others to make up the difference. A
lack of optimal funding for science will not mark the end of rational agency
(or civilization as we know it). The same point can be made regarding many
other nonessential public goods, including Nozick's neighborhood entertainment association.

In contrast, those who refuse to fund national defense place the remainder of society in an intolerable dilemma: either make up the deficit or risk
a moral catastrophe. These free riders, sincere or not, collapse the moral
space of their fellow citizens.[64] They commit a passive form of aggression,
and accordingly, it is legitimate for a relatively just and peaceful state to
compel them to pay their fair share of the cost of military defense. In light
of the above and informed by the moral principles defended in Chapter 1,
I claim that the principle of fairness is limited to the obligation to support
public goods necessary for the preservation of rational agency.

We have thus arrived at the "libertarian principle of fairness," viz., that if the benefits and burdens of cooperating with the state in a program necessary to secure our rational agency are fairly distributed, then all rational agents are morally obligated to participate.[65] We now turn to the question of whether the libertarian principle of fair play can be extended to vindicate the internal protective functions of the minimal state.

A defense of the minimal state's exclusive role in supplying domestic security

It is important to recognize at the start that the justification of the minimal state's monopoly in the supply of protective services, i.e. law enforcement, criminal and civil adjudication, and punishment, presents a different challenge than does the case of national defense. The issue with respect to domestic security is not simply dealing with the problem of free riders (discussed in the previous section), but the right of competing PAs and independents to operate outside the control of the state. The anarchist's position is that she *will* contribute to the cooperative venture of securing "law and order," but on her own terms.

The case for coercion in the cause of internal protective services is tougher to make than for military defense because the former goods are, to a large extent, excludable. In other words, those who refuse to pay for law enforcement or the courts could be denied the benefits thereof: for example, the police could be instructed not to respond to calls for help that originate from their residences, perpetrators of aggression against them would not be prosecuted in the criminal courts and they could be denied the right to file civil lawsuits. If free riders are cut off from the benefits of a good, there is clearly less justification for imposing on them the unwanted costs.[66]

As in the case of national defense, not all states are entitled to monopolies in the provision of domestic protective services. A state might be minimal, but nevertheless may supply goods in a manifestly corrupt or discriminatory manner. Accordingly, we will restrict our claim of justifiable monopolies to those states that operate substantially in accordance with F. A. Hayek's construal of the rule of law, discussed below. My claim is that only in a society roughly organized along these lines will its members have the right to exclude private PAs and independents from the unauthorized administration of justice.

When politicians and media commentators speak of a society that is governed by the "rule of law," they are typically referring to a democracy that exhibits a host of familiar legal institutions and procedures, including "due process," "equal protection," and the "separation of powers" (or political "checks and balances"). While Hayek would agree that these features characterize societies operating under the rule of law, his understanding of this concept differs from the conventional one in two fundamental respects.

First, Hayek appreciates that the rule of law cannot consist merely of the sorts of constitutional protections mentioned above because the ultimate legislator can always abrogate them. For these formal safeguards to actually protect our moral space, something must stand *behind* them. Accordingly, for Hayek the rule of law is "not a rule of the law, but a rule concerning what the law ought to be, a meta-legal doctrine or a political ideal."[67] Critically, our constitutional protections will be maintained only if our commitment to them forms "part of the moral tradition of the community, a common ideal shared and unquestionably accepted by the majority."[68]

Second, for Hayek a community governed by the rule of law will adhere to two key legal principles.[69] The first of these is that its legislation must be "abstract" (or "general") in nature.[70] Hayek uses the example of the traffic code to illustrate the "flavor" of this crucial distinction. This system is designed to maximize safety for all travelers, without commanding motorists to travel to particular locations, at particular times, for particular purposes, and so forth.[71]

For Hayek, enactments that comport with the rule of law inform

people in advance what action the state will take in certain types of situation, defined in general terms, without reference to time and place or particular people. They refer to typical situations into which anyone may get and in which existence of such rules will be useful for a great variety of individual purposes.[72]

Accordingly, when our lawmakers decided that we should all drive on the right, it was not because they sought to advance the interests of any class or group, but simply to establish the sort of rule of universal application that is required under such circumstances.

In contrast, when the legislature prohibits an employee from directly bargaining with her employer because a majority of her co-workers wish to be represented by a union, the law has lost its abstract character and is being used to advance the interests of one constituency at the expense of another. Here, the law becomes, instead of a "roadmap" to be used by all, an instrument of coercion.

Since legislation that appears on its face to be "abstract" may be designed to have a disproportionate impact on a particular group or community,

Hayek introduces a second, complementary principle, that of "equality."[73] This principle demands that we "ask whether we can or cannot foresee how a law will affect particular people."[74] If there is disproportionate impact, "equality" can only be satisfied if the members of the group singled out acknowledge the legitimacy of the distinction. Finally, this principle demands that legislation apply equally to all, including the legislators.[75]

In Hayek's schema, a "government which cannot use coercion except in the enforcement of general rules...cannot determine the material position of particular people or enforce distributive or 'social' justice."[76] Hayek recognizes that the state might pass laws that are unwise and unjust, yet still comport with the rule of law. However, in a society committed to Hayek's political ideal, the "fact that all rules apply equally to all, including those who govern...makes it improbable that any oppressive rules will be adopted."[77]

It should be understood that a society governed by this "meta-legal doctrine" would not necessarily conform perfectly to libertarian principles. The electorate might pass legislation that is both abstract and in compliance with Hayek's other criteria for consistency with the rule of law, yet unjust from the libertarian perspective. For example, the voters might mandate the supply of discretionary public goods, funding them with a tax scheme that doesn't discriminate against any particular group. However, this would violate the side constraint against coercion because such programs are not essential for the preservation of rational agency.

Rational agents should, subject to the above exception, prize the rule of law because, when internalized, it shields the individual from aggression by others or the state. However, and this is a critical point, as noted above the rule of law will be maintained only if it is engrained in the community. Accordingly, while democracy is a necessary means for achieving and maintaining the rule of law, Hayek stresses that,

> the authority of democratic decision rests on its being made by the majority of a community which is held together by certain beliefs common to most members; and it is necessary that the majority submit to these common principles even when it may be in its immediate interest to violate them.[78]

The point of this exegesis is that unlike in Nozick's invisible hand narrative, those living in a society substantially governed by Hayek's rule of law are *justified* in rejecting legal procedures and punishments employed by outsiders, even if they are formally the "same" procedures. As indicated above, one of the central characteristics of governance in conformity with this ideal is equality before the law. In other words, all members of the society must play by the same rules, and the rules will be administered impartially. In such a society unreliable procedures or barbaric punishments will not be tolerated because everyone, and everyone's friends, family and affiliates, will be subject to them.

Moreover, malfeasance in the operation of the legal system is subject to continuing supervision and rectification by the political process, so that, for example, incompetent, corrupt or malicious judges and prosecutors can be impeached or voted out of office. The fact that all aspects of the legal system are subject to political review in a society committed to the rule of law gives them legitimacy. The members of such a state have, I claim, a morally justified expectation that they not be required to submit involuntarily to autonomous procedures.

Accordingly, it is possible to apply the libertarian principle of fair play to the supply of protective services. Without "law and order" the exercise of our rational agency will be severely constrained or even eliminated. The supply of this good benefits all persons. To secure it, the citizenry of a state governed by the rule of law have collectively foregone the opportunity to employ their individually preferred legal procedures.

They do so in exchange for a reciprocal commitment by their fellow citizens, and this arrangement ensures that the justice system is, within tolerable limits, fairly and impartially administered. The anarchist claim is that private PAs and independents are entitled to exercise a privilege surrendered by the rest of society. The above argument shows that, to the contrary, members of a reasonably just state have the right to demand that such parties submit to its rules.

We would expect that in a society that has internalized the rule of law there would be a substantial accommodation of members' desire for alternatives to the state system. Just as our far-from-libertarian polity allows the middle class and wealthy to escape the public educational system by sending their children to parochial or private schools, it has gone some distance toward permitting and even encouraging the emergence of private competitors to the state's protective services.

Thus, one can hire private forensic specialists and detectives, security guards and consultants, and arbitrators whose decisions have the force of law. The last option is the most significant because binding arbitration is only an effective substitute for the state's civil litigation system because our courts generally enforce both agreements to arbitrate and the judgments rendered by arbitrators pursuant to such arrangements. But we are only willing to authorize this private competition because the political process ensures that it produces outcomes consistent with our values.

Our state, like all past, present, and (in all probability) future states is, at best, imperfectly committed to the rule of law. The question then presents itself as to the extent of our political obligation to such a flawed enterprise. In response, I would note that there is no reason to think that political obligation operates in a binary manner; that is, we either have it or we don't. To the contrary, we should suppose that political obligations, like moral duties generally, come in varying degrees of stringency.

Thus, with respect to "ideal" states—in which virtually all members fully embrace Hayek's political ideal—we might have not only a strong obligation to obey their laws but also a duty to take other positive actions to support them, i.e. voluntary participation in civic organizations, service in the armed forces, active participation in the political process, and so on. On the other hand, with respect to states where only a majority of members are weakly committed to the rule of law, perhaps our duty is limited simply to obeying the rules. Therefore, we may have meaningful political obligations even to seriously flawed states, provided that they generally safeguard our rational agency.[79]

In summary, in response to the challenge posed by the anarchist, we have established a role for the relatively just and peaceful state as provider of national defense and as the exclusive supplier of domestic protective services. Alternatively, if either the Holcombe or Cowen thesis described above is true, then the debate regarding the intrinsic immorality of the state turns out to be irrelevant for all practical purposes, and we should turn our attention to shaping the institutions of our society so that the state governs in a manner respectful of libertarian rights.

We will touch on one final topic before concluding our defense of the minimal state. As mentioned at the beginning of this chapter, Nozick skirts the question of whether the role of the minimal state should be expanded to include such additional functions as environmental regulation, infrastructure construction, public health (enforcing mass vaccinations and the like), and so forth. As will be seen momentarily, he had good reason to steer clear of this difficult issue.

This debate is usually framed in terms of whether it is "necessary" for the state to perform the functions referenced above. But if the use of "necessary" implies that the state's involvement in these activities is justified if its absence would cause a substantial drop-off in overall societal welfare, then this approach presupposes the soundness of consequentialism. Clearly, from the natural rights libertarian perspective, this is the wrong question. Just as we rejected a hypothetical policy of state-compelled organ transplants, even if such a program would save lives, we should on these same principles reject state compulsion generally even if the outcome does not maximize utility.

In place of this consequentialist analysis, we defended above a libertarian principle of fairness that would justify state coercion only in support of those functions necessary to secure our rational agency. However, we cannot exclude the possibility that this principle will saddle us with gross inefficiencies or serious hardships. For example, it is often claimed that without the benefit of the state's power of eminent domain it will be prohibitively expensive to build roads or other infrastructure projects because of the problem of holdouts.[80] In other words, the owners of key parcels of land will either refuse to sell at any price because they sincerely prefer owning their land to any amount of money or will demand exorbitant sums because they recognize that they have a chokehold over a project of great economic value.

A number of libertarian economists have argued that there are free market solutions to this difficulty and that the magnitude of the problem, if any, has been greatly exaggerated.[81] Still, there is simply no way to adjudicate this dispute in advance of solid evidence, which unfortunately will be unavailable until the state gets out of the eminent domain business. Accordingly, as acknowledged above, it is at least theoretically possible that adherence to libertarian principles might impose serious hardships on the citizenry in various ways. At some point, such deprivations will amount to the sort of "moral catastrophe" that Nozick cites as a possible exception to the inviolability of rights. As argued in Chapter 6, natural rights libertarians can, consistently with their core principles, accommodate such cases.

Chapter 5

Property Rights, Capitalism, and the Rule of Law

In this sense, the theory of the Communists may be summed up in the single sentence: Abolition of private property.

Karl Marx, the Communist Manifesto [1848]

The Founding Fathers knew a government can't control the economy without controlling people. And they knew when a government sets out to do that, it must use force and coercion to achieve its purpose. So we have come to a time for choosing.

Ronald Reagan, Nationally Televised Address [1964][1]

In this work we have so far focused on those issues of political philosophy that are particularly relevant to Nozick-style libertarianism. Thus, we have explicated the ethical foundation of natural rights, traced the implications of such rights for egalitarian principles of justice, and considered whether libertarian rights are compatible with the coercion required to enforce the dictates of even the most minimal state. We now come to an important idea that is broadly embraced by libertarians of all stripes, i.e. the tight connection between property rights and liberty generally.

The Libertarian Thesis Regarding Property and Freedom

Richard Pipes, a prominent historian known for his studies of Russia, nicely summarizes the libertarian view of economic rights: "there is an intimate connection between public guarantees of ownership and individual liberty; that while property in some form is possible without liberty, the contrary is inconceivable."[2] We will refer to this claim as the "libertarian thesis." This theory clearly cannot be validated (or discredited) by philosophical analysis since it is essentially an empirical claim. Thus, it can only be tested by examining the dynamics of actual societies. And, since the theoretical relationship between secure property rights and personal freedom manifests itself over long time horizons, only historical investigation will do.

Having stated the libertarian thesis, and having noted its empirical nature, we could just leave well enough alone. That is, I could simply acknowledge that it is not an appropriate subject for *philosophical* analysis, and leave the reader to fend for him or her self. However, given its central place in libertarianism, I believe it would be negligent to leave this case unprosecuted.

Accordingly, we will illustrate the libertarian thesis by means of a three-nation historical survey encompassing England, Germany, and Mexico. I hope in this way to identify and describe the actual transmission mechanisms that connect property rights with individual liberty. The central idea is that the successful defense by one or more strata of society of their property against the arbitrary intrusions of the state triggers a "chain reaction" of social developments that have, under favorable circumstances, evolved into industrial capitalism.

A market economy in turn further widens the ambit of prosperity by creating a powerful middle class, thereby strengthening the appeal of the rule of law. In contrast, when the state comes to dominate both the political and economic domains, the stage is set for disastrous outcomes. We will briefly address the methodological issues raised by my defense of the libertarian thesis at the end of our mini-survey.

Before concluding this chapter, we will apply the libertarian thesis to our own polity. Sadly, our electorate appears oblivious to the lessons of history, and has partially demolished the wall that separates the political and economic worlds, threatening grave mischief by enabling the state to use economic rewards to further political ends.

The rule of law

While the libertarian thesis asserts a connection between a state's protection of property rights and the existence of freedom generally, it does not on its face specify the means by which this link is established. My hypothesis is that secure property rights lead over time to the development of those societal attitudes that produce the rule of law.

As you may recall from our discussion in Chapter 4, when Hayek's political ideal—the rule of law—is internalized it constrains the state by preserving "a private sphere clearly distinct from the public sphere [in which] the private individual cannot be ordered about but is expected to obey only the rules which are equally applicable to all."[3] Moreover, the abstract nature of the rule of law would preclude its use as a tool for social engineering or redistribution. I am sure that Hayek would be the first to acknowledge that no current or past society has ever totally committed itself to the rule of law.

We should also note here that while Hayek acknowledges that the democratic process plays an essential role in the maintenance of the rule of law, he understands its value to consist solely in its role as a means to this end. He is highly critical of what he terms the dogmatic or doctrinaire democrat who seeks to submit every question of policy to the vote:

> The crucial conception of the doctrinaire democrat is that of popular sovereignty. This means to him that majority rule is unlimited and unlimitable. The ideal of democracy, originally intended to prevent all arbitrary power, thus becomes the justification for a new arbitrary power.[4]

The lynchpin of Hayek's political ideal is that "the power of the majority ultimately derives from, and is limited by, the principles which the minorities also accept."[5]

It should be evident from the above that the rule of law is not only distinct from representative democracy, but that the practice of the latter may endanger the existence of the former. Political theorists have long recognized the danger of "tyrannies of the majority" arising within democracies.[6] Such coalitions may turn the state's monopoly on force against disfavored groups. A number of our familiar political institutions were consciously designed by the Founding Fathers to minimize this danger, which history has proven to be all too real.[7]

For example, the original leaders of the French Revolution were sent to the guillotine by the vote of the National Assembly, which came to be dominated by an even more radical, second generation of revolutionaries. Closer to home, as Thomas Sowell has observed: "The systematic denial of rights to American blacks in the Southern states during the Jim Crow era was a classic example of democratic despotism."[8] During WWII, American citizens of Japanese ancestry were shipped off to internment camps without even the semblance of due process, and this gross violation of the Constitution was perpetrated or approved by all three branches of the federal government.

As of this writing, something approaching a durable tyranny of the majority is developing in Venezuela, where most of the populace appears willing to surrender their rights to an autocrat in exchange for the mirage of economic security.[9] Similarly, following the collapse of the former Soviet

Union, it appeared that Russia was set on a democratic path. Yet in recent years free and fair elections have given way to an increasingly repressive political structure. Now, only Vladimir Putin's party, United Russia, has the means to promote its candidates, freedom of the press has been severely curtailed, and the judicial system is used to punish and intimidate the opponents of the regime.[10] The experience of Venezuela and Russia reminds us that democracy can slide into dictatorship in relatively short order. It is thus apparent that the mere existence of democratic institutions will not guarantee our liberties.

Indeed, as strange as this may sound to many of my readers, because all modern democracies, including our own, exercise their monopoly of force to determine many matters properly left to the individual, they function as tyrannies of the majority to this extent. The Social Security system is a single example of this phenomenon amongst the countless others that could be cited. Under this program, workers entrust the federal government with 12.4 percent (6.2 percent from both employee and employer) of their earnings (up to cutoff of $106,800 as of 2010) to support an older generation's retirement. In exchange, they get an *unsecured* promise that several decades later a new generation will do the same for them. I do not object, of course, to my fellow citizens freely participating in this arrangement, but I think it outrageous that I (and millions of other Americans) have been *involuntarily* tied to the mast of this sinking financial ship. Much the same could be said of the Medicare program.

It is the general absence of coercion and not the existence of a particular form of government that characterizes the rule of law. Since the democratic process imposes the will of the majority on the minority, it should be invoked only to decide those matters for which it is impossible to accommodate individual choice. The history of Great Britain illustrates the distinction between democracy and liberty.

Before the expansion of suffrage to the (male) middle class in 1867, only one in six adult males had the vote; even afterwards, the working classes, the poor, and all women were still excluded.[11] Moreover the value of the franchise was limited by the fact that only the ministers of the House of Commons were elected; the other two branches of government, the executive and the House of Lords, remained hereditary. Clearly, prior to 1867 our mother country was not a "representative" democracy in any meaningful sense, and the expansion of the franchise that year could only be said to modestly affect this assessment. Nevertheless, as discussed later in this chapter, there is no doubt that Britain substantially enjoyed the rule of law for over 150 years prior to the 1867 Reform.[12]

In short, democracy is a double-edged sword that may serve as a tool of oppression as well as a mechanism for protecting individual rights. Whether it will be employed for good or ill in any given society will depend on the extent to which it has ingrained Hayek's political ideal. This observation naturally gives rise to an inquiry regarding the socioeconomic conditions that promote the rule of law. It is to this question that we now turn.

Private property and the rule of law—three cases

I hope to show the connection between private property rights and the Hayekian rule of law by comparing the modern histories of Great Britain, Germany, and Mexico. The former narrative will illuminate the mechanisms by which a society's commitment to individual rights is strengthened by its respect for economic liberty, while the latter two examples will illustrate the pernicious and even catastrophic consequences that may ensue when the state comes to dominate both the political and economic spheres.

Historians generally hold that with the "Glorious Revolution" of 1688 England became the first state to achieve some rough approximation of the rule of law. The English Bill of Rights, adopted the following year, was rightly celebrated as a profoundly significant milestone by the intelligentsia of that time, not just in Britain but throughout Europe.[13] The significance of this achievement, imperfect as it may have been, can perhaps be best appreciated in contrast to the histories of other traditional European powers: Spain was ruled by a dictator as recently as 1975; Germany did not achieve the rule of law until the post-WWII reconstruction under Allied tutelage; and it cannot be said that Russia enjoys the rule of law even today.

Therefore, we are prompted to ask whether it was simply a historical accident that English society embraced individual liberty before others or whether the libertarian thesis may be the best explanation for this development. Here, we are particularly indebted to Professor Pipes, whose *Property and Freedom* (quoted above), artfully makes this case.

However, while Pipes more or less ends his analysis of English history with the Glorious Revolution, we will continue the narrative into the Victorian era, while supplementing his work with other sources. Moreover, while *Property and Freedom* is primarily devoted to a comparison of English and Russian history, I have elected to include two additional "case studies." While I cannot claim any especially compelling justification for the selection of Germany and Mexico, the former nation played a momentous and incredibly destructive role in the history of the twentieth century, and thus seems worthy of our attention.

On the other hand, while Mexico may have had a less consequential role in world history, it shares a long border with us and its national experience is intertwined with our own in a number of significant ways. Furthermore, our southern neighbor is blessed with abundant natural resources, yet there are some 10 million or more Mexicans currently seeking a better life in the United States. Inquiring minds want to know: why is the flow of humanity in this direction, rather than the other way around?

Britain

Any analysis of the evolution of the rule of law in England must begin with the feudal system imported by William after the Norman Conquest, which resembled a sort of grand "pyramid scheme." At the apex was the king, who enfeoffed (leased) lands to the great barons, who in exchange swore their undying loyalty to the monarch and, more tangibly, agreed to supply a nego-tiated number of suitably equipped knights in time of war. Additionally, the nobles undertook certain financial obligations to their ruler.[14]

The great lords in turn "sub-leased" their vast land holdings to *mesne* (midway) lords, who in exchange undertook parallel military and finan-cial obligations to their overlord. The *mesne* lord was permitted to and did divide his property among his vassals, who assumed corresponding obliga-tions to him.[15] However, while feudalism endured for centuries, the variable quality of the monarch was the system's "Achilles heel."

England's King John lost Normandy to King Philip of France in 1204, and until his death in 1216 was determined to regain these lands. In order to do so, the king "imposed an ever-increasing burden of taxation upon England to provide funds for the hiring of mercenaries on a grand scale" and gener-ally abused his feudal prerogatives.[16] As a consequence, the great barons felt insecure in their lives and property and so in 1215 imposed the Magna Carta on King John by force.[17]

The nobles "were primarily intent on removing the vagueness which sur-rounded feudal relations, on re-stating and re-asserting the feudal law and compelling the king to acknowledge its authority."[18] Its most familiar and perhaps most significant provision is that: "No freeman shall be imprisoned or disseised or exiled or in any way destroyed, nor will we go upon him nor will we send upon him except by the lawful judgment of his peers or (and) the law of the land."[19]

By compelling the monarch to agree to abide by existing feudal law and custom, this Ur-constitution established the precedent that the ruler could not levy new taxes without the consent of the nobles and later their representatives in parliament.[20] All subsequent English kings accepted this precedent as binding until the advent of the Stuart dynasty at the beginning of the seventeenth century.[21] The first Stuart king, James I (reigned 1603–25) brought with him from Scotland notions of royal absolutism that had long been foreign to English soil.[22] However, it was James' son and successor, Charles I who, in dire need of revenues to prosecute first continental wars and then a conflict with Scotland, openly defied the long-established prerogatives of parliament in the matters of taxation and the independence of the judiciary.[23]

Parliamentary resistance to Charles I was based, in additional to his Catholicism, on notions of property rights which were, by then, gaining currency amongst the educated classes. As Pipes notes:

> [T]he political resistance to early Stuart absolutism was driven by the defense of property, which acquired a political dimension. The parliamentary opposition...did not so much insist on the king's convening parliament and honoring their authority in taxation on the grounds of historical precedent or constitutional principle, but rather invoked these precedents to ensure the inviolability of property.[24]

The critical development here was not simply the determination of the nobles and gentry to defend their property against the Crown, but the growing conviction that they had a God-given *right* to do so, whether recognized in the statute books or not. The leading proponent of this natural law doctrine was the great jurist Sir Edward Coke, who "conceived of law as having an independent existence of its own, set above the King as well as his subjects, and bound to judge impartially between them."[25]

The triumph of the parliamentary forces in the Civil War, and the execution of Charles I in 1649, brought to an end the absolute monarchy in England.[26] With the ascension to the throne of William of Orange in 1688 as part of what was even then called the "Glorious Revolution," a critical milestone was achieved. The Bill of Rights not only delineated the respective powers of the parliament and the crown (including an acknowledgment that the sovereign could not levy taxes without parliamentary consent), but also guaranteed freedom of expression, religious liberty (subject to certain civil disabilities), habeas corpus, and an independent judiciary.[27]

The Glorious Revolution is comprehensible only as the product of fundamental developments in the economic sphere. By the end of the sixteenth century, England was a dominant maritime and trading power.[28] As a result, for the century leading up to the Bill of Rights, London functioned as a gigantic Petri dish for the cultivation of entrepreneurial activity. Its port facilitated the import and export of goods on a grand scale, while the City served as the center of banking and foreign exchange, communications, commodity trading, and mercantile activity of all kinds.[29]

In sum, late-seventeenth-century English economic elites were in a position exactly the opposite of that described by Bob Dylan in *Like a Rolling Stone*, i.e. "when you ain't got nothing, you got nothing to lose." In fact, the most powerful and influential sectors of English society had everything to lose from the unrestrained exercise of executive power and were thus motivated to hem it in by promoting the authority of parliament, the independence of the judiciary, and the Bill of Rights. As described below, this "virtuous circle" of secure property rights and the rule of law continued to unfold throughout modern British history.

By the middle of the eighteenth century much of the population had shed its agricultural roots and was available for employment in manufacturing or trade.[30] During that era approximately one in ten Britons lived in London, compared to one in forty Frenchmen who were Parisians.[31] The cultural, demographic, and technological changes that occurred in the first half of the eighteenth century set in motion the "Industrial Revolution," the term coined by Arnold Toynbee to describe the economic transformation of Britain between 1760 and 1840.

It was not by chance that this economic boom first occurred in Great Britain. In explaining this fact, one prominent historian cites a number of institutions that were present in British society to a unique degree, including "rights of private property," the ability of parties to "[e]nforce rights of contract," and "stable government, not necessarily democratic, but itself governed by publicly known rules (a government of laws rather than men)."[32] The spike in productivity resulting from this industrialization dramatically raised living standards in Britain. *Laissez faire* prevailed during this period, not as deliberate economic policy, but because of both political inertia and the absence of the necessary regulatory apparatus.[33]

As a result of these developments, by the late eighteenth century vast wealth was held in private hands.[34] The rich and super-rich demanded new categories of goods and services that would be supplied by small business owners, professionals, artisans, and other members of society's middle stratum.[35] As a consequence, the growing middle class owed its livelihood not to the state, but to private employers or their own efforts. (Adam Smith famously referred to late-eighteenth-century Great Britain as "a nation of shopkeepers.") Robert Heilbroner describes the transformational effects of capitalism as follows:

> Under capitalism two realms of authority existed where there had for-
> merly been only one—a realm of political governance for such purposes
> of law and order and a realm of economic governance over the processes
> of production and distribution. Each realm was largely shielded from
> the other. The capitalists who dominated the market system were not
> automatically entitled to governing power, and the members of the gov-
> ernment were not entrusted with decisions as to what goods should be
> produced or how social rewards should be distributed.[36]

In addition to the impulse to protect one's property against arbitrary
confiscation or taxation, there is a more subtle mechanism by which free
markets produce resistance to state coercion. As Hayek observes, those who
are forced to fend for themselves, rather than rely on the state for their
livelihoods, will come to prize

> independence and self-reliance, individual initiative and local responsi-
> bility, the successful reliance on voluntary activity, noninterference with
> one's neighbor and tolerance of the different and the queer, respect for
> custom and tradition, and a healthy suspicion of power and authority.[37]

Persons so disposed will generally resist the intrusion of the political authorities into their private spheres. On the other hand, those who depend on
the government for sustenance are more likely to develop a different set of
values, including an acceptance of the legitimacy of state action in a much
wider variety of circumstances.

It should be apparent from the preceding that the expansion of the
franchise in the United Kingdom to the *nouveau riche* in 1832 and then
more broadly in 1867 did not create the rule of law, but was its byproduct.
While a century and a half of scientific and technological progress has provided the current generation of Britons with a standard of living unimagi-
nable by their Victorian counterparts, it can scarcely be doubted that the
great queen's subjects enjoyed a freedom quite unknown in contemporary
England in being spared the ubiquitous governmental meddling of the sort
that they (and we) are now forced to endure.

The American colonists absorbed the natural rights philosophy that prevailed in the mother country, as shown most directly in the profound influence of John Locke's writings on the Founding Fathers.[38] Their demand
for "no taxation without representation" and other liberties simply asserted

their entitlement to rights that Englishmen had secured generations earlier.

Germany's tragic history

The course of German history is profoundly different from Britain's with respect to the independence of the political and economic realms. The critical feature of the English narrative from the Magna Carta through the Victorian era was the ever-increasing autonomy of the private sector relative to the authority of the state, while the decisive feature in the German experience was the unification of political and economic control in the hands of the executive until this unfettered power culminated in the absolute tyranny of the Third Reich.

We may start our review of German history with the conclusion of the Peace of Westphalia in 1648, which marked the end of the Thirty Years' War. At this time, "Germany" consisted of some 300 large and small, secular and ecclesiastical, Catholic and Protestant principalities loosely organized under the banner of the German Empire, also known as the Holy Roman Empire. Brandenburg, in northern Germany, was one of the "mini-states" destined to play a critical role in this nation's history.

This principality was at the time of Westphalia ruled by Frederick William (reigned from 1640–88), a descendant of the Hohenzollern dynasty. In addition to Brandenburg (and other minor territories), Frederick governed the distant Duchy of Prussia (now, Kaliningrad, Russia), which he held as a fief under the King of Poland.

As part of the Peace of Oliva in 1660, which settled the First Northern War (1655–60), Polish sovereignty over the Duchy of Prussia ended and it became a possession of the Hohenzollerns. Thus a major political force was born, rivaled only by Austria in the German-speaking world.[39] The history of Brandenburg-Prussia (which through territorial accretion evolved into modern Prussia) was driven for the next 126 years by its three powerful kings: Frederick William (the "Great Elector"), his son Frederick William I of Prussia (ruled 1688–1740), and his grandson, Frederick the Great (ruled 1740–86).

Brandenburg-Prussia did not enjoy the large population or economic strength of rival European powers. Accordingly, in order to compete with them on the geopolitical chessboard, Frederick William and his progeny focused their energies on increasing the state's military might. As one authority puts it, "the army was the beginning and end of all policy."[40] Thus, at the time of Frederick's death in 1688 he had built Brandenburg- Prussia's army up to some 30,000 men.[41] By the end of his grandson's reign, a century later, the Prussian army numbered almost 200,000 men and was the strongest in Europe.[42]

In order to finance this expansion, the three monarchs sought to strengthen their kingdom's economy by delegating its management to a huge professional bureaucracy. These administrators pursued a mercantilist (export-driven) trade strategy coupled with interventionist domestic economic policies, including "the exclusion of competitive production, either by limiting the number of producers or the grant of exclusive market rights."[43] From the death of Frederick the Great until the ascension to power of Otto von Bismarck in the middle of the following century, nothing occurred in Prussia to threaten the state's grip on the economy.

The price of Prussian central planning was retarded economic development. While the Industrial Revolution was largely completed in the United Kingdom by 1840, industrialization did not begin in earnest in Germany and Prussia until after 1850.[44] Accordingly, the available evidence is that in the middle of the nineteenth century the British standard of living was at least 50 percent higher than the German.[45]

Bismarck, the Prussian Prime Minister, promoted economic liberalization in the late 1860s in order to foster industrialization and to channel the energies of the educated classes away from political agitation.[46] Acting through the parliament of the newly created Northern German Confederation (consisting of the northern states that had fought with Prussia against Austria in the war of 1866), he won approval of legislation that broke the power of the guilds, allowed the unregulated formation of corporations, established a Northern German code of commercial law, and removed other obstacles to *laissez faire*.[47] However, as we shall soon see, Germany's flirtation with free enterprise was to be brief and unfruitful.

The nationalist fervor aroused by the German states' decisive defeat of France in the war of 1870, in which the Prussian army fought side-by-side with troops from all other German principalities, set the stage for national unification.[48] Bismarck achieved this goal the following year, under terms that left Prussia as the dominant political power in the new Germany; a fact underscored by the proclamation of the Prussian king as "German Emperor."[49] The new state's response to the worldwide economic crash of 1873 would have profound implications both for this nation's future and for the world at large.

In response to and for decades following this major depression Prime Minister Bismarck and his successors abandoned the free market principles of the late 1860s, particularly with respect to tariffs and cartels. The distinguished English historian A. J. P. Taylor describes the impact of these policies, which is of such significance that I will quote him at length:

> Without protection, Germany would have had a less grandiose production of iron and steel, would have imported more, and would have concentrated instead on the more profitable finishing industries. She would have had a higher standard of life, a better and more fully developed system of transport, and every step in her economic advance would have promoted the prosperity and peacefulness both of Germany and other countries. In fact, Germany would have been so deeply bound to the world market as to be incapable of war. This was the vital consideration that made Bismarck's conversion to Protection inevitable... *The price was paid by the mass of German people who did not reap the full benefit of the great industrial advance...* The method of the 'eighties was economic conflict; fast on the heels of the tariffs came the Kartells, the great trade associations which fixed prices—high for the home market, artificially low for export—and which went from price-fixing to the regulation of production.[50] (Emphasis added)

Accordingly, despite the explosive industrialization that occurred in Germany from 1870 until the Great War, the average German never enjoyed during these decades the standard of living of his British counterpart.[51] Predictably, the tenor of German politics grew increasingly anti-capitalist from unification to Hitler's rise to power. In 1878, Bismarck reacted to the rising popularity of the Social Democratic party (which advocated a Marxist program of nationalizing all major industries) by persuading the parliament to pass legislation designed to cripple the party by preventing it from holding meetings and suppressing the publication of its literature.[52] In 1890, this legislation lapsed, and the popularity of "workers" parties continued to grow.

In addition to outright repression, Bismarck launched a more oblique attack on his leftist adversaries by implementing his famous social security programs. Between 1883 and 1889, Germany adopted compulsory employee insurance plans for health, accident/disability and retirement. Two-thirds of the cost of the health insurance system was borne by the workers, while the employers contributed the remainder; the accident/disability insurance program was funded entirely by employers; and the funding of pensions was divided between employers and employees, with the government also contributing.[53]

German leaders hoped that these "progressive" programs would take the wind out of the sails of the Social Democrats by demonstrating to the masses that they need not pursue a radical agenda in order to achieve material progress. However, as Taylor concludes,

> Social security did not achieve its immediate aim; it did not arrest the growth of the Social Democratic party. In a more profound sense it was successful; *it made the German workers value security more than liberty and look to the state rather than their own resources for any improvement in their condition.* The German workers came to feel that they too were receiving Protection and that the Reich was, in some sort, doing their work for them—the very feeling that had earlier been the ruin of German liberalism.[54] (Emphasis added)

The Social Democrats captured 34.8 percent of the vote in the national elections of 1912, the last before the Great War.[55] This made it the strongest German party, a status it held until 1932. In the November 1932 national elections, the last "free and fair" one in Germany before Hitler seized power, the Social Democratic party's vote fell to 20.7 percent, but the Communist party received 16.9 percent. The National Socialists received 33.1 percent.[56]

The full name of Hitler's party was the "National Socialist German Workers' Party," known by its infamous acronym, "Nazi." This name was not accidental. The Party's 1920 platform advocated a highly interventionist role for the state in the economy, including maintenance of full employment; the confiscation of all incomes not derived from labor (capital gains, dividends, interest, etc.); the nationalization of trusts; the abolition of land rents and speculation in land; and the communalization of department stores and their lease at cheap rents to small traders.[57]

Hayek, in *The Road to Serfdom*, explores in some detail the socialist roots of Nazi ideology. He quotes the writings of such prominent German intellectuals as Oswald Spengler and Arthur Moeller van der Bruck, who he describes as the "patron saint" of National Socialism, to establish the Nazis' widespread antipathy to the classic liberalism that was associated with the hated English.[58] While Hitler was a consummate political opportunist who cared about economics only as a means of achieving and maintaining total power, National Socialism's appeal to the masses was largely based on its overt hostility to capitalism (identified with the Jews) and Hitler's willingness to trample the rule of law in order to resolve the economic crisis facing the German people.[59] As Taylor observes: "In the beginning, anti-Semitism was an easy outlet for the vague socialism of the National Socialist rank and file, the destruction of Jewish shops a showy substitute for social change. As always, anti-Semitism was the socialism of fools."[60]

The course of modern German history validates Hayek's conclusion that the existence of ostensibly rights-preserving legal institutions is insufficient to safeguard the rule of law. While the 1871 German constitution designed by Bismarck was structurally deficient and thus incapable of checking a powerful executive,[61] the same could not be said about the 1919 Weimar constitution. Under this charter, universal suffrage was instituted and power dispersed among four distinct organs of government: an elected president (who appointed the chancellor, and had a veto right over the chancellor's ministerial appointments); the *Reichstag* (parliament); the *Reichsrat* (which represented the German states); and the chancellor, together with the ministries he supervised.[62]

Therefore, the Weimer constitution embodied the concepts of "separation of powers" and "checks and balances" characteristically found in societies that substantially honor the rule of law.[63] If what is committed to paper is decisive, the Third Reich would have been impossible. However, as both Marx and Hayek understood, the character of a nation's politics will be driven by the organization of its economy and not by the formal structure of its governance.[64]

Mexico

Mexico is a nation not so much younger than our own, endowed with great petroleum and other natural resources.[65] Yet, to this day our southern neighbor does not enjoy the rule of law and, not coincidentally, its citizens endure a standard of living (measured in terms of GDP per capita) less than one-third our own.[66] As a result, at least 10 million Mexicans have uprooted themselves from their family, culture, and language in order to enter the United States, often at great physical peril, in search of the economic opportunities denied them at home. Our media and academic elites have, perhaps because they are afraid of the answer, studiously avoided the question of what accounts for the glaring disparity in the quality of rights and standard of living that exists in these two nations.

Part of the explanation must lie in our respective national genealogies. While the United States had the good fortune of being colonized by the state that was the first to achieve a fair approximation of competitive capitalism, Mexico had no such luck. While the leaders of the Glorious Revolution were deeply imbued with Lockean notions of natural rights, autocrats ruled Spain and its precursor kingdoms from medieval times through most of the twentieth century.

It is difficult to pin down the impact of something as amorphous as political culture, but one scholar made the following comparison between the elites of early-nineteenth-century England and Mexico:

> When the old authoritarian system of Spain collapsed, it left no body of citizens, in the Peninsula or in America, trained to assume the responsibility of government...Autocracy was irresponsible and it came to foster irresponsibility. The so-called ruling class in New Spain was not a ruling class in the sense that it could take over the machinery of government and run it, say, as the upper and middle classes of England did. The wealthy and privileged of New Spain were as irresponsible as the Indians they despised...It was this recklessness and frivolity that made it impossible to set up a working government after Independence.[67]

This observation dovetails nicely with Hayek's hypothesis, discussed above, that *laissez faire* produces a distinctive set of social attitudes relative to economies that are heavily manipulated by the state.

In any case, after four decades of great political instability and violence it appeared that things were looking up for Mexico in 1857. In that year, a group of democratic reformers, including the future president, Benito Juarez, triumphed over General Santa Anna and the conservatives after a bitter, three-year civil war. The liberals passed legislation and adopted a new constitution that in their totality were known as "La Reforma." These measures abolished the jurisdiction of the ecclesiastical courts over the clergy in civil cases and prohibited corporations of any type from owning property not essential to their current operations (in effect, forcing the Church to auction off its massive real estate holdings).

Juarez was installed as president in 1861, but his government was overthrown almost immediately thereafter by the intervention of the French ruler, Napoleon III, who saw Latin America as a geopolitical prize that could be claimed by France. However, the liberal government eventually won its struggle with the French puppet, Emperor Maximilian, and after a semblance of order was restored, Juarez was elected president in 1867 and reelected in 1871.

It is difficult to characterize the economic policies of the two Juarez administrations along neat ideological lines. While the liberals supported and sought to encourage private enterprise within a democratic framework, the Reforms were premised on the idea that "the soil and subsoil are property of the nation, granted for use by the state as a concession, with the state retaining the option of expropriating it in the national interest."[68] Clearly, this philosophy was blatantly at odds with classical liberalism.

It also appears that Juarez was influenced by the "positivist" doctrine of Auguste Comte, who held that society should be governed by a scientific-industrial elite that would base policy on the "invariable laws" they would divine—hardly a *laissez faire* philosophy.[69] Comte merits a brief mention by Hayek in *The Road to Serfdom* as "that nineteenth-century totalitarian."[70] It is possible that Mexico's political culture would be materially different today if Juarez had governed for a longer period, but he died suddenly in 1872.

Porfirio Diaz's seizure of power in 1876 from Juarez's democratically elected successor, Sebastian Lerdo de Tejada, marked the beginning of over 30 years of political stability, albeit under dictatorial rule (often referred to as the "Porfiriato"). Here, it is possible to speak of a coherent economic policy, directed from the center. As one authority notes:

> Around him Diaz gathered many intellectuals (the *cientificos*). They were positivists who stressed the need for rational planning and development. The emphasis was on economic development to assure social progress. How such development was to be achieved was translated into one of Diaz' political slogans, "pan o palo" ("bread or the club"), meaning that acquiescence to official policies would ensure livelihood, even wealth, but failure to agree would bring sure reprisals—harassment, imprisonment, death. Another slogan was "few politics, much administration." Liberty was dropped from the earlier positivist triad of liberty, order and progress.[71]

Diaz's growth strategy relied on the *selective* recognition and protection of property rights. Stanford historian Stephen Haber describes the Porfiriato as

> a canonical example of crony capitalism. Crony capitalism is a system in which those close to the political authorities who make and enforce policies receive favors or entitlements that have economic value... One very common form that these favors take is to award some favored economic group with an official or quasi-official monopoly.[72]

This perversion of *laissez-faire* economics aligns the interests of the leaders of the political and economic spheres "in such a way that the political elite has no incentive to abrogate the property or special entitlements of the economic elite."[73] However, according to Haber, this arrangement produces "very skewed distributions of income and wealth" whereby the affluence of the few is achieved at the expense of the many, and "give[s] rise to disaffection from other members of the economic elite, who are not closely linked to the political elite."[74]

While crony capitalism under the Porfiriato sustained growth and stability for several decades, it bore the seeds of its own destruction. According to one source, as a result of the inflation produced by the narrowly focused boom economy, "the buying power of wage earners declined by as much as half during the Diaz years."[75] Under such circumstances, we should anticipate social unrest. The revolution of 1910 was the explosion of the pent-up resentments of those broad segments of society locked out of the Porfiriato's inner circle.[76]

This struggle, led by Francisco L. Madero, lasted several years but ultimately resulted in victory of the disparate revolutionary forces and the adoption of the Constitution of 1917. The charter enshrined a highly interventionist economic philosophy. For example, Article 27 interjected concepts of social utility and national benefit to limit the untrammeled use of private property, asserted state ownership of subsoil resources, and established land reform and government-directed agrarian programs. Article 123 included 31 separate provisions regulating employment in the private sector, and an additional 15 provisions relating to government employees.[77]

Mexico's government continued to practice crony capitalism following the revolution, but now embraced organized labor as its primary crony. As one might anticipate from the tenor of the Constitution, the labor laws that emerged in the decade following the revolution represented a capitalist's worst nightmare.[78] The 1927 contract that governed the nation's textile mills—the nation's most important industrial sector—was not only administered by a vast bureaucracy that was subject to union political manipulation, but worse,

> Law and contract transferred from owners to unions both hiring and firing. Supervisors could run factories only through the acquiescence of unions. The industry-wide contract specified the conditions of work. Paternalism rested with the union bosses rather than the factory owners.[79]

Mexican labor unions exploited their political power in the 1920s and beyond to extract above-market wage rates from the textile industry, while the authorities protected the mills from foreign competition by raising tariffs.[80] In addition, the mill owners were dissuaded from introducing new technology because their union contracts prevented them from realizing any cost savings.[81] The "odd man out" in this anti-competitive fandango was, of course, the hapless consumer. In the long run, an entire, once-promising industry was condemned to obsolescence.

Even greater damage was caused in the 1930s when the Mexican government took state control of the economy a critical step further by seizing key industries outright. In 1938, during the rule of General Cardenas (1934–40), the railroads were nationalized and given to the labor unions to manage. That same year, the Cardenas administration, in an action that would have disastrous long-term consequences for both the nation's economy and respect for the rule of law, expropriated the assets of foreign petroleum companies and nationalized the industry. Petroleos Mexicanos ("Pemex"), then a small agency, was delegated to manage the nation's energy resources.[82]

Pemex has, in its eight decades of operation, achieved a spectacular record of inefficiency and corruption, serving as "a cash machine for the government, a slush fund for politicians and a patronage mill for party loyalists."[83] State prosecutors have alleged that tens of millions of dollars were diverted from Pemex to fund the PRI's (unsuccessful) 2000 presidential campaign. Its own executives estimate that Pemex "loses more than $1 billion a year to fraud, theft, tax-evasion schemes and clandestine fuel sales by its workers and distributors," which have created illicit fortunes for Pemex managers and union bosses.

It is impossible to even estimate the economic loss suffered by Mexico as a result of this agency's inefficiency. Some hint of the gravity of this self-inflicted wound is provided by the following comparison. In 2004, Pemex had $69 billion in sales and 137,722 employees, while Exxon Mobil had $291 billion in sales and 85,900 employees.[84] Not surprisingly, a clear majority of Pemex's workers are unionized, while Exxon Mobil's are not. Shielded from the "ravages" of competition, Pemex did not until recently maintain even a rudimentary accounting system for tracking its expenses.[85]

Pemex was but one of 1,155 state-owned enterprises ("SOE") operating in Mexico during the early 1980s, including television channels, the telephone industry, railroads, airports, mining operations, and the entire banking system.[86] By the end of 1982, the SOE accounted for 4.4 percent of the nation's labor force, 30 percent of its long-term capital borrowing, and received subsidies equivalent to a crippling 18.5 percent of the state's GDP.[87] Finally recognizing the need for reform, in 1982 Mexico instituted a privatization program that reached its peak in 1988 under the Salinas administration. By 1993, the number of SOE had been reduced to 258.[88] However, while this policy is generally considered to have been an economic success, most of Mexico's major firms continue to operate in state-sponsored monopolies or oligopolies, shielding them from competition, while oppressive regulation stifles entrepreneurial activity.[89]

The state's history of economic intervention has not only provided a vast array of tools with which the political authorities can reward their allies and punish their foes, but has also stunted growth. Thus, the Mexican middle class is still relatively small and impotent. Moreover, workers employed by state owned or controlled businesses depend upon the authorities for their livelihood. In such circumstances, we can hardly expect the population to internalize the rule of law.

This economic backdrop explains Mexico's historically sclerotic and oppressive political superstructure. The Institutional Revolutionary Party ("PRI") ruled for 71 consecutive years, from 1929 to 2000, maintaining itself in power through massive political corruption and fraud that terminated only with the victory of the rival PAN party and the Vicente Fox presidency. In light of the relatively peaceful, if very contentious, transfer of power to a second democratically elected PAN president in 2006, there is some reason to hope that the rule of law might begin to take hold in this troubled nation. However, Mexico's commitment to this ideal is still quite tentative.[90]

Conclusions

Our mini-survey tends to validate Pipes' claim that:

> The right to property in and of itself does not guarantee civil rights and liberties. But historically speaking, it has been the single most effective device for ensuring both, because it creates an autonomous sphere in which, by mutual consent, neither the state nor society can encroach: by drawing a line between the public and the private, it makes the owner co-sovereign, as it were. Hence it is arguably more important than the right to vote.[91] (Footnote omitted)

The paradigmatic example of this process is the transformation of feudal England into first, the mercantilism of the Elizabethan era, followed by the emergence of "industrial capitalism" in the mid-to-late eighteenth century and finally into a modern, market economy. At each stage of this sequence, the balance of economic power shifted in favor of the private sector relative to the state, and the circle of prosperity expanded to include additional elements of society. One key byproduct of Britain's capitalist economy was the creation of a powerful middle class committed to the rule of law.

In contrast, Germany never achieved a bifurcation of the political and economic realms until the post-WWII era. Like Great Britain, Germany experienced the Industrial Revolution, but its entrepreneurs never held their wealth independently of the state, and the absence of a market economy left its middle class relatively small and feeble. Because the "ersatz-capitalism" experienced by German society did not bring peace and prosperity, the liberal values propagated by *laissez faire* in Great Britain were largely discredited in Germany. As a result, at its critical moment Germany was riven by deeply felt antagonisms between its propertied classes and the powerful trade unions, both seeking to turn the apparatus of the state against their enemy. Hitler exploited masterfully this complete breakdown in the rule of law.

Mexico's governments have been hostile to capitalism for more than 130 years and have not even today allowed the emergence of a truly independent private sector. Despite being blessed with great natural resources, its neo-socialist policies are responsible for its citizens having a standard of living far below that of the United States. Until 2000, Mexico endured a suffocating one-party rule for seven decades and continues to suffer from endemic corruption at all levels of government. There is a rueful saying in vogue south of the border to the effect that Mexico is "so far from God, so close to the United States." More accurate would be "so close to socialism, so far from prosperity and the rule of law."

Before concluding this short survey, I should say something about methodology. If there is a single quotation regarding history known to virtually every educated person it is surely George Santayana's warning that, "Those who cannot remember the past are condemned to repeat it." Most modern philosophers who have examined the traditional methods of historians would contend that Santayana, in making this statement, is implicitly adopting a number of dubious assumptions.[92]

Very briefly and somewhat crudely, these would include the idea that there are "lessons," i.e. general laws that may be learned (or "remembered") by means of historical analysis. Perhaps each historical event is the product of a unique set of causes or conditions, so that, like snowflakes, no two situations are identical. Thus, even if we remember the past, it will not be prologue to the future.

There is also serious doubt that it is possible to make any objective analysis of the past; that is, the historian's own conscious and unconscious biases will infect her understanding of the data. Moreover, there is the problem of separating what might be regarded as objective reality from our subjective understanding or representation of past events. Thus, we can well question whether there was any such "thing" as the "French Revolution," or whether historians have simply created it conceptually out of a series of discrete actions and events.[93] If this is true, it may only be possible to view the past through the lens of our construction of it, which will necessarily involve an interpretive (subjective) component.

I mention these objections to naïve historiography simply to acknowledge the impossibility of "proving" the libertarian thesis in the way that scientific theories may be validated. I will not wade any further into these controversies, since whatever obstacles they pose for the libertarian they pose equally for any competing interpretation of history. In any case, the purpose of this historical survey is not to prove this thesis, but merely to show that it is plausible.

I have sought to do this by demonstrating that the libertarian interpretation of history meshes well with the modern narratives of the three nations we have studied. I am happy to have my readers evaluate it for themselves using the standards described by Daniel Little, who holds that even in light of the contemporary critique:

> Historical knowledge depends on ordinary procedures of empirical investigation, and the justification of historical claims depends on providing convincing demonstration of the empirical evidence that exists to support or invalidate the claim. There is such a thing as historical objectivity, in the sense that historians are capable of engaging in good-faith interrogation of evidence in constructing theories of the past. But this should not be understood to imply that there is one uniquely true interpretation of historical processes and events.[94]

State Intervention in the Economy and the Rule of Law in Our Democracy

If the libertarian thesis is true, it has significant implications for our own governance. In the section below, we review what I contend is our democracy's ever-growing disregard of the salutary boundary between the political and economic spheres, which threatens the rule of law. In the name of social justice and in order to protect the citizenry against its own bad judgment, our government has, principally from the New Deal onward, asserted new powers and undertaken functions that were traditionally left to the private sector.[95]

Accordingly, we are subject to overreaching administrative regulations of every imaginable variety, confiscation of property by means of eminent

domain, redistributive and social welfare taxes, massive entitlement programs, agricultural subsidies and other forms of "corporate welfare," the
coercive labor code, paternalistic legislation of every stripe, restrictions on
international trade, and more. While liberals may defend such developments on egalitarian and other grounds, it is undeniable that they have
profoundly altered the relationship between citizen and state.

In democracies, if the authorities are able to determine economic outcomes, well-organized groups will use the political process as a means of
advancing their own ends at the expense of others. They will be met halfway
in this invidious enterprise by our politicians, who will surely bid against
each other for the support of such constituencies by offering ever more
generous terms.

Thus, if wages, prices, trade flows, capital allocation, and other economic
outcomes are not determined by the impersonal, "invisible hand" of the
marketplace, they must be fixed by the very personal and visible hand of
government officials. As Thomas Sowell puts it, "the power to select beneficiaries is an enormous power, for it is also the power to select victims—and
to reduce both to the role of supplicants of those who hold this power."[96]
While some of the results produced by the free market may seem bizarre, for
example the incredible wealth achieved by mediocre entertainers, nobody
has ever been compelled to buy Madonna's recordings or attend a Tom
Cruise movie. On the other hand, the state can pursue its vision of social
justice only by disregarding the rule of law, i.e. by employing the threat of
force to achieve its purposes.

In our society the beleaguered taxpayer/voter is the only counterweight
to the never-ending demands by innumerable constituencies for various
forms of governmental largess. However, economic outcomes generated
by the political process are unacceptable substitutes for the marketplace
because they are arbitrary and coercive. When the school board and the
teachers' union agree to a new contract, the terms thereof cannot be
defended on any principled basis, i.e. as reflecting what the teachers are
"worth."

Even if we were to concede for the sake of argument that there is some
scale of social utility on which the respective contributions of (say) firefighters and schoolteachers could theoretically be weighed, no individual
or committee would have the requisite knowledge and expertise to successfully administer this process. It should be obvious, however, that as a practical matter no such effort is made. Rather, teachers' pay is solely the product
of the competing political pressures generated by the union and its allies
on the one side, and (primarily) reluctant taxpayers on the other. Voters

who do not wish to support our failed social experiment in publicly funded education are nevertheless compelled by the state to pay up; the majority simply imposes its will on the minority.

Even worse, a majority of the voters imposing school levies may be exempt from paying them. The public education system in this country is generally financed by local property taxes. Approximately 70 percent of eligible voters own their own homes, and will thus pay the tax, while renters will not. Using some very simple math, it is clear that if all renters (30 percent of the electorate) combine with 30 percent of homeowners (21 percent of voters), they can levy a tax that *all* property holders must pay.

When the authorities boost the salaries of teachers, there are naturally howls of protests from police, firefighters, and other state employees, who contend that it is unfair to raise teacher pay while leaving theirs in place. Therefore, financial pandering has a tendency to spread beyond its initial beneficiaries. In other words, once a "command and control" philosophy is applied to one segment of the economy, it is difficult to limit the spread of this infection.

Consider a second example. The left wishes us to adopt a "single-payer," government-administered healthcare system in this country. Such a plan will do for medicine what the public schools have done for education. Just as the "rich" abandoned the public system by sending their children to private academies and parochial schools, single-payer will accelerate the existing trend of physicians refusing to accept Medicare patients in favor of a fee-for-service model.

This exodus of providers from the state system will cause further deterioration in the quality of care provided. Rather than repeal its floundering social program the government may follow Canada's lead and criminalize private medicine. As Nozick quipped, the state "will have to forbid capitalist acts between consenting adults" (*ASU*, 163).

If politicians are permitted to reward their favored constituencies with economic favors, there will be an irresistible temptation for interest groups not only to obtain direct financial benefits, but also to manipulate the system in less obvious ways, such as subsidies, tariffs, regulations (think taxi "medallions"), and so forth. However, as Hayek explains, increased economic security for some can only be obtained at the expense of others:

[W]ith every grant of complete security to one group the insecurity of the rest necessarily increases. If you guarantee to some a fixed part of a variable cake, the share left to the rest is bound to fluctuate proportionately more than the size of the whole. And the essential element of security which the competitive system offers, the great variety of opportunities, is more and more reduced.[97]

Hayek cites Social Security as a program ripe for political demagoguery. President Roosevelt promoted the program in the mid-1930s as a government-enforced self-insurance mechanism, whereby the worker would be protected against disability and poverty in old age. However, if this was the sole objective it could have been accomplished, as Milton Friedman notes, with much greater efficiency simply by requiring workers to purchase retirement annuities from private insurance companies.[98] While this would entail some enforcement mechanism, the scale and cost of this would be miniscule in relation to the massive bureaucracy that now exists.

As most people now know, payments to social security recipients do not come out of any trust fund created from their own withholdings, but from payroll taxes paid by current employees and matched by their employers. Payments under the system are heavily redistributive, i.e. high-income employees who have had over the course of their careers three times the amount of withholdings as low-wage workers, do not receive anything like three times the retirement benefits. As a consequence of demographic trends, and the program's faulty actuarial assumptions, the social security tax rate has gradually but inexorably increased from 2 percent at inception (1937) to the present 12.4 percent (including the employer's matching contribution).[99]

The net result of the structure of the program is that to date retirees have taken much more out of the system than they have paid in, even including imputed interest.[100] Even the dramatic tax increases described above have proven insufficient to stabilize the program, as retirees are still living (and drawing benefits) longer than expected, and are being supported by a smaller than anticipated base of current employees. Clearly, something will have to give. Benefits to the next generation of retirees will have to be cut drastically and/or the retirement age raised quite significantly and/or payroll taxes increased even further.

As shown above, there is little relationship between what a worker contributes in payroll taxes and what he or she receives during retirement. One's fate under this system is determined by a generational lottery and where one stands in relation to the government's social policy.[101] However, all efforts to reform this program in a fundamental way have failed, as retirees are convinced that they are *entitled* to their benefits, and they vote! The evolution of the program away from self-insurance to a mechanism for redistribution has made it vulnerable to political manipulation, as Hayek observed 50 years ago:

> It is easy to see how such a complete abandonment of the insurance charac-
> ter of the arrangement…must turn the whole system into a tool of politics,
> a play ball for vote-catching demagogues. It is vain to believe that any objec-
> tive standard of justice will set a limit on the extent to which those who have
> reached the privileged age…can insist on being "adequately" maintained by
> those still at work—who in turn will find consolation only in the thought that
> at some future date, when they will be proportionately even more numer-
> ous, and possess correspondingly greater voting strength, they will be in a
> better position still to make those who work provide for their needs.[102]

Every governmental program that benefits one group at the expense of
another creates a dependency relationship. The more extensive the state's
control over the economy, the larger the pool of voters whose livelihoods
depend in one way or the other on the "benevolence" of the political
authorities. Inevitably, interest groups will form coalitions to protect each
other's "pork."[103] Each such constituency will sincerely believe, of course,
that it is entitled to its governmental "goodies."

Returning again to our scheme of public education, let us imagine that
we poll the teachers, administrators, and bureaucrats who operate and
administer this quasi-monopoly for purposes of ascertaining their attitude
toward it. How many would respond along these lines: "I am ashamed to
owe my livelihood to an idiotic system that robs millions of parents of their
freedom of choice and provides their children with an inferior education
that will leave them unprepared to compete for employment in a global
marketplace." Answer: damned few. Social psychologists have invented the
term "cognitive dissonance" to describe the reluctance of individuals to
acknowledge painful truths.

Thus, the commingling of the political and economic realms permits the
development of a vicious circle in which constituencies use the apparatus of
the state to achieve illegitimate financial advantages and the authorities use
their ability to provide such rewards as leverage to further erode our free-
doms. Just as the human body can tolerate extremely low doses of arsenic
and other toxins (do not try this at home!), societies with deeply ingrained
traditions supportive of the rule of law can withstand a substantial level of
state interference in their economic lives without collapsing into outright
tyranny. However, even "minor" abridgements of liberty are pernicious
in and of themselves, and if such cancers are allowed to metastasize, the
"patient" will eventually succumb.

Chapter 6

Answering the Critics: The Implications and Boundaries of Natural Rights

A foolish consistency is the hobgoblin of little minds, adored by little statesmen and philosophers and divines.
                    Ralph Waldo Emerson, Essays: First Series [1841]

The Lord will help the poor, but not the poor lazy.
                    Louis ("Satchmo") Armstrong, TV Interview [1961][1]

In this chapter we shall consider what I take to be the most salient and commonly heard objections to the individualist philosophy. We shall review four complaints: (i) that the stringency of libertarian property rights renders them implausible, (ii) that the doctrine has morally unacceptable consequences for the most vulnerable members of society, (iii) that the Nozickian conception of autonomy is morally inferior to other forms of self-determination possible only under more egalitarian institutional arrangements, and (iv) that natural rights are too blunt an instrument to resolve the complex social problems present in modern societies, such as air pollution. At the conclusion of this chapter I will offer some final comments on where these criticisms and my responses leave libertarianism as a political philosophy.

Before proceeding further, I should note that although, as explained in Chapter 1, Nozick-style libertarianism is built on the foundation of deontological moral principles, I am not addressing here the various objections that have been raised against the plausibility of this ethical theory or its basic assumptions. My justification for this omission is that this work is not intended as study of normative ethics generally, but is a focused defense of natural rights.

I note that deontologists and consequentialists have been locked in an intractable ideological struggle for centuries, and the literature on this subject is so vast that it is impossible to do it justice in the space available here. Moreover, it is not practical to simply defend deontology against a sampling of the most prominent criticisms, since much of the discourse between the two camps is unavoidably comparative. In other words, any intellectually honest moral philosopher will admit that no single ethical theory is perfectly coherent and persuasive in every respect, so the controversies end up revolving around which theory has relatively fewer flaws, their respective gravity, and so on.[2] Accordingly, we will now proceed to consider four of the "standard" challenges to libertarian principles.

The Stringency of Property Rights

As should be clear by now, it is libertarianism's commitment to the stringency of property rights that has generally drawn the most intense fire from its philosophical foes. As noted in Chapter 1, Nozick holds open the possibility that side constraints might be justifiably violated in order to avoid "catastrophic moral horror." We will now examine certain cases of the sort he may have had in mind and trace their implications for libertarian rights. However, before proceeding further, I believe we need to stop and carefully investigate the very idea of "property rights."

Liberals tend to speak of economic liberty as if it refers to a distinct class of (inferior) rights that exist quite separate and apart from their political, social, or expressive counterparts. But is this view coherent? For one thing, as James Buchanan has observed, the exercise of rights generally presupposes a permissive use of property for that particular purpose.[3] For example, I do not have a "disembodied" right of free expression or free association that I can exercise as I like on *your* front yard or in *your* home. This recognition prompted Hayek's well-known warning regarding the connection between guarantees of property rights and freedom generally:

> there can be no freedom of the press if the instruments of printing are under the control of government, no freedom of assembly if the needed rooms are so controlled, no freedom of movement if the means of transport are a government monopoly, etc.[4]

Notice also that it is often difficult to even classify a right as one of property or belonging to some other sphere. If, for example, the government arbitrarily regulates commercial advertising in such a way that I can no longer effectively promote my services, the state has clearly trampled my rights, but it is impossible to separate the violation into distinct economic and expressive components. These considerations establish, at a minimum, that property rights and individual liberty are tightly intertwined.

The recognition that property and other rights are interrelated and mutually dependent should cause us to question the liberal assumption that the former are categorically inferior to the latter. Imagine that a person, A, relies on a certain drug to treat a particular chronic, life-threatening medical condition. Unbeknownst to A, a thief breaks into his residence and steals this medication. Subsequently, A experiences the onset of his symptoms, reaches for his pills, discovers too late that they are missing, and dies. At one level, the thief has violated a "mere" property right, but I believe that this example shows—as Nozick intended by his "taxation as forced labor" argument—that such rights often implicate our most fundamental values.

In my judgment, the idea that property rights differ in some morally significant way from other rights is indefensible because all rights ultimately rest on the same foundation, i.e. respect for rational agency. And, the different labels we typically place on our rights simply refer to the various aspects of our autonomy that are being protected.

Shelly Kagan summarizes this idea as follows, and (correctly in my view) attributes it to Nozick:

> Now if there is such a moral prohibition [against interfering with an agent's autonomy], then other prohibitions might be derivable from it. That is, it might be that interference with another's autonomy is the form of harm that is most fundamental from the moral point of view. Other familiar forms of harm—inflicting pain, causing bodily damage, murder, theft and so on—might matter (when they do) just by virtue of the fact that normally such acts interfere with, or destroy, autonomy.[5]

Because the violation of different rights will have, depending on the circumstances, more or less serious implications for the exercise of rational agency, we may reasonably hold that not all violations are equally pernicious. But this is a far cry from holding categorically that economic rights are generally inferior to others, or that they must generally give way in order to realize patterned principles of justice.

For ease of exposition, I will continue to use the term "property right(s)," adopting Eric Mack's definition: "the right of property is a right to others' compliance with a system of rules under which individuals may peacefully acquire, transform, and otherwise exercise exclusive and discretionary control over extrapersonal objects [in addition to rights over one's body]."[6]

However, the reader should bear in mind that I do so in the context described above.

The claim that the moral foundation for all rights is their essential role in safeguarding our rational agency is not to say that they must be considered absolute; that is, they outweigh all other values that may be at stake in particular circumstances. One widely discussed case, proposed by Joel Feinberg, which we will call "Cabin," involves an individual ("hiker") lost in a blizzard who discovers a cabin in the mountains. The hiker can only survive by ignoring the "No Trespassing—This Means You!!" sign posted by the owner, breaking into the cabin, burning the furniture for heat and eating the stored food.[7]

David Friedman imagines a similar example, but one that plays out on a global scale. In his case ("Asteroid"), the Earth is directly in the path of a large asteroid. The only way to save our world is to use a piece of equipment whose ownership rightly and unquestionably rests in the hands of a miserable misanthrope, who is quite happy to see the entire population (including himself) perish.[8] He will not sell or lease this equipment for any price.

Two things need to be said about such cases. First, they clearly demonstrate that our commonsense intuitions do not permit us to assign a conclusive priority to property rights over the entire range of their possible application. Second, for the reasons discussed below, this acknowledgment should not undermine our confidence in the stringency of such rights in general. This claim may be vindicated in two independent ways, both of which appropriately circumscribe property rights within the limits set by competing moral values.

The Lockean proviso and property rights

In our discussion of Locke's theory of original acquisition in Chapter 2, we saw that Nozick interprets Locke's famous proviso as conditioning *just* initial appropriation on the claimant improving the property in some significant fashion and not worsening the position of others. The latter qualification would preclude an agent from appropriating all the water in the desert or the like. We noted the existence of certain complications relating to the selection of the appropriate baseline to be used to test the "no worse off" condition, which Nozick himself calls attention to by asking at one point, "Lockean appropriation makes people no worse off than they would be *how?*" (*ASU*, 177). Although Nozick is less than clear on this point, he appears to think that the proviso's antimonopoly prohibition rests on the circumstance that in such cases the owner's full capitalist property rights are making people worse off than they would be under other forms of ownership that might have evolved from a state of nature (see *ASU*, 177).[9]

The Lockean proviso also has implications for Nozick's principle of "justice in transfer." For example, not only would it be unjust to initially appropriate all the water in the desert, it would also be morally illegitimate to first appropriate some of it and then, through a series of subsequent purchases, to acquire the rest (see *ASU*, 179). Therefore, the Lockean proviso casts what Nozick calls a "historical shadow" on property, such that it,

> excludes [the owner from] transferring it into an agglomeration that does violate the Lockean proviso and excludes his using it in a way, in coordination with others or independently of them, so as to violate the proviso by making the situation of others worse than their baseline situation. (*ASU*, 180)

Nozick holds that the proviso would apply even if the monopolist corners the market in a critical resource as a consequence of circumstances outside of his or her control. Accordingly, if as a result of natural causes all the water holes in the desert dry up but one, the owner of the remaining one may not charge what he likes, because:

> This unfortunate circumstance, admittedly no fault of [the owner], brings into operation the Lockean proviso and limits his property rights (footnote omitted). Similarly, an owner's property right in the only island in an area does not allow him to order a castaway from a shipwreck off the island as a trespasser, for this would violate the Lockean proviso. (*ASU*, 180)

In light of this comment, Nozick may have anticipated the sort of counterexamples to libertarian property rights conceived by his critics and sampled above. It is tempting to conclude that just as the owner of the island may not order the castaway back into the sea, the owner in Cabin may not prevent the hiker from using it to survive. By the same logic, the owner of the asteroid-destroying devise cannot deprive humanity of its use.

However, upon further reflection, the Lockean proviso (as construed to this point) is not clearly applicable in Cabin and Asteroid. As you may recall from Chapter 2, Nozick argues that Lockean appropriation does not leave subsequent generations worse off because capitalism's economic vitality, relative to *any* non-capitalist alternative, provides at least an equal range of economic opportunity for those who did not acquire natural resources in the initial round. We must, therefore, assume that this is exactly what has happened in these two scenarios.

Accordingly, in Cabin, but for the virtues of private property the cabin might not exist, and hiker is *not* necessarily made worse off (relative to a noncapitalist baseline) by being denied access.[10] Furthermore, in Asteroid we may suppose that Lockean appropriation created the economic conditions that made the development of the equipment possible, and so society is not necessarily made worse off (relative to a noncapitalist baseline) by being denied its use. Thus, neither hiker nor the general public respectively would, under the proviso, have an unambiguous right to the Cabin or the equipment.

I believe there is a plausible response to this challenge. The answer relies on the fact that as discussed early in Chapter 2, the proviso has its origin in Locke's insistence that original appropriation not violate any other party's natural right to self-preservation. It is this concern that causes him to impose the condition that any reduction to private property leave "enough and as good" for others.

This principle of "equal right" is an inescapable aspect of our ordinary moral consciousness and is acknowledged by Nozick in his argument for side constraints (see Chapter 1). Therefore, the appropriate question in Cabin and Asteroid is not whether those in danger would fare better relative to a noncapitalist baseline, but whether their equal right of self-preservation is being violated. Clearly, the owners are abusing their property rights in Cabin and Asteroid, and thus come within reach of the proviso, properly understood.

Note that Nozick need not appeal to hypothetical non-capitalist welfare baselines in order to resolve the "all the water in the desert" and the castaway cases. When the original owners of these natural assets privatized them, they did so subject to the condition that they respect the equal right of others to self-preservation. At the time of first acquisition, this obligation was satisfied by the availability of other unclaimed land or water holes. However, since each subsequent transferee of these resources inherits the advantages of individual ownership, Nozick recognizes, that: "Each owner's title to his holding includes the historical shadow of the Lockean proviso on appropriation" (*ASU*, 180). Thus, there is no need to make welfare comparisons to solve such cases; the continuing obligations of those who acquired property from the original appropriator will do the trick.

On the other hand if, contrary to fact, collective forms of property ownership actually did outperform "pure" capitalism in terms of the standard of living enjoyed by most members of society, then privatization would clearly worsen the position of others and be morally bankrupt. Therefore, Nozick's principle of justice in acquisition must as a general matter rely on the assumption of capitalism's economic superiority. Thus, Cabin, Asteroid and similar examples should be seen as special cases where the economic advantages of capitalism are insufficient by themselves to satisfy the "no worse off" requirement.

Finally, note that at least with respect to his justification of private property, Locke recognized only an equal right of self-preservation and not a general right to welfare. Accordingly, in construing cases like Cabin, the owner's full property rights would be limited only when the threatened loss of life or serious injury is clear, immediate and avoidable only through the use (or if absolutely necessary, the destruction) of private property. It would also require that the beneficiaries of any emergency appropriation of private property fully compensate the owner for its use or destruction.

Rights as pluralistic values

A second rationale for assigning less than decisive weight to property rights in all possible contexts is based on moral (or value) pluralism, which John Kekes helpfully describes as the view that "there are no states of mind, values, or conceptions of the good life that should always override whatever comes in conflict with them."[11] This notion is not only a fixed part of our commonsense morality, but is prevalent in normative philosophy. Matt Cavanagh has articulated a strong statement of this idea:

> There is of course good reason to think that, if we are theorizing about the way the world is, then everything we say must be consistent with everything else we say...But the same does not apply when we are theorizing about what we ought to do...To take just one example, consider the kind of situation in which you want to be truthful to someone, but also want them not to be unhappy, and realize that telling them the truth would make them unhappy. The undeniable fact that such situations exist does not undermine the thought that both these aims—being truthful and making people happy—are aims we ought to have. The same is true of our political aims.[12]

Many, if not most, moral philosophers are value pluralists. Ready examples are found amongst the various egalitarian theories of justice, Nozick's main foil in *ASU*. The central tenet of this doctrine is that equality, in whatever measure it is to be achieved (resources, welfare, opportunity for welfare, etc.), is intrinsically valuable. However, advocates of this view were soon challenged with the argument that their doctrine has the disturbing implication that an equal sharing of misery is to be preferred to an unequal sharing of riches. This is known as the "leveling down" problem.[13]

Accordingly, egalitarians have had to admit other values into their moral calculus in order to address this issue. As Stefan Gosepath has noted, "Most of today's egalitarians are pluralistic... Many egalitarians regard the moral significance of choice and responsibility as one of the most important other values besides equality... [and] therefore they strive to eliminate involuntary disadvantages for which the sufferer cannot be held responsible."[14] A similar trend can be identified amongst consequentialist philosophers. According to one authority, "many consequentialists deny that all values can be reduced to any single ground, such as pleasure or desire satisfaction, so they instead adopt a pluralistic theory of value."[15]

Finally, W. D. Ross, a highly influential deontological philosopher of the first half of the twentieth century whose views are often identified with commonsense morality, formulated an early version of what is now called "moral pluralism." Ross's basic conception was that we are to be guided by a handful of irreducible, objective moral principles, what he called "prima facie duties," consisting of such qualities as fidelity, gratitude, promoting justice, beneficence, and so forth.[16]

The obvious relevance of value pluralism to the challenge posed by such cases as Cabin and Asteroid is that libertarianism can acknowledge that the moral force of consequentialist values limit the scope of the property owner's rights. Note that the libertarian acceptance of value pluralism implies that, given appropriate circumstances, *all* rights and not just so-called property ones may be overridden. For instance, if we knew that allowing a prominent politician to give a particular speech (ordinarily protected by the First Amendment) would trigger a nuclear exchange costing millions of lives, we would be justified in suppressing it. For our present purposes, value pluralism allows us to resolve the two above cited cases (and similar ones) by holding that the owners' rights are not absolutely inviolable.

An evident difficulty with this approach is the danger that there will be no rational way to delineate the defensible scope of property rights once we acknowledge competing values. In other words, once we concede that rights are not absolute, what principled reason can we give for not permitting the state to seize property whenever necessary to realize a "desirable" pattern of holdings?

There are two things to say about this problem. First, libertarians face no greater difficulty with the integration of disparate values than do proponents of any other theory that incorporates value pluralism. Shelly Kagan, in discussing what he calls "moderate deontology," i.e. the view (defended here) that deontological constraints are binding up to a certain point and then yield to consequentialist considerations, observes that whatever threshold is set will appear arbitrary. Nevertheless, Kagan argues that "such an appearance of arbitrariness will be present *whenever* a theory needs to trade off two factors against each other," and therefore concludes that "moderate deontology is—on the face of it—no worse off than any other form of pluralism."[17]

Kagan's conclusion appears sound in light of the analog problem faced by those egalitarians that alloy their intuition that equality is intrinsically desirable with considerations of responsibility and choice. They must articulate a defensible notion of what constitutes an *undeserved* advantage (that may be nullified) and a means of balancing these values.[18] Our discussion of this issue in Chapter 2 should illustrate the immensity of this challenge.

Second, as argued above, the notion that rights exist to allow the expression of our rational agency offers substantial guidance in reconciling them with other moral values. Clearly, the gravity of an interference with a right is highly sensitive to the particular context in which it occurs. For example, the close relationship between our body and our sense of personal identity and autonomy renders forced organ transplants, even if they would save lives, morally repulsive. Similarly, I suggest that what makes the Supreme Court's infamous decision in *Kelo v. New London, Connecticut*, 545 U.S. 469 (2005), upholding the state's exercise of its power of eminent domain in favor of a commercial developer seem especially outrageous is that the properties being seized were family residences, i.e. the location central to our most deeply personal relationships and choices.[19]

In contrast, were the state to use its power of eminent domain to seize, for purposes of transfer to a private party, property held by the owner purely as an investment vehicle, I believe we would feel somewhat less offended. This is not to say that such seizures would be justified in other than extreme or unusual circumstances. Our commonsense moral judgment informs us that it is wrong to steal even a small sum of money, and that a compelling reason would be required to justify it. Similarly, it would take very strong consequentialist considerations to override the prohibition on the coercion of innocent rational agents even when the circumstances render it *relatively* innocuous.

Clearly, in Cabin, Asteroid and similar cases there are quite powerful ethical considerations favoring a limitation on the scope of property rights. Hiker will loose his life if he does not break into the cabin, while the owner will suffer at most a trivial reduction of his own moral sovereignty if he forfeits the right of exclusion. The same logic applies on a massively larger scale in Asteroid.

In light of the above, I believe our recognition of limitations on the absolute nature of property rights will not result in the "exception swallowing the rule." I contend that the tension between property rights and consequentialist considerations is fundamentally of the same nature as exists with respect to deontological constraints generally, e.g. the "kill one to save five" scenario discussed in Chapter 1. Few people would endorse killing the one innocent person to save five others, but even fewer I suspect would spare the one if the consequences were the loss of a million innocent lives. The fact that it is impossible to say exactly where the deontological constraint breaks down does not diminish the force of our intuitions regarding the first example. Similarly, I believe it would require quite powerful utilitarian considerations to justify the coercion of innocent rational agents.

In describing conflicts between rights and other moral values, I have remained neutral amongst the different theories of rights that would account for the trade-offs called for by our moral intuitions. One popular theory, specificationism, is based on the idea that rights are absolute or conclusive within their defined limits.[20] This preserves the inviolability of rights by restricting their scope to those circumstances where they are entitled to prevail over all other normative considerations.[21] Thus, when we limit the maximal claims of property holders in cases like Cabin and Asteroid, we should not see this outcome as a defeat for property rights, but rather a case of them butting up against the boundaries of other values. On this view, the cabin owner simply did not *have* the right to exclude hiker.

One rival opinion conceives of rights as having only prima facie status. A prima facie right is a claim that, if regarded as valid in light of all the relevant moral considerations that bear on that particular case, is recognized as an actual right.[22] Rights may be overridden because competing claims have greater moral weight.[23] So, on this account, in Cabin, hiker's actual right to use the structure and consume its contents overrides the cabin-owner's prima facie property rights.

A second alternative to specificationism, associated most closely with Judith Jarvis Thomson, has been called the "infringement theory." Here, rights are regarded as actual and full-fledged, but subject to justifiable infringement.[24] A right is violated when it is infringed under circumstances that, in light of all of the relevant moral factors, do not justify this action. Accordingly, in Cabin, we would conclude that the owner's right was infringed but (assuming compensation is paid) not violated.

A great deal of philosophical energy has been spent debating the relative merits of these theories. Fortunately, it does not seem necessary for me to enter the fray because we can defend the *substantive* libertarian commitment to rights using the vocabulary of any of them. For example, using the terminology of prima facie rights, we could simply hold that property rights are generally actual rights, but can be overridden in Cabin and Asteroid and in any other circumstance necessary to make the prima facie theory coextensive with the specificationist position. This possibility should not surprise us because, as noted by Russ Shafer-Landau:

> the problem of specifying the content of a right is the very same problem as that of balancing prima facie rights or knowing when a right is permissibly infringed. In each case, conflicting moral considerations generate a moral conclusion either about what a full-fledged right contains, or about the circumstances under which a full-fledged right can be permissibly infringed.[25]

The Needs of the Most Vulnerable

Having addressed above the relationship between property rights and other moral values, both as a gloss on the Lockean proviso and more generally by means of value pluralism, we now shift our focus to what will turn out to be a closely related iss⸻   ⸻ most commonly heard objections to natur⸻⸻   would require the state to stand by as
                ⸻tarily unemployed starve or go with-
    ; ba⸗   as we will demonstrate below, this is
    ⸗⸗⸗   onstraints.

                        ⸻embers of society

                        ⸻biguity in the Lockean proviso's
                        ⸻id. There is a parallel ambiguity
                        ⸻ice of capitalism with respect to
                        ⸻ociety. As we have seen, Nozick's
                        ⸻on-appropriators is that a mar-
                        ⸻rd of living relative to *any* rival
                        ⸻ersons not able to originally
                        ⸻unity for welfare equal to or

The comparative affluence of nations that have organized their economies along capitalist lines versus those that have not strongly supports this claim. However, not all members or groups will benefit to the same extent from this system, and the Entitlement Theory as interpreted to this point is completely insensitive to any distribution of holdings that may arise from its operations. While we need not be concerned regarding the welfare of the "winners" under capitalism, this aspect of the Entitlement Theory raises an issue regarding the justice of original appropriation for those in future generations who end up on the lowest rung of capitalism's economic ladder.[27]

As discussed in the prior section, Nozick interprets Locke's proviso to impose a constraint on the operation of an entitlement-based system with respect to certain innocent persons who might be victimized by it, i.e. those who are unable to obtain water in the desert due to the existence of a monopoly and castaways whose only hope for salvation is an island owned by someone who would deny them access. Therefore, it does seem likely that Nozick is interested in exonerating his theory of justice with respect to the innocent needy.[28]

As indicated above, Nozick seems to suggest that this could be accomplished by comparing the position of non-appropriators under capitalism with their situation under other forms of ownership. If the most disadvantaged group would fare worse under unrestricted capitalism than they would under some other system, then they are entitled to relief. But, unfortunately, there are virtually an infinite number of theoretical ownership arrangements occupying the spectrum between a pure Nozickian entitlement-based system at one extreme and a rigidly egalitarian one at the other. The fact presents what I regard as an insurmountable obstacle to the use of this strategy, because there is no principled way to select any one of these models to function as the baseline.

Of course, the deserving poor will fare much better under some of those non-entitlement-based systems than others, thus potentially establishing a very high baseline of welfare that unfettered capitalism would be required to match. But, I see no reason why, in order to satisfy the demands of justice, Lockean appropriation must provide the *optimal* arrangement for the least well-off group in society. This is the political ideal that Rawls argues for in *A Theory of Justice*, but as previously noted, this effort is widely regarded as a magnificent failure. Moreover, picking as our baseline the economic arrangement that represents the "best case" for the least advantaged group implies, contrary to our intuitions, that we should accept a massive loss of welfare on the part of a slightly better-off group if this would produce a trivial improvement in the condition of the worst-off.

Once this point is grasped, it should be clear that the selection of any non-libertarian system of property as the baseline for the welfare of the innocent poor under the Entitlement Theory is arbitrary.[29] The choice of any particular form of ownership would only be justified if we first knew what the deserving poor are deserving of. But as should be clear by now, there is a fierce, ongoing philosophical debate on this subject. Thus, we have no warrant for selecting any of these alternatives.

There is a second, even more fundamental problem. *All* of the ownership structures on offer are inconsistent with the ethical foundation of the Entitlement Theory, that is respect for persons, expressed in the form of side constraints. Accordingly, grafting a patterned principle of justice onto the Entitlement Theory without formally endorsing value pluralism would render the theory objectionably *ad hoc.*

Rather than deriving a welfare baseline for the disadvantaged based on a comparison of an entitlement-based system with one founded on an alternative model of property, I believe that a libertarian standard of justice for the innocent needy can be derived from considerations internal to the Entitlement Theory. As argued in the previous section, the moral legitimacy of Lockean appropriation is grounded in a natural right of self-preservation, but one subject to the equal rights of others. There, we showed that a system of property rights based on this principle does not include the "right" to deny innocent persons life-saving access to property in exigent circumstances. On the same logic, the right of original appropriation comes attached with certain potentially broader obligations to innocent non-appropriators.

These obligations arise from the fact that the institution of secure private property takes all other forms of (non-capitalist) property ownership off the table. By doing so, it eliminates certain liberties only available to people in a state of nature, e.g. to graze one's cattle on the commons, the freedom to travel without having to contend with fences and trespass laws, and so on.[30] While most members of society will benefit from this transformation, some might not, and they did not get to choose.

Nozick appears to acknowledge that those persons for whom the advantages of life under capitalism do not outweigh the loss of liberty incurred thereby are entitled to compensation (see *ASU*, 178–9n). This rationale does not require us to select (without justification) a particular counterfactual welfare baseline for the "losers" under an entitlement-based system. Rather, we can view the requirement of a guaranteed minimum as the appropriate moral deference owed to persons for having been involuntarily thrust into the entitlement system. In this light, it is reasonable, I believe, to view the appropriators' implied commitment to provide a social safety net as a condition precedent for privatization to proceed.

This interpretation of Nozick's views is consistent with his justification for modifying property rights in the "all the water in the desert case." There he notes that he is not asserting that the monopolist's rights are overridden by other, external considerations, such as positive claims by others to the water. Rather, "Considerations internal to the theory of property itself, to its theory of acquisition and appropriation, provide the means of handling such cases" (*ASU*, 180–1). Similarly, we are not claiming here that the innocent needy under capitalism have some independent right to assistance, but instead have it as a condition of Lockean appropriation.

Jonathan Wolff acknowledges that minimal welfare benefits can be derived from the Locke/Nozick model of appropriation in the manner described above.[31] However, he levels two criticisms against the idea that this feature of original appropriation rebuts the claim that Nozickian libertarianism is an implausibly cruel theory of justice. First, he notes that there will be some not covered by the social safety net because their situation arises not from being deprived of the liberties they enjoyed in the pre-property world, but because of their own irresponsibility. Accordingly, he says, "the undeserving poor, whose plight is the consequence of their own fecklessness, would have no claim even on the surplus of others."[32]

In response, I claim that the distinction drawn here between the deserving and undeserving poor is a verdict of our ordinary moral consciousness. Claims for assistance by children and responsible persons exert a significantly greater normative pull on us than those asserted by irresponsible individuals. In fact, even most egalitarian-minded theorists make this distinction.[33] This is not to say that the affluent should ignore the suffering of the irresponsible, merely that the case for coercing such support is dramatically weaker.

Second, Wolff suggests that if we interpret the Lockean proviso in the way described above, it would "severely weaken Nozick's claim to have produced an entirely unpatterned theory."[34] But although Wolff's comment is undoubtedly correct, I am unclear as to why this should count as a defect in Nozick's theory of justice. Nowhere does Nozick assert that we should prefer an unpatterned to a patterned theory *simply* on this basis. Rather, the former is to be preferred because it alone instantiates the Entitlement Theory, the plausibility of which depends on the formulation of a satisfactory principle of "justice in acquisition." Since the interpretation of this principle as just described would shape it in a way consistent with both its underlying Lockean values and with commonsense morality, this modification can hardly count against the Entitlement Theory.

Value pluralism and the needy

As suggested earlier in this chapter, a pluralistic understanding of moral values would, by accommodating competing considerations, provide a second rationale by which natural rights libertarianism could acknowledge the needs of the "deserving poor," children, and so on. However, the obvious problem with this notion is that without much more elaboration it will appear to be a purely artificial, *ad hoc* solution to an embarrassing problem for libertarianism. Furthermore, in its naked form it provides no reason to believe that its recommendations would be compatible with the picture of libertarian rights we have drawn so far. In other words, once we acknowledge the existence of positive rights, how are they to be limited in any principled way? Accordingly, we are obliged to address this question in substantially more detail.

One way to make progress on the substance of positive rights is to follow a line of thought prominent in Kantian ethics. Kant draws a sharp distinction between the nature of an agent's obligation with respect to what he calls our "duties of omission" (not to lie, steal, etc.) and our positive duties of virtue.[35] Since the former are the product of the Categorical Imperative (pure reason) their violation would contravene universal moral law. Therefore he characterizes them as "strict," "rigorous" and "perfect." Indeed, many critics of Kant cite the rigidity of such negative duties (e.g. we must *never* lie) as evidence of the implausibility of his moral system.

On the other hand, the Categorical Imperative is indeterminate with respect to the fulfillment of our positive duties of virtue, such as beneficence, because their execution depends on the specific, empirical circumstances facing the agent, and thus inevitably involves moral judgment. In other words, our general obligation to help others in need might be satisfied in a variety of different ways and we must have latitude to select the most appropriate means in light of our individual circumstances, commitments, talents, resources, and so on. Moreover, our duty of beneficence is qualified by more specific obligations we may have to those closest to us, such as spouses, children, and parents. Accordingly, Kant characterizes our positive duties as "wide," "broad," "limited" and "imperfect."

Even (or perhaps particularly) when stripped of its accompanying metaphysical assumptions, Kant's distinction between the limited nature of our duties to strangers on the one hand, and our more stringent obligations to those closest to us on the other hand, fits nicely with our common-sense moral intuitions. Few of us believe or act on the proposition that our obligations to the starving of Africa have the same moral weight as those we owe to our spouse, children, friends, or even, to a lesser extent, our countrymen.[36]

Moreover, as Kant also holds, our general duty of beneficence does not require us to substantially sacrifice our own happiness in order to meet the needs of others. In other words, it is generally felt that we have a broad moral license for selfishness, i.e. a right to pursue those goals, projects, and pleasures that are important to us, even if this consumes resources that might be directed to alleviate the acute needs of others. Indeed, one of the most frequently heard criticisms of consequentialism is that most versions of this doctrine are "overly demanding." In plain English, the objection is that since this theory commands us to maximize the total quantity of good in the world, it implies (implausibly) that we should devote almost *all* our energy and resources to those (likely strangers) in desperate need.[37]

The relevance of the Kantian distinction between wide and narrow duties to our present task is that the wide, limited, and imperfect nature of our duties of virtue may provide a principled basis for curtailing the scope of positive rights. If we have only limited duties of beneficence, perhaps only dire need by other innocent persons is sufficient to remove the matter from our moral discretion and ground an actual positive right to assistance.

To see this, recall that we started our analysis of rights in Chapter 1 with the idea that they are justified moral claims. Moreover, we noted there that rights and duties stood in a correlative relationship such that the possession of a right by one party implies corresponding obligations on the part of other agents. An implication of the notion of "correlativity" is that rights must be sufficiently clear and definite in content so as to give rise to a specific duty on the part of others. This concept limits what can count as a "right."

Thus, for example, it would be implausible for people to have a general right to "happiness," since this means radically different things to different people, i.e. close and satisfying personal relationships, material wealth, spiritual fulfillment, self-esteem, accomplishments, and so on. Moreover, given that the realization of this good will largely depend on our individual dispositions and psychologies, it is unclear how a society would go about providing "happiness" to its discontents, or how we would determine that this right has been vindicated. Additionally, given our intuitive commitment to the idea that we possess (at least a substantial) moral license for selfishness, we should be highly skeptical that the moral weight of a general claim to "happiness" is sufficient to overcome our right to pursue our own ends.

In contrast, it is perfectly coherent to speak of a right to "the *pursuit* of happiness," since it seems plain that this right can be satisfied by the simple noninterference by other persons with the right-holder's innocent activities. Similarly, if blameless members of a particular community are facing imminent death by starvation or from an easily curable disease, or are experiencing acute suffering, it is easy to both comprehend the substance of a positive right to help and how it should be honored. Moreover, if the members of this community have sufficient resources to provide life-saving assistance without making major sacrifices in the quality of their own lives, then the claims of the desperately needy have overwhelming moral weight. Indeed, the gravity of this claim is such that it is plausible that it must override our general unwillingness to coerce persons, even to do the right thing.

While the claims of those in dire need are compelling, it seems equally plain that a purported right to relief from mere deprivation, i.e. the desire for *better* food, shelter, medical care, and so forth, is both less clear as to content and has less moral weight. First, we are faced with the challenge of determining what level of assistance is obligatory once the community has obviated the threat to life itself, i.e. how do we select a nonarbitrary level of assistance.[38] For example, assuming that both options are fully adequate with respect to nutritional requirements, must society provide the needy with a tasty and varied (but more expensive) diet of fresh produce, fish, and meat—or will adequate portions of pasta, "mac and cheese," and frozen or canned vegetables satisfy our obligation?

Second, Kant's attractive idea that rational agents have wide moral discretion in determining how they will exercise their positive duty of beneficence limits the circumstances where coercion can be justified. Specifically, appropriate respect for autonomy would constrain the use of force to compel persons to honor a positive "right" that is not based on any superior claim to assistance relative to other pressing needs. And, it is doubtful that a supposed right to relief asserted by members of our community takes moral precedence over a variety of such other noble endeavors, such as scientific research directed at horrible diseases like Alzheimer's, AIDS, and cancer; protecting the environment; ending cruelty to animals; and eliminating mass famine in the third world.

Moreover, it seems intuitively clear that the moral discretion described immediately above justifies agents in supporting causes of particular salience to them, even if doing so is less cost-effective than other choices on some objective scale of utility (if one exists). So, it should be morally permissible for an agent to prefer, for example, making a large donation to his alma mater in gratitude for the scholarship that allowed him to attend, or funding research into a rare disease that took a loved one, over improving the living standard of the deserving poor.

Finally, there is an additional complication. It seems plausible that our wide and imperfect duty of beneficence encompasses values that are not measurable on any common scale, i.e. they are incommensurable.[39] In other words, how does one evaluate the merits of saving the polar bears from extinction versus incrementally improving the quality of life for the needy? If our duty of beneficence can legitimately be expressed by supporting a variety of worthy but incommensurable causes, how can we rationally impute a right of assistance for some beneficiaries and not others?

In light of the above, the recognition of a right of innocent persons to be lifted out of unpleasant, but not exigent, living conditions would rob moral agents of the legitimate discretion they have to exercise their duty of beneficence in a way that expresses their individual judgments and values. Accordingly, on the basis of respect for rational agency we may limit the scope of positive welfare rights to assisting the innocent out of truly desperate circumstances, and do so in a way that is both principled and consistent with underlying libertarian values.[40]

Liberal versus Libertarian Self-ownership

As discussed in Chapter 3, G. A. Cohen has formulated an influential objection to libertarian rights that purports to show that they yield a form of self-ownership that is "merely formal" in the same way that self-ownership is rendered useless in one of his jointly owned worlds. Since we would find the ideal of self-ownership unattractive in the latter, we should also reject the former. Although we previously rebutted Cohen's specific argument, other critics have adopted his strategy of attacking libertarian self-ownership as merely formal.

Although economists such as Milton Friedman, Thomas Sowell, and Richard Epstein have given us good cause to believe that unrestricted free markets actually do maximize utility, this system cannot *guaranty* that there will not be in Cohen's terminology "abject Zs." In fact, Nozick acknowledges this. Recall his "marriage lottery" scenario (described in Chapter 2) from which he argues that no injustice arises from the fact that the free choices of some persons (e.g. selecting mates) eliminate desirable alternatives for others. Nozick immediately follows this example by noting:

> Similar considerations apply to market exchanges between workers and owners of capital. Z is faced with working or starving; the choices and actions of all other persons do not add up to providing Z with some other option. (*ASU*, 263)

Accordingly, left-leaning political philosophers have argued that Nozick arbitrarily privileges "formal" self-ownership over "substantive" self-ownership, meaning that persons such as Z may be free from others' interference, but too poor to have effective control over their lives. Will Kymlicka sets forth an extended (and representative) argument of this sort, which starts by defining substantive self-ownership in terms of self-determination, which he understands to mean that "in the central areas of one's life, in our most important projects, we should be free to act on our own conception of the good."[41] While negative rights safeguard formal self-ownership, they may deny substantive self-ownership to others:

> [T]he difficulty, of course, is that in a libertarian regime not everyone can parlay their formal self-ownership into substantive self-determination. Libertarianism cannot guarantee each person substantive control over their lives... Thus [a worker] may be forced to agree to whatever terms the capitalist is offering her in order to survive.[42]

Such one-sided agreements, says Kymlicka, "might well, as in Victorian England, be essentially equivalent to the enslavement of the worker."[43] Since self-determination "requires resources as well as rights over one's physical being," the state is free to promote it by redistributing holdings arising from (undeserved) inequalities in natural abilities.[44] Kymlicka then asks rhetorically, "Is there any reason for self-owners to prefer libertarian regimes over liberal-egalitarian ones?"[45]

He considers three possible arguments. First, that the choice of an economic system should be based on the consent of self-owners, which he quickly dismisses for reasons that need not detain us further. Second, that self-ownership would be thwarted by societal recognition of anything less than full capitalist property rights. In response, Kymlicka argues that a liberal-egalitarian regime will better promote substantive self-ownership, since, as just noted, self-determination requires at least a basic level of resources."[46] We will return to this argument below.

The third argument he considers comes closest to Nozick's actual position:

> Nozick might argue that welfare redistribution denies people's dignity...But why is taxation an assault on my dignity? Nozick often ties dignity to self-determination, but if so, then one could argue that it is liberal regimes not libertarian ones, which best promote each person's dignity, since they ensure that everyone has the same capacity for self-determination. In any event, dignity is predicated on, or a byproduct of, other moral beliefs. We only feel something to be an attack on our dignity if we are already convinced it is wrong...If we believe instead that redistribution is a required part of treating people as equals, then it will serve to promote, rather than attack, people's sense of equal dignity.[47]

When we are done unpacking the different threads of this argument we will understand that while there may not be good cause for "self-owners" to prefer libertarian regimes to liberal-egalitarian ones, there are compelling reasons for those who value rational agency to do so.

As discussed at the end of Chapter 1, Nozick posits rational agency, and particularly *moral* agency, as the attribute that confers value on persons, and not self-ownership. However, by formulating "substantive self-ownership" in terms of "self-determination" or having "effective control over one's life," Kymlicka at least gestures toward the core libertarian idea. Therefore, we will interpret his attack on what he calls "formal" self-ownership as directed against the sufficiency of libertarian rights as respecting the idea of rational agency.

I believe that there are several things that need to be said in response to Kymlicka's argument. First, the short answer to his rhetorical challenge is that rational agents should prefer a libertarian regime because only it is consistent with the moral framework propounded in Chapter 1. As you may recall, for Nozick moral agency consists of the capacity of persons to recognize and conform their behavior to the moral law.

Hence, for Nozick the material conditions under which we exercise our autonomy are, within very broad limits, of no consequence. To use a metaphor, I may play golf on a poorly maintained public course, using borrowed clubs and without the benefit of lessons. This course may be the only one I can afford to play. Nevertheless, I am just as much a *golfer* as the super-wealthy members of the Augusta National or Winged Foot country clubs. It is worth noting that the perfect, narrow, and rigorous obligations described by Kant as "obligatious of omission" apply equally to rich and poor alike, i.e. *all* persons are subject to the prohibition on lying.

Kymlicka correctly notes that a regime that enforces respect for Nozickian rational agency is compatible with persons leading very unhappy lives i.e. they may suffer deprivations "as in Victorian England" (whose workers, incidentally, enjoyed the highest standard of living in the world).[48] However, since political theories generally attempt to identify those legal and institutional arrangements that the proponent regards as ideal, they are not intended to answer the empirical question of which theory, if implemented, would *in fact* maximize welfare.

Thus, Kymlicka's point that libertarianism is "compatible" with extreme poverty is true of *any* political theory, including strict egalitarianism. If the economic pie produced by such a system is tiny, then everyone will lead lives of equal misery. Therefore, in comparing Nozick's ideal of "respect for persons" and Kymlicka's notion of self-determination, I suggest that the key question is which theory is based on the most attractive and plausible ethical foundation.

For Nozick, the appropriate moral responsive to the dignity due persons is noninterference, including specifically their use solely as a means for the realization of ends not of their own choosing. In contrast, when in the lengthy passage quoted above Kymlicka praises liberal regimes for better promoting the "capacity for self-determination," he means the possession of sufficient resources to allow an agent to exert effective control over his/her life and not the capacity for moral agency, which will exist even in impoverished circumstances. Therefore, while Kymlicka's ideal of substantive self-ownership (i.e. self-determination) is semantically similar to the language Nozick uses to describe rational agency, it differs in basic respects from his notion of respect for persons.

Unfortunately, Kymlickian "self-determination" is not anchored to any more comprehensive ethical theory, at least not one that he articulates and defends. Thus, he does not explain *why* we should we care about self-determination, in Kymlicka's sense, at all. To paraphrase Nagel's criticism of Nozick (referenced in Chapter 1), Kymlicka offers us "self-determination without foundations." Clearly, we cannot evaluate the soundness and implications of the ethical presuppositions that justify the value he attaches to self-determination until they are spelled out.

And, crucially from the libertarian perspective, Kymlicka does not address the origins and stringency of the constraints (if any) that limit how people may be treated in pursuit of the so-called greater good. Plainly, Kymlicka contemplates that, in violation of Nozickian side constraints, some persons may be used against their will solely as a means of enhancing the self-determination of others. Perhaps, on its own terms, this doesn't seem so dreadful; but how and where does Kymlicka draw the line between what he apparently regards as a benign exception to Kant's second formulation of the Categorical Imperative, and those cases (if any) where it would be respected?

Rather than attempt to justify the coercion required to realize the patterned principle of self-determination he envisions, Kymlicka asserts that Nozick should on his own principles actually welcome welfare redistribution. He contends that this follows from the fact that Nozick's version of self-ownership (rational agency) is premised on our capacity "to act in terms of some overall conception of the life one wishes to lead" (quoting *ASU*, 50).[49] And, says Kymlicka, while "a liberal regime which taxes the unequal rewards of undeserved talents does limit some people's self-determination... [it] does not unfairly disadvantage anyone in their substantive self-ownership— i.e. in their ability to act according to their conception of themselves" (footnote omitted).[50] In other words, even after redistribution the wealthy will have sufficient resources for self-determination, while the disadvantaged will now also enjoy this privilege.

But Nozick's objection to redistribution has nothing to do with its effect on self-determination as Kymlicka understands it. Rather, he holds that it is morally impermissible to coerce a moral agent, through redistributive taxation or otherwise, because such treatment violates a basic ethical principle, i.e. respect for persons. By assuming that we should judge the moral permissibility of redistribution based on its impact on "self-determination," Kymlicka begs the question against Nozick's argument. Kymlicka's analysis also, as just noted, begs the question of why, if it is legitimate to take resources from some in order to realize a more just pattern of self-determination, it is not also permissible to (say) take organs from unwilling donors in order to realize a more just pattern of kidneys.

Now, Kymlicka might fairly respond to this by pointing out that rational agents who happen to be starving in the street will not in practice have much opportunity to express their agency. And, if it were the case that the realization of Nozick's moral ideal implied that they must be allowed to starve, Kymlicka's argument for redistribution as a means of securing "self-determination" would have some teeth. But, I note that the previous two sections of this chapter were dedicated to showing that this is not true.

As shown above, if you start with an entirely different understanding of what attributes (if any) confer dignity upon human beings (Kymlicka does not articulate his views on this subject), and ignore Nozick's arguments for the inviolability of rights, you can derive a political theory that justifies the redistribution Kymlicka envisions. But the cost of abandoning the deontological constraints that arise from the supreme normative weight that Nozick assigns to moral agency is that everyone loses the status of highly inviolable persons (see the Kamm quote at page 23). We become the sort of beings who *can* legitimately be sacrificed to achieve a much wider variety of objectives.

So, Nozick's moral framework presents a compelling reason for those who subscribe to its basic assumptions to prefer the side-constraint view of political authority to liberal egalitarianism. Note, I do not contend that anything said above establishes that Nozick's moral theory is superior to its many competitors, but I do claim that I have provided a satisfactory affirmative answer to Kymlicka's challenge regarding whether there is "any reason for self-owners [read moral agents] to prefer libertarian regimes over liberal-egalitarian ones."

Apart from this, Kymlicka's competing notion of substantive self-ownership is objectionable on a number of fronts. First, Kymlicka's concept of self-determination is complicated and indeterminate in a way that Nozickian rational agency is not. For one thing, it does not appear that an egalitarian share of resources is even *necessary* for self-determination as this concept is commonly understood. It seems obvious that people who freely choose to lead lives of poverty (in monasteries, for example), to accept low wages in order to satisfy other preferences, or to "drop-out" and become slackers, are, despite their lack of resources, exercising a full measure of self-determination.

Moreover, we can also ask, "What level of resources is sufficient to confer substantial self-ownership?" While having $50,000 in the bank provides a certain menu of choices with respect to the realization of our "conception of the good," $100,000 provides a much larger selection, and so on. Any level of resources selected by Kymlicka will surely be arbitrary. Accordingly, we are left to wonder about the nature of the relationship between resources and substantive self-ownership. In contrast, for Nozick almost all adult human beings are rational agents.

The uncertain nature of the connection between wealth and self-determination is not only interesting in its own right, but is relevant in another way. If you were to enact the redistribution Kymlicka imagines, it is unclear that you would enhance autonomy even in the sense favored by him. If history is any guide, egalitarian economies produce more equal distributions of much smaller pies. At some point, according to Kymlicka's own logic, each piece becomes too small to support substantive self-ownership. Thus, a liberal-egalitarian society might have dramatically fewer substantive self-owners than an unfettered capitalist one.

In summary, Kymlicka does not show that concern for self-determination should lead us to favor egalitarian regimes over libertarian ones, both because he fails to confront Nozick's actual case for libertarian rights, and because his own notion of self-determination is not justified from the moral perspective, nor fully coherent.

The Alleged Inability of Libertarianism to Deal with "Externalities"

The final objection to natural rights libertarianism that we will consider is the claim that its insistence on stringent property rights would produce implausible results if used to arbitrate complicated interactions among members of modern societies. One frequently cited shortcoming is in dealing with what economists call "externalities," defined as "an effect of one economic agent's activities on another agent's well-being that is not taken into account through the normal operations of the price system."[51] Air pollution and the imposition of nonconsensual risk are often cited as examples of problematic externalities. Peter Railton's influential essay, "Locke, Stock and Peril: Natural Rights, Pollution, and Risk,"[52] presents an extended critique of Nozickian libertarianism with respect to both these items, so we will direct our attention to his article.

Although he does not use these exact words, Railton interprets Nozickian libertarianism as based on the idea that all rights are, in effect, like those governing real property, and that the owners have posted threatening "No Trespass!!" signs at the boundaries.[53] Thus, he writes: "From this Lockean view emerges an image of moral space akin to a map at a registrar of deeds. Individual entitlements or rights determine a patchwork of boundaries within which people are free to live as they please so long as they respect the boundaries of others."[54] And, "When we apply the Lockean framework to social policy... the image of individuals holding rights against individuals, and of individual trespass as the paradigm of impermissible action ceases to be illuminating."[55]

If, as Railton suggests in the language quoted immediately above, all libertarian rights are property rights, then by definition any violation must resemble a trespass, theft or some other act cognizable under the laws of property. Starting with this understanding of natural rights, Railton asserts that libertarians (or "Lockeans," as he prefers to call us) are unable to provide a satisfactory rationale for the regulation of externalities such as pollution and risk. With respect to pollution, the problem is that libertarianism is too restrictive, since even a few atoms of pollution landing on a noncon-senting owner's property would constitute an impermissible "trespass" that would require that the offending activity be terminated without regard to its potentially great economic value.[56]

Conversely, with respect to the non-consensual imposition of "pure risk," i.e. endangerment unaccompanied by any actual boundary crossing, the Lockean paradigm is, according to Railton, too lax. As he interprets liber-tarianism, until another party's property boundaries are actually crossed, agents may do whatever they wish on their own property, including even "operating an unsafe miniature fission reactor."[57]

The "all rights are property rights" thesis was propounded by Murray Rothbard and is held by many anarcho-capitalists, and I will leave it to them to defend this position against Railton's critique.[58] However, while it is true that Nozick speaks of natural rights as defining an individual's "moral space" (*ASU*, 57) and of rights violations as "boundary crossings" (*ASU*, 57, 71–3), it is not true that he regards these boundaries as akin to actual prop-erty lines such that *any* crossing (and *only* a crossing) constitutes a rights violation. Not only did he expressly reject this idea in conversation with a prominent libertarian writer, but as demonstrated below it is inconsistent with what he has to say about rights at various points in *ASU*.[59]

Recall from Chapter 4 that Nozick describes the legitimate functions of the minimal state as "protecting all its citizens against violence, theft, fraud, and . . . the enforcement of contracts and so on" (*ASU*, 26). Since "fraud" is the act of obtaining a person's property by trickery, deceit or the like, it is difficult to assimilate the right not to be maliciously *deceived* to a property right and (if Nozick holds the view Railton ascribes to him) puzzling that he should think we are entitled to be protected against it.

Moreover, in his "invisible hand" derivation of the minimal state, Nozick invokes the idea of a right not to be subjected to unreliable criminal proce-dures (see *ASU*, 102). Here again, it is difficult to conceive of this right as one logically tied to any useful notion of "property," and unclear as to how Nozick could hope to justify it in those terms.

Finally, as described in Chapter 1, Nozick expressly embraces the idea of deontological constraints in opposition to the less stringent idea of a mere "utilitarianism of rights." The latter principle would permit a right to be violated if doing so would prevent a greater number of rights violations of the same kind (see *ASU*, 28–9). For Nozick it is wrong to kill one innocent person to save five others because the dignity possessed by a moral agent requires that she not be used solely as a means, even a means to save oth-ers. It is difficult, I think, to derive this constraint from the premise that all rights are property rights—for the five potential victims are just as much property owners as the single person we refuse to sacrifice.

On the other hand, if as suggested in Chapter 1, we interpret Nozick's metaphorical "moral space" as being circumscribed by Kantian principles regarding respect for persons, we will have an easier time understanding his views about the subjects identified immediately above. All these positions can be grounded in the root idea that natural rights express the appropriate deference due moral agents. By the same token, any common-sense interpretation of this principle will cause us to reject the idea that I have "disrespected" my neighbor if I allow a leaf from one of my trees to blow onto his property or that, conversely, I am showing appropriate respect by (using Railton's example) building an unsafe nuclear reactor on my property.[60]

However, even if we reject Railton's construal of libertarianism and instead accept the understanding of moral space suggested above, we are still left with the problem of application. That is, how do natural rights libertarians, consistent with the tenets of their doctrine, draw the line between harmless boundary crossings and those that constitute a rights violation, and acceptable and unacceptable levels of risk imposition?

As defended below, my general thesis with respect to the problems cited by Railton is that decisions rendered pursuant to a fairly administered cost-benefit analysis ("CBA") satisfy the Kantian values that stand at the core of Nozickian side constraints. CBA is designed to quantify, in terms of monetary value, all costs and benefits associated with a particular decision or policy, thus allowing the analyst (in theory) to make an objective choice between alternatives. The monetary values assigned to costs and benefits are intended to reflect people's actual preferences, based either on prevailing market prices or derived indirectly from observations of their "willingness to pay."[61]

Thus, if building a water treatment plant would cause consumers to purchase one million fewer bottles of water a year, and if each bottle costs $1, then the decision to construct the facility would produce, in this regard, a benefit of $1 million/year. On the other hand, certain goods are not directly traded in the market, and in such cases economists attempt to infer the value of such goods through behavioral evidence. For example, in attempting to price clean air, economists have compared the prices paid for otherwise identical residences located in neighborhoods with substantially different levels of smog. Given a sufficiently large sample size, and assuming the *ceteris paribus* condition is satisfied, the average price difference should reflect the value people place on better air quality.

This method can also be employed to measure the value individuals assign to avoiding risk, including the risk of death. To understand this, it will be helpful to briefly explain the concept of the "value of a statistical life," or VSL. One authority has summarized this idea as follows:

> The VSL should roughly correspond to the value people place on their lives in their private decisions.... [W]e do not all drive armored trucks to work, but instead drive somewhat less safe—and considerably less expensive—cars. Our willingness to accept some risk in exchange for a more easily affordable vehicle suggests there is some limit to how much we will spend to protect our lives.[62]

In other words, VSL measures the trade-offs that members of a society actually make between cost and safety. It does not render metaphysical judgments about the "value" of life, but quantifies people's actual behavior. This measurement is made by observing their employment choices in terms of the compromises they make between compensation and risk, their purchase patterns with respect to optional safety equipment in vehicles, and so on. Accordingly to one recent meta-analysis (review of existing studies) by a panel of experts, the most reliable estimate for VSL in the United States is between $5.5 and $7.5 million.[63]

I wish to pause here to make the point that I do not believe I am obligated for purposes of meeting Railton's critique to show that CBA is a flawless or morally pristine decision-making procedure. The crux of Railton's complaint against (his interpretation of) libertarianism is that its conception of rights is too rigid and monolithic to generate, consistent with its core principles, a rational method for regulating externalities. Therefore, I believe that it is sufficient to show that CBA is available to libertarians as a rational decision procedure, not that it is a perfect one.

Since much of Railton's critique of libertarianism focuses on its alleged inability to explain why the imposition of high levels of nonconsensual risk should count as a "border crossing," and since he appears to regard this as the more difficult issue (relative to regulating pollution itself) for libertarians to resolve, I will focus on risk management. The strategy I am adopting to answer Railton's critique appears to have originated with Charles Fried in his book *An Anatomy of Values*, where he suggests that nonconsensual endangerment might usefully be viewed in terms of a "risk pool."[64]

By analogy, the risk pool is like a community loan fund that members may access as they need it, except that in Fried's concept, risk has replaced money as the commodity that may be borrowed and repaid:

> This notion holds that all persons by virtue of their interactions contrib-
> ute, as it were, to a common pool of risks which they may impose upon
> each other, and on which they may draw when pursuing ends of the
> appropriate degree of seriousness.[65]

Fried elucidates the ethical foundation of this principle as follows:

> [P]ersons are justified in imposing risks of death upon each other by
> reference to the principle of equal right, that is the principle of moral-
> ity. This would mean that all persons may impose risks of death upon
> each other for their ends and to the extent that all other persons may
> do so. This, then, would be a special case of the Kantian principle of
> right, that a person is entitled to the fullest amount of freedom com-
> patible with a like freedom for all other persons according to general
> laws.[66]

In the absence of such a right rational agency would be paralyzed, since
many of our necessary day-to-day activities impose *some* involuntary risk of
harm on others.[67]

Although Fried does not pursue this idea, it is possible, as discussed
above, to apply CBA as a means of calibrating tolerable risk imposition. An
acceptable level of risk would be derived from society's existing norms with
respect to comparable activities. If the economic benefit of the risky activity
exceeds our VSL standard, then it should be permitted. A similar calcula-
tion could be made with respect to the trade-offs we make between risk and
the freedom to engage in pleasurable activities.

Railton does, to his credit, consider CBA as a possible libertarian solution to
the problem of risk regulation. He acknowledges that if "a threshold level of
acceptable risk could be established" this would address the problem of involuntary endangerment, and suggests that one strategy would be to "observe
what levels of risk people do in fact accept in their daily lives without taking
special precautions or demanding special compensation and then infer that
this level must not be intolerable."[68] Moreover, he even acknowledges that
this proposal appears to be consistent with the libertarian notion of respect
for persons, since "to respect a person involves (among other things) refrain-
ing from exposing him to unusual ('unacceptable') levels of risk."[69]

However, he finds this concept problematic in multiple respects, deem-
ing it "deeply confused."[70] He offers three reasons for this conclusion. First,

he argues that the fact that individuals tolerate a certain level of risk ("r") "does not establish that they are indifferent about whether an additional risk of magnitude r is imposed on them, yet the right at issue concerns increments of risk."[71] Thus, even if people may in general willingly accept a certain level of danger, we cannot assume that any particular person will voluntarily accept this level of risk every time we wish to act. Therefore, each discrete imposition of risk would require a separate consent from each potentially affected individual, and the nonconsensual use of a CBA standard would be impermissible.

But Railton is wrong to assume that the moral plausibility of the CBA/ risk pool concept depends on obtaining the consent of those involuntarily exposed to risk. As Fried articulates this idea, people have the *right* to impose risks on others up to a certain limit. Without such a right, the exercise of rational agency would be severely hindered. Therefore, if Fried's basic concept is sound, nonconsensual risk imposed pursuant to a CBA standard no more depends on the consent of others than does the exercise of any other right. Let us, then, examine the moral necessity of consent.

I claim that we are appropriately troubled by Railton's example of the *unsafe* nuclear reactor (and like cases) not because of the absence of consent by those exposed to the danger, but simply because of the unacceptably high chance that the risk eventuates and its catastrophic consequences. To see this, consider another risk imposition case at the opposite end of the spectrum. Suppose *A* and *B* are neighbors somewhere in suburbia. *A* wishes to conduct some activity on his property, say a BBQ, which imposes an infinitesimal, one-in-a-billion risk of damage to *B*'s property. *B* is hypersensitive to risk of any sort and sincerely objects to *A*'s plans.

As Railton recognizes in connection with his unsafe nuclear reactor example, under a traditional Lockean analysis *A* would *not* need *B*'s consent because he is not trespassing on *B*'s property. If, against all odds, *A*'s BBQ did damage *B*'s property, *A* would be liable in trespass. I believe that this result is entirely consistent with our commonsense judgment about situations of this sort. The problem, then, that Railton identifies with respect to Lockean rights is not that they permit the nonconsensual imposition of risk, but that they allow an *unreasonable* level of exposure.

However, since natural rights libertarians are not committed to the "all rights are property rights" thesis, they may consistently uphold a moral right, premised on "respect for persons," not to be involuntarily exposed to levels of risk greater than people in that community ordinarily accept in their day-to-day activities, as measured by CBA. Risk-imposition at lower levels shows sufficient "respect for persons," and therefore does not violate the rights of others or require their permission. Whatever the merits of this idea, I do not see that it runs aground on the issue of consent.

Railton's second objection to the libertarian reliance on CBA is that there are fatal problems of application, even assuming that we are able to agree on a level of tolerable (what he calls "trivial") risk exposure that persons could be exposed to involuntarily. He describes a situation where a polluter exposes many people to a permissibly trivial risk, but (somehow) there is a virtual certainty that someone, perhaps a hypersensitive individual, will be seriously wronged. Here, the problem is that this act "should be impermissible even though it violates no individual's Lockean rights."[72]

Alternatively, many people might each pollute in a way that creates only a trivial risk, but the combined, interactive effect is sure to harm someone in a serious way. Here again, "no individual violates another individual's rights, but non-trivial risk—indeed arbitrarily great risk—has been imposed."[73] These scenarios are supposedly a *special* problem for libertarians because "Lockean rights characteristically apply between individuals."[74] It is here that Railton makes the above-quoted comment regarding the futility of "individual trespass as the paradigm of impermissible action."

I believe that Railton's point is that libertarians are committed to allowing the imposition of unacceptable levels of nonconsensual risk when we are unable to identify (in his first case) a particular rights-holder or (in his second case) a particular rights-violator. In other words, if all rights violations must be assimilated to trespassing, then we will need to know the identity of the trespasser and the trespassed upon if we wish to enjoin or punish this conduct. But, as argued above, Nozickian libertarians are not committed to this idea. If, instead, our rights stem from our status as moral agents, they are violated whenever insufficient respect for persons is shown, without regard to the number of polluters or the interactive effects of the pollutants.

Thus, I see no convincing basis for Railton's claim that libertarianism is analytically paralyzed by cases involving thousands of potential victims or multiple polluters. CBA could certainly be applied in cases of the sort he describes because it registers a 1 percent chance of a single person dying or a .001 percent chance of each of a thousand people dying, as the same cost. CBA would also be indifferent between risks imposed by a single or multiple actors—only the magnitude of the risk relative to the benefit would be relevant. It seems to me that Railton's argument is effective, if at all, only against those who deny the existence of any rights other than property ones.

Finally, Railton contends that even if a serviceable "acceptable risk" model could be developed, Lockeans are not entitled to use it. He bases this argument on the idea that the notion of a threshold level of risk "has no answer in traditional property rights."[75] Since, he claims, Lockeans are committed to the idea that "it is morally impermissible for me to commit trivial theft," the consistent Lockean cannot explain why it is "permissible for me to endanger others to a small degree."[76]

However, I do not think that libertarians are trapped by this alleged moral parallelism. Theft is a zero sum game, benefiting the thief at the expense of the property owner. It is almost always morally impermissible because it fails to accord rational agents the respect due them; a thief uses the victim *solely* as a means of advancing his or her own illicit ends. In contrast, if I expose others involuntarily to a level of risk that falls within the standard set by a fairly administered CBA process, I am showing them the same deference customarily shown all members of the community with respect to acts of this sort, and thus I do not run afoul of "respect for persons."

The use of "fairly administered" in the preceding sentence acknowledges that CBA can be abused or skewed in various ways to unfairly sacrifice the legitimate interests of certain citizens or groups.[77] But the fact that CBA can be manipulated to produce biased results does not disqualify it as a rational decision procedure any more than the jury system is disqualified by the fact that judges and jurors can be bribed or intimidated.

Even when CBA is administered in an impartial manner, it is subject to a number of serious moral objections.[78] A far from exhaustive list would include the argument that the extreme difficulty if not outright impossibility of assessing the costs and benefits of a decision or policy whose effects will typically reverberate far into the distant future renders the process fatally unreliable. Second, the fact that people's behavior indicates that they assign a particular value to a good does not establish that this judgment is defensible from the moral point of view. Perhaps our collective values are warped in some substantial way and (for example) polar bears have an intrinsic value in excess of whatever we would collectively be willing to pay to preserve them.

Last but not least is the seeming impossibility of making valid interpersonal comparisons of utility.[79] For example, if a particular social policy results in *A* increasing his income by $1,000 and *B* having her income reduced by $1,000, has there been a net gain or loss of utility, or no change at all? How would we determine this? In the light of these apparent difficulties it may seem strange that that libertarians should be reduced to relying on a dubious, consequentialist methodology. Moreover, doesn't the nonconsensual application of CBA violate side constraints by *forcing* persons to conform their conduct to standards that they may sincerely reject?

I think not. It seems apparent that there is simply no viable alternative to CBA when we are required to make rational decisions regarding externalities that will affect all or most members of a community. Social cooperation will be difficult if not impossible if each member of a community may freely impose the level of risk (or pollution) that she deems optimal—even if she is willing to subject herself to the same standard. Accordingly, we are in need of a decision-making tool that does not arbitrarily favor one person or group's values over others.

CBA fits the bill. As Richard Langlois has argued, it is the only method of public decision-making that is "liberal" in the classic sense, meaning that it does not impose any particular conception of the good.[80] Langlois notes that CBA is neutral in this way because it registers only people's *actual* purchase decisions or their "willingness to pay," while excluding politicians' or citizens' *moral* judgments "about what constitutes the good for someone else;" for example, "the socialist intellectual from Berkeley who is offended because a New York landlord charges a rent above the 'just price.'"[81] Thus, he concludes:

> [I]f we must make a centralized decision about "public" resources, then we should prefer something like utilitarianism to a criteria involving the decision-maker's perception of "social values" or of the "higher preferences" the citizen would like to see emphasized in public policy but which, alas, he is unable to incorporate into his own decisions.[82]

In short, a reliance on CBA to resolve issues arising from the existence of externalities is consistent with the values that underlie natural rights. As noted earlier, rights are not themselves the foundation of libertarian theory, but are derived from the respect due rational agents. Their derivative status explains why libertarians and egalitarians have starkly opposing positions regarding the substantive content of rights.

On an intuitive level it is clear that "respect for persons" is not offended when the conduct of a suitably beneficial activity exposes people to a trace level of pollution that poses *no* realistic threat to their health. Similarly, it is obvious that it is violated when persons are involuntarily subjected to a substantial risk of death, unless this exposure is unavoidably necessary to save a much greater number of innocent human lives. Therefore, it does no violence to the logic and justification of rights that I have previously advanced to interpret them in a manner that is in harmony with their *raison d'etre*.

The use of CBA, therefore, should be seen as part of a process by which rights are shaped to render moral judgments that are defensible in terms of the values that generate them.

Conclusion

As described in *Genesis,* God created the world *ex nihilo,* out of nothing. Rights do not come into existence this way. As we have just seen, any effort to evaluate the existence or stringency of particular rights in isolation from the underlying values that animate them is doomed to failure. For example, strict egalitarians will respect rights claims only to the extent that they advance the moral imperative of achieving social equality. On the other hand, if we accept the paramount value of rational agency as a first principle, then a robust and stringent set of rights, including economic ones, is implied.

As we have argued to this point, rights function to safeguard our moral space, so that unless we have violated the rights of other persons, or unreasonably threaten to do so, we cannot permissibly be *coerced,* even to do the right or socially acceptable thing. In Chapter 1, we showed how this prohibition was implied by Nozick's arguments, which are themselves based on the Kantian notion of respect for persons, an enormously attractive ideal for moral philosophers and thoughtful people across the ideological spectrum.

Because the material world provides the means by which our rational agency is exercised, libertarians hold that what are sometimes dismissively referred to as property rights must be taken seriously. It is here that the battle is usually joined between libertarians and liberals. Philosophers holding what Nozick called "patterned" principles of justice have traditionally argued that absolute property rights produce absurd or monstrous results of the sort described in this chapter, and are thus radically implausible.

In response, we have argued that libertarian philosophy can, in harmony with its core principles, resolve such cases in a satisfactory way. Specifically, we have tried to show that by accurately describing the source and function of *all* rights, we can maintain their stringency while integrating them with other moral values. If so, then natural rights libertarianism should have wide appeal.

Libertarians are not oblivious to the fact that many people are adversely affected by bad luck or other circumstances beyond their control. And, there is nothing in this doctrine inconsistent with the affirmation of a stringent moral duty to assist the less fortunate. But, other than in a narrow range of circumstances, we firmly oppose the *imposition* of any patterned principle of justice because any such distribution can only created and maintained by force.

When the state compels persons to contribute their labor or resources to a cause to which they do not subscribe (other than in support of irreducible governmental functions that establish the preconditions for rational agency), it treats them as mere tools to accomplish some greater good. But since persons *are* the greatest good, they cannot legitimately be used in this fashion.

The contrast between natural rights libertarianism and its liberal competitors could not be starker. The individualist philosophy holds that persons do not exist to advance the goals of others, or the state, but that the state exists to safeguard the autonomy that each of us requires to exercise those capacities that define us as rights-bearing beings. As argued herein, only a political philosophy that, in Talmudic terms, builds fences around our human dignity can claim the moral high ground.

Notes

Epigraphs

[1] Trevor Royle, ed., *A Dictionary of Military Quotations*, 1st American edn (New York: Simon & Schuster, 1989), 37. Unless otherwise indicated, all epigraphs are from Emily Morison Beck ed., *Bartlett's Familiar Quotations*, 15th edn (Boston, MA: Little, Brown, 1980).

[2] Royle, *Dictionary of Military Quotations*, 8.

Introduction

[1] This quotation is found at *Bartlett's*, 746, but no source or date is provided. In any case, it is certainly consistent with Churchill's mature political philosophy.

[2] See Brian Doherty, *Radicals for Capitalism: A Freewheeling History of the Modern American Libertarian Movement* (New York: PublicAffairs, 2007), 484 and Barbara H. Fried, "*Anarchy, State and Utopia* at Thirty Years," in Ellen Frankel Paul, Fred D. Miller, Jr. and Jeffry Paul, eds. *Natural Rights Liberalism from Locke to Nozick* (Cambridge: Cambridge University Press, 2005), 226. Doherty's tome is an indispensable reference for those interested in the history, politics, personalities and sociology of the twentieth-century libertarian movement.

[3] Peter Singer, "The Right to be Rich or Poor," in Jeffrey Paul, ed. *Reading Nozick: Essays on Anarchy, State, and Utopia* (Oxford: Basil Blackwell, 1982), 37–53 [originally published in *The New York Review of Books*, March 6, 1975].

[4] Thomas Nagel, "Libertarianism without Foundations," in Paul, *Reading Nozick*, 191–205 [originally published in *The Yale Law Journal*, vol. 85 (1975)].

[5] Bernard Williams, "The Minimal State," in Paul, *Reading Nozick*, 27–36 [originally published in *Times Literary Supplement*, January 17, 1975].

[6] Fried, "*ASU* at Thirty Years," 221.

[7] Philip Pettit, "Non-Consequentialism and Political Philosophy," in David Schmidtz, ed. *Robert Nozick* (Cambridge: Cambridge University Press, 2002), 83.

[8] Robert Nozick, *Anarchy, State, and Utopia* (New York: Basic Books, 1974), ix.

[9] This point is defended eloquently and in depth by Tibor R. Machan in *Generosity: Virtue in Civil Society* (Washington, DC: Cato Institute, 1998).

[10] It has sometimes been suggested by critics of libertarianism that Nozick's brief comments in two of his subsequent books (on subjects unrelated to political theory) amount to a repudiation of the basic views expressed in *ASU*. This claim is simply false. For the details, see Edward Feser, *On Nozick* (Toronto: Wadsworth,

2004), 7–8. At the same place Feser also reports Nozick's stated reasons for not returning to political philosophy.

11 Eric Mack comes to mind as a possibility, but describing the complex relationship between his rich and deep body of work and Nozick's thinking would take us too far afield.

12 Nagel, "Libertarianism without Foundations."

13 Most economists are careful to distinguish in their work between empirical observations and normative conclusions. For example, economists generally recognize that even accurate predictions of the following sort: "if the federal government raises the minimum wage by X amount, the economy will lose Y number of jobs," do not by themselves tell us what the state should do under such circumstances. See, for example, John C. Harsanyi, "Value Judgments," in John Eatwell, Murray Milgate, and Peter Newman, eds. *The New Palgrave: The World of Economics*, 1st American edn (New York: W. W. Norton & Company, 1991), 704–5.

14 Friedrich A. Hayek, *The Road to Serfdom*, anniversary edition, with a new introduction by Milton Friedman (Chicago: University of Chicago Press, 1994), 101.

15 See Shelly Kagan, *Normative Ethics* (Boulder, CO: Westview Press, 1998), 11–17. John Rawls prescribed a highly influential method of testing our moral judgments that has come to be known as "reflective equilibrium." See John Rawls, *A Theory of Justice* (London: Oxford University Press, 1971), 20. One authority describes this process as consisting of,

> working back and forth among our considered judgments (some say 'intuitions') about particular instances or cases, the principles or rules that we believe govern them, and the theoretical considerations that we believe bear on accepting these considered judgments, principles or rules, revising any of these elements wherever necessary in order to achieve an acceptable coherence among them. The method succeeds and we arrive at an acceptable coherence among these beliefs. (Norman Daniels, s.v. "Reflective Equilibrium," sec. 1, in Edward N. Zalta, principal ed., *Stanford Encyclopedia of Philosophy* [Stanford, CA: Centre for the Study of Language and Information, Stanford University, available online at http://plato.stanford.edu/])

Because the reflective equilibrium process justifies moral conclusions at least partially on the basis of their compatibility with a person's other beliefs, it is a "coherentist" account of moral knowledge.

An opposing view, "foundationalism," maintains that, as Kasper Lippert-Rasmussen expresses it, "A's moral belief that p is epistemically justified if, and only if, p is either foundational or based on an appropriate kind of inference from one or more foundational beliefs" (Kasper Lippert-Rasmussen, *Deontology, Responsibility, and Equality* [Copenhagen: University of Copenhagen, 2005], 441–2). For purposes of this study, it does not matter which of these theories is the more persuasive account of moral judgment, so long as it is indeed possible without the benefit of any special training or esoteric knowledge.

16 By "comprehensive normative theory" I mean one that "provide[s] reasons for adopting a system of moral principles or standards of virtue and defend[s] claims about the range of their applicability" (Tom L. Beauchamp, *Philosophical Ethics: An Introduction to Moral Philosophy*, 3rd edn [Boston, MA: McGraw-Hill, 2001], 17). Examples include deontology, consequentialism, and virtue theory.

Chapter 1

1 Translated in Abraham Cohen, *Everyman's Talmud* (New York: Schocken Books, 1975), 67.
2 See Leif Wenar, s.v. "Rights," sec. 2, in Zalta, *Stanford Encyclopedia of Philosophy* and Jan Narveson, *The Libertarian Idea* (Philadelphia, PA: Temple University Press, 1988), 41–2.
3 John Hospers, "What Libertarianism Is," in Tibor Machan and Douglass Rasmussen, eds. *Liberty for the Twenty-First Century: Contemporary Libertarian Thought* (Lanham, MD: Rowman & Littlefield, 1995), 5–7.
4 Ibid., 11–12. See also Narveson, *Libertarian Idea*, 57–61.
5 Larry Alexander and Michael Moore, s.v. "Deontological Ethics," sec. 1, in Zalta, *Stanford Encyclopedia of Philosophy*.
6 Ibid., sec. 2. As noted there, "deontology" is derived from the Greek words *deon* (duty) and *logos* (science or study of).
7 W. H. Walsh, "Immanuel Kant," in Paul Edwards, general ed., *The Encyclopedia of Philosophy*, reprint edn, 8 vols (New York: Macmillan, 1972), vol. 4, 317. Very briefly and hopefully without introducing too much distortion, Kant's fundamental goal in ethics was the identification of moral principles that were true both necessarily and unconditionally for all rational agents, and thus he accepted as fundamental only those propositions that could be established a priori, by the use of what he termed "pure reason." His survey of our universal moral consciousness revealed to him that the touchstone of our morality is a "good will," understood as a will "whose decisions are wholly determined by moral demands or as he refers to this, by the Moral Law." See Robert Johnson, s.v. "Kant's Moral Philosophy," sec. 3, in Zalta, *Stanford Encyclopedia of Philosophy*.

The essence of this Law is that it functions as a constraint on our desires, which necessitates acting pursuant to *duty*, even when this conflicts with our self-interest. A deeper analysis of this idea leads Kant to the conclusion that to act from duty is to be "motivated by the thought that, insofar as we are rational beings, we must act only as the fundamental law of (practical) reason prescribes, a law that would be…universally valid" (ibid.). And, "only a universal law could be the content of a requirement that has the reason-giving force of morality" (ibid.). For Kant, this analysis demonstrates that only a "Categorical Imperative" can ground our moral duties, i.e. a general command that is unconditionally binding on all rational agents simply by virtue of their reason.

This Kantian formula finds expression in T. S. Eliot's famous stanza from *Murder in the Cathedral:* "The last temptation is the greatest treason, to do the right deed for the wrong reason." In the course of researching this book I learned that Eliot pursued graduate studies in philosophy at Harvard, focusing on Kantian ethics. On the subject of Eliot's philosophical studies, see M. A. R. Habib, "The Prayers of Childhood: T. S. Eliot's Manuscripts on Kant," *The Journal of the History of Ideas* 51, no. 1 (1990): 93–114.
8 Johnson, "Kant's Moral Philosophy," sec. 3.
9 Alexander and Moore, "Deontological Ethics," sec. 2. Here, as in many other places, I am simplifying what is an enormously complex subject. There is a great deal of philosophical controversy as to what features actually distinguish deontological

and consequentialist ethical systems. Those interested in a more in-depth analysis may consult Gerald F. Gaus, "What is Deontology? Part One" and "What is Deontology? Part Two," *Journal of Value Inquiry* 35 (2001): 27–42 and 179–99.

[10] Gaus, "What is Deontology? Part Two," 189–90.

[11] The use of the qualification "so far as we can tell" in the text is required in order to reflect the fact that it is arguably never possible to know with certainty what the outcome of a particular act will be, since the (often unforeseen) consequences will play out into the indefinite future. For this and other reasons, while some consequentialists conceive of their doctrine as a decision procedure, i.e. they hold that moral judgments should be guided by the agent's evaluation of the expected outcomes of the available alternatives, the majority interpret the doctrine solely as a criterion for judging the rightness of actions. This second approach leaves open the possibility that, given time constraints and imperfect knowledge, the best outcomes might generally be produced by following deontological principles. As Peter Railton noted in his important essay on this question, "it becomes an empirical question (though not an easy one) which modes of decision making should be employed and when." (Peter Railton, "Alienation, Consequentialism and Morality," *Philosophy and Public Affairs* 13, no. 2 (1984): 134–71). For a trenchant criticism of Railton's "objective consequentialism," see Lars Bergstrom, "Reflections on Consequentialism," *Theoria* 62, no. 1–2 (1996): 74–94.

[12] John Locke, *Two Treatises of Government*, student edition, edited with an introduction by Peter Laslett (Cambridge: Cambridge University Press, 1988). All citations herein to the *Two Treatises of Government* are (unless otherwise stated) to the *Second Treatise* in the referenced edition.

[13] Locke, *Two Treatises of Government*, chapter V, sec. 27, 271.

[14] See James Clapp, s.v. "John Locke," in Edwards, *Encyclopedia of Philosophy*, vol. 4, 498–503. According to Locke, since the aggressor potentially threatens the entire community, the right to punish aggressors in a state of nature actually extends beyond the victim and encompasses society at large.

[15] Locke, *Two Treatises of Government*, chapter V, sec. 26, 286–7.

[16] Ibid., chapter V, sec. 27, 287.

[17] Ibid., chapter V, sec. 27, 287–8 and sec. 32, 291.

[18] Ibid., chapter V, sec. 37, 294.

[19] Ibid., chapter VI, sec. 57, 305–6.

[20] Here is as good a place as any to briefly take up the question of whether Locke is properly regarded as a "proto-libertarian." This is a controversial claim, which cannot be fully explored here. I believe that such an interpretation is warranted by Locke's (i) elucidation and defense of the notion of natural rights; (ii) formulation of the concept of "self-ownership," discussed in Chapters 1 and 2; (iii) justification of the reduction of common property to private ownership (discussed in Chapters 2 and 3); and (iv) insistence that the tacit consent of those in a state of nature to the formation of political society does not subject them to the *arbitrary* will of the state, meaning that the legislature must follow proper procedures in the enactment and enforcement of the law, and that the political authorities are constrained in their activities by the natural law.

For contrary arguments, see Jeremy Waldron, "Nozick and Locke, Filling the Space of Rights," in Paul et al., *Natural Rights Liberalism*, 88–97; Alex Tuckness, s.v. "Locke's Political Philosophy," sec. 4, in Zalta, *Stanford Encyclopedia of Philosophy*; and Laslett, *Two Treatises of Government*, 93–122. For my purposes, nothing of substance hangs on the outcome of this debate.

[21] Note the echoes of Locke's natural rights thesis in the Declaration of Independence:

> We hold these truths to be self-evident: that all men are created equal; that they are endowed by their creator with certain unalienable rights; that among these are life, liberty and the pursuit of happiness; that to secure these rights, governments are instituted among men, deriving their powers from the consent of the governed; that whenever any form of government becomes destructive to these ends, it is the right of the people to alter or abolish it...

[22] Mark Murphy, s.v. "The Natural Law Tradition in Ethics," sec. 1.2, in Zalta, *Stanford Encyclopedia of Philosophy*. See also Richard Wollheim, s.v. "Natural Law," in Edwards, *Encyclopedia of Philosophy*, vol. 5, 450–4. Wollheim describes the central assumptions of the Thomist view as follows: "That phenomena are divided into natural kinds, that each natural kind is distinguished by the possession of an essence, that the essence stipulates an end, [and] that virtue and goodness are necessarily linked with the fulfillment of these ends" (ibid., 452).

[23] For more detailed critiques of Locke's derivation of natural rights from the natural law doctrine, see John Hasnas, "Toward a Theory of Empirical Natural Rights," in Paul et al., *Natural Rights Liberalism*, 118–22; W. T. Jones, *A History of Western Philosophy: Vol. 3 Hobbes to Hume*, 2nd edn (New York: Harcourt, Brace & World, 1969), 263–6; and Laslett, *Two Treatises of Government*, 67–92.

[24] To the best of my knowledge, Rand never literally speaks of "natural rights," but (for reasons that will become clear) instead used the cognate locution, "the source of rights is man's nature" (Ayn Rand, "Man's Rights," in *The Virtue of Selfishness*, by Ayn Rand, with additional articles by Nathan Brandon [New York: Signet Books, 1970], 94). Nevertheless, she clearly adopts the concept of *negative* rights outlined above:

> No man can have a right to impose an unchosen obligation, an unrewarded duty or an involuntary obligation on another man....A right does not include the material implementation of that right by other men; it includes only the freedom to earn that implementation by one's own effort. Observe in this context, the intellectual precision of the Founding Fathers: they spoke to the right of *the pursuit* of happiness—*not* of the right to happiness; it does *not* mean that others must make him happy. The right to life means that a man has the right to support his life by his own work (on any economic level, as high as his ability will carry him); it does *not* mean that others must provide him with the necessities of life. (Ibid., 96–7)

[25] John R. Searle, "How to Derive 'Ought' From 'Is,'" in Wilfrid Sellars and John Hospers, eds. *Readings in Ethical Theory*, 2nd edn (New York: Appleton-Century-Crofts, 1970), 63. For Hume's original argument, see David Hume, *A Treatise of Human Nature*, 1739, in V. C. Chappell, ed. *The Philosophy of David Hume* (New York: Random House, 1963), 247.

26 See Jonathan Harrison, s.v. "Ethics, Naturalism," in Edwards, vol. 3, *Encyclopedia of Philosophy*, 70.

27 For a summary of the variety of Randian views that have evolved, see David D. Gordon, "Bibliographic Essay: Contemporary Currents in Libertarian Political Philosophy," *Literature of Liberty: A Review of Contemporary Liberal Thought* 4, no. 1 (1981): 7–35.

28 Rand, "Objectivist Ethics," in Rand, *The Virtue of Selfishness*, 16.

29 Ibid., 17.

30 Ibid.

31 Ibid., 19–20.

32 Ibid., 24.

33 Ibid., 27.

34 Ibid.

35 The Randian model resembles the recently fashionable (although still a distinctly minority-held) moral theory known as "virtue ethics." This theory follows Aristotle in rejecting the idea that the fundamental purpose of morality is to provide rules or guidance regarding what we ought to do or abstain from doing, in favor of an emphasis on the cultivation of virtuous traits of character, where "virtue" is not characterized in primarily moral terms. As one philosopher describes this view:

> A virtue should not be thought of as a moral *requirement*, because this confuses it with a principle or statement of what ought to be done. It is better to say that a virtue is, at a minimum, a character trait that is socially valued. Patience, attentiveness, concern, humility, graciousness, and the like are examples. A *moral* virtue is a character trait that is morally valued—for example, truthfulness, honesty, gentleness, and the like. Virtues can be other than moral: they can be nonmoral and even immoral. (Beauchamp, *Philosophical Ethics*, 184 [footnote omitted])

Since proponents of virtue-based theories generally have a wider array of virtues in mind, including benevolence, than Rand's singular focus on "rationality," they would generally reject Rand's version of ethical egoism.

36 John Hospers, *An Introduction to Philosophical Analysis*, 2nd edn (Englewood Cliffs, NJ: Prentice-Hall, 1967), 592. Hospers gives a very sympathetic account of Rand's ethical system in this textbook. Ibid., 591–4, 602–3.

37 Ibid., 92.

38 Rand, "Man's Rights," in Rand, *The Virtue of Selfishness*, 97.

39 See James Lenman, s.v. "Moral Naturalism," sec. 4.1, in Zalta, *Stanford Encyclopedia of Philosophy*.

40 Murphy, "The Natural Law Tradition," sec. 2.4.

41 I owe this point to Matt Zwolinski.

42 See, e.g., Beauchamp, *Philosophical Ethics*, 69 ("Egoism has received favorable treatment from many academic psychologists and political theorists, but this theory has never fared well among moral philosophers, who have variously judged it to be unprovable, false, inconsistent, or irrelevant to morality.")

43 Robert Shaver, s.v. "Egoism," introduction, in Zalta, *Stanford Encyclopedia of Philosophy*.

44 Rand, "The Ethics of Emergencies," in Rand, *The Virtue of Selfishness*, 45.

45 See, e.g., Rand, "'Conflicts' of Man's Interests," in Rand, *The Virtue of Selfishness*, 50–60; Hospers, *Introduction to Philosophical Analysis*, 606; and Tibor R. Machan, *Individuals and Their Rights* (LaSalle, IL: Open Court, 1989), 58–60.

46 Alternatively, ethical egoists could argue that if everyone pursued their own self-ish goals, this would (serendipitously) produce the best overall consequences; but not only would this outcome be the purest coincidence, but if the *reason* we should pursue our selfish interests is because acting on this principle would produce the greatest good, then this is an argument for consequentialism, not egoism.

47 Kai Nielsen, "Why Should I Be Moral?" In Sellars and Hospers, *Readings in Ethical Theory*, 49.

48 Nozick expressly rejects Objectivist ethics in "On the Randian Argument," in Paul, *Reading Nozick*, 206–31. For a Randian rebuttal to Nozick's critique, see Douglas Den Uyl and Douglas Rasmussen, "Nozick on the Randian Argument," in Paul, *Reading Nozick*, 232–69.

49 Immanuel Kant, *Groundwork of the Metaphysic of Morals*, 1785, translated and edited by H. J. Paton (New York: Harper & Row, 1964), 96.

50 In outlining his argument for side constraints, Nozick cites Gilbert Harman's essay, "The Inference to the Best Explanation," *The Philosophical Review* 74, no. 1 (1965): 88–95.

51 Ibid., 89.

52 Ibid.

53 Nozick is clearly channeling Kant here. As Roger Sullivan has noted, for Kant persons are "rational agents" who are "by nature free and rational, able and obli-gated to set goals, to recognize the existence of objective ends, to make genuine choices, and to enact and act on genuinely universal laws of conduct for them-selves and all others." Roger Sullivan, *Immanuel Kant's Moral Theory* (Cambridge: Cambridge University Press, 1989), 197.

54 Matt Zwolinski in "The Separateness of Persons and Liberal Theory" provides an excellent comparative analysis of the use of the "separateness of persons" idea by both Nozick and John Rawls. In this essay, he explains that these two philosophers make radically different uses of this concept in their political theo-ries not because they disagree about its meaning in some fundamental way, but that "the difference, instead, lies in their understanding of what a person is—or, more precisely, what the normatively significant aspects of a person are" (ibid., 154). Zwolinski interprets Nozick as holding that our personal identities are to a major extent defined by the projects we elect to pursue. And, since such projects require external goods, property rights are a "normatively significant" aspect of personhood (ibid., 155). Accordingly, to seize a person's property for the benefit of another is to impinge their "separateness." I agree with this analysis, but also believe that Nozick's bedrock moral commitment, on which his notion of separ-ateness rests, is respect for rational agency.

55 See, e.g., Nagel, "Libertarianism without Foundations," 192–3; Robert Paul Wolff, "Robert Nozick's Derivation of the Minimal State," in Paul, *Reading Nozick*, 78–80; and Jonathan Wolff, *Robert Nozick: Property, Justice and the Minimal State* (Stanford, CA: Stanford University Press, 1991), 27–33. To say that Nagel's review of *ASU* is "uncomplimentary" would be a major understatement. His

verdict was that *ASU*

> attempts to set forth the libertarian position in a way that will persuade some of those who do not already accept it. Despite its ingenuity of detail, the effort is entirely unsuccessful as an attempt to convince, and far less successful than it might be as an attempt to explain to someone who does not hold the position why anyone else does hold it. (Nagel, "Libertarianism without Foundations," 192).

[56] Nagel, "Libertarianism without Foundations," 193.

[57] Ethical arguments usually proceed by building on some normative proposition that seems as ironclad as possible, such as "it is wrong to wantonly kill human beings." However, even here the moral skeptic can at least pretend to be unconvinced, and demand of the proponent that he prove this proposition as well. At this point the dialog ends because there is no even more fundamental ethical truth to which the defender of objective morality can make appeal. So the skeptic apparently emerges victorious.

However, the tables are turned if basic moral judgments are self-evident, in the same way we regard it as obvious that in two dimensional space the shortest distance between any two points is a straight line or that if all men are mortal and Socrates is a man, then it *must* be the case that Socrates is mortal (this basic rule of logic is known as *modus ponens*). In other words, the truth of basic ethical propositions might be knowable through reason alone (what philosophers call a priori knowledge).

This idea, applied to ethics, is known as ethical intuitionism ("EI"). It was quite mainstream in academic philosophy through the middle of the twentieth century. However, this view then fell far out of favor for at least two reasons. First, philosophers had become convinced that no non-tautological (i.e. "synthetic") truths could be known a priori and second, because they developed what they regarded as plausible, non-objective accounts of moral judgments. In the last two decades there has been a renewed interest in EI, as many philosophers concluded that the case against the possibility of synthetic a priori knowledge was less airtight than first thought and that "subjective" explanations of our moral judgments were less persuasive than they originally appeared. See Philip Stratton-Lake, "Introduction" to Philip Stratton-Lake, ed. *Ethical Intuitionism: Re-evaluations* (Oxford: Oxford University Press, 2002), 1–28.

For ethical intuitionists, the truth of moral propositions does not lie in their stating some fact about the natural world, but in their mind-independence. On this account, our understanding of the ethical universe cannot be empirical. Rather, we come to know moral propositions in the same way we know the truths of mathematics or logic. While ethical intuitionism holds that at least some normative truths are self-evident, it is not committed to the questionable view that our ethical intuitions are infallible. While self-evidence may only be appropriately claimed for basic ethical truths, one can argue deductively or dialectically from them to broader claims, as we have done for natural rights.

EI is no less controversial than other meta-ethical theories, and a fair and reasonably thorough analysis of the variety of objections and rebuttals that have been propounded in the academic literature would be well beyond the scope of this work. The point of discussing the doctrine to this extent is simply to show that Nozick's reliance on his first premise is not only justified by its central place in our ordinary moral consciousness, but may plausibly be said to be known in the same way we know *modus ponens*. For a survey of contemporary EI positions, see the essays collected in Stratton-Lake, *Ethical Intuitionism: Re-evaluations,* and for an articulate, book-length defense of this view, see Michael Huemer, *Ethical Intuitionism* (New York: Palgrave Macmillan, 2005).

[58] Here, Nozick took a stab at resolving philosophy's "big questions," which have bedeviled theorists for centuries: the identity of the self, how knowledge is possible, free will, the foundations of ethics, and the important role that philosophy can play in enabing persons to live meaningful lives. In this impressive tome he addresses the foundations of morality in far greater depth than in *ASU*.

Nozick's analysis of the objective/subjective nature of morality is quite complex and moreover occurs against the backdrop of what one commentator describes as "a new way of doing philosophy" (Alasdair MacIntyre, "Pluralistic Philosophy," Review of *Philosophical Explanations* by Robert Nozick, *New York Times,* Late City Final Edition, September 20, 1981: sec. 7, p. 7). According to MacIntyre, the approach advocated by Nozick in *Philosophical Explanations* ("*PE*") would have philosophers, rather than striving to demonstrate the exclusive truth of their views, provide explanations "that enable...us to understand how certain things are possible, given other beliefs or suppositions" (ibid.). This method does not require theorists to adhere solely to a single account of the phenomena in question. Thus, while Nozick's account in *PE* of the foundations of morality differs from the one I have proposed, it is not necessarily in conflict with it.

Nozick's meta-ethical views defy easy summary. Simplifying a great deal, he does not seek to overcome the is/ought gap, but instead seeks to show that we can "live with" the uncertainty we have regarding the ultimate nature of ethics (*PE,* 567–70). In his judgment, what makes values possible is that "we choose that there be value but do not choose its character" (*PE,* 558 [footnote omitted]).

[59] Bertrand Russell, "The Elements of Ethics," in Sellars and Hospers, *Readings in Ethical Theory,* 4.

[60] It is also apparently intuitively obvious to Nozick, since he endorses the potentiality view without offering any argument for it. See Nozick, *PE,* 457–8. I do not claim, nor do I believe that my argument depends on showing, that potentiality is the *only* reason that killing the immature is wrong. This position is consistent with, and is perhaps compelled by, my endorsement of moral pluralism in Chapter 6.

In any case, it should be recognized that the difficulty of giving a satisfactory account of the moral status of newborns, infants and children is not a *special* problem for libertarians. For example, for purposes of judging the rightness of actions or policies most consequentialists would like to assign a far greater importance to the impact of such acts or rules on infants relative to primates. Yet, primates are more "advanced" in most measures of intelligence than infants, and are (it seems) equally capable of feeling pleasure and pain. Accordingly, unless they wish to acknowledge the moral equivalence of infants and primates, consequentialists must articulate some principled basis for making this distinction that is consistent with the other tenets of their doctrine.

[61] See, e.g., Frances Kamm, "Non-consequentialism, the Person as an End-in-Itself, and the Significance of Status," *Philosophy and Public Affairs* 21, no. 4 (1992):

354–89, and Thomas Nagel, "Personal Rights and Public Space," *Philosophy and Public Affairs* 24, no. 2 (1995): 83–107.

⁶² Kamm, "In Search of the Deep Structure of Morality: An Interview with Frances Kamm by Alex Voorhoeve," *Imprints* 9 (2006): 93–117. Nagel endorses this argument in "Personal Rights," where, he sees inviolability as a "nonderivative and fundamental element of morality" (Nagel, "Personal Rights," 89). This is the same Thomas Nagel who in his scathing review of *ASU* rejected the inviolability of rights out of hand. However, he falls off the libertarian bandwagon by failing to accord property rights the respect they deserve.

⁶³ Peter van Inwagen, "The Mystery of Metaphysical Freedom," in Peter van Inwagen and David Zimmerman, eds. *Metaphysics: the Big Questions* (Oxford: Blackwell, 1998), 373.

⁶⁴ Kagan, *Normative Ethics*, 280.

⁶⁵ The literature on this subject is now quite voluminous. For a brief introduction, see Sharon Begley, "What Your Pet is Thinking," *Wall Street Journal*, October 27, 2006, W1.

⁶⁶ Judith Thomson, *The Realm of Rights* (Cambridge, MA: Harvard University Press, 1990), 215.

⁶⁷ Nozick, *PE*, 500–1.

⁶⁸ See Troy Jollimore, s.v. "Impartiality," sec. 2.1, in Zalta, *Stanford Encyclopedia of Philosophy*; and Brad Hooker, *Ideal Code, Real World: A Rule-Consequentialist Theory of Morality* (Oxford: Oxford University Press, 2003), 23–9.

⁶⁹ Jollimore, "Impartiality," sec. 3.1. Consequentialists who hold that the appropriate moral inquiry is the search for optimal *rules* of conduct might endorse particular ones that accord a disproportionate moral weight to the interests of those closest to the agent, if this would maximize overall welfare. For rule consequentialists, "impartiality" consists of the identification of "an impartial perspective for selecting moral rules" (Hooker, *Ideal Code, Real World*, 28).

⁷⁰ Charles Fried, *An Anatomy of Values: Problems of Personal and Social Choice* (Cambridge, MA: Harvard University Press, 1977), 42.

⁷¹ Jollimore, "Impartiality," sec. 4.2. Note that I am not invoking "impartiality" to directly fix the *content* of morality, as Kant famously proposes with his Categorical Imperative, i.e. we must only act pursuant to maxims that could consistently be willed as a universal law. See Sullivan, *Immanuel Kant's Mortal Theory*, 49. Rather, I am starting with a particular moral perspective, and using what Jollimore calls the "minimal version" of impartiality to impose "formal consistency" on agents. See Jollimore, "Impartiality," sec. 4.2.

⁷² There has been substantial confusion on this point in the literature. See, e.g., Will Kymlicka, *Contemporary Political Philosophy: An Introduction*, 2nd edn (New York: Oxford University Press, 2001), 108 ("For Nozick, on the other hand [versus Rawls] the most important rights are rights over oneself—the rights which constitute 'self-ownership'"); Kasper Lippert-Rasmussen, "Against Self-Ownership: There Are No Fact-Insensitive Ownership Rights Over One's Body," *Philosophy and Public Affairs* 36 (2008): 87 ("Among recent proponents of the self-ownership thesis, the most prominent is Robert Nozick"); Edward Feser, "There is No Such Thing as an Unjust Initial Acquisition," in Paul et al., *Natural Rights Liberalism*, 56 ("Nozick does seem to assume that most of the rights he ascribes

to individuals follow from the thesis of self-ownership"); Wolff, *Robert Nozick*, 8 ("Nozick is distinctive in the emphasis he puts on self-ownership"); and G. A. Cohen, *Self-Ownership, Freedom, and Equality* (Cambridge: Cambridge University Press, 1995), 13 ("in Nozick's case...the self-ownership principle was thought to imply a principle which readily permits formation of unequal property in portions of external nature").

For interpretations of Nozick's views along Kantian lines, as defended herein, see Gordon, "Book Review, *Robert Nozick*," 129–33; Wenar, "Rights," sec. 6.1; Hasnas, "Empirical Natural Rights," 120; and H. Tristram Engelhardt, Jr, *The Foundations of Bioethics* (New York: Oxford University Press, 1986), 113–14, 353.

73 Wolff, *Robert Nozick*, 8.

74 This argument is closely associated with Murray Rothbard and the anarcho-capitalists, although as noted its roots extend at least as far back as Locke. See Murray N. Rothbard, *For a New Liberty: The Libertarian Manifesto*, rev. edn (New York: Macmillan, 1978), 39–44. Libertarians who subscribe to the self-ownership thesis typically also hold, in order to banish positive (welfare) rights from the moral landscape, that "all rights are property rights."

75 There are other serious objections to grounding libertarian rights in self-ownership. See, e.g., Lippert-Rasmussen, "Against Self-Ownership." See also Gerald F. Gaus, "Property, Rights, and Freedom," in Ellen Franken Paul, Fred D. Miller, Jr. and Jeffry Paul, eds. *Property Rights* (Cambridge: Cambridge University Press, 1994).

76 See Kymlicka, *Contemporary Political Philosophy*, 110–27.

Chapter 2

1 *The Chumash: The Torah, Haftors and Five Megillos with Commentary Anthologized from the Rabbinic Writings*, ed. Rabbi Nosson Scherman, 11th edn (Brooklyn, NY: Mesorah Publications, 2000), 661. According to the commentary by Rashi cited there, the import of this command is that a judge should not favor a poor person in a dispute with a rich one on the ground that the rich litigant owes a duty of charity to the poor anyway, so that a verdict in favor of the latter would simply be enforcing a pre-existing obligation.

2 Available in English at http://english.peopledaily.com.cn/constitution/constitution.html

3 In the context of political theory, "egalitarian" is a description that applies to a very broad range of views that differ in substantial ways. One specialist defines the concept as follows:

An egalitarian favors equality of some sort: People should get the same, or be treated the same, or be treated as equals in some respect. Egalitarian doctrines tend to express the idea that all human persons are equal in fundamental worth or moral status...Egalitarianism is a protean doctrine, because there are several different types of equality, or ways in which people might be treated the same, that might be thought desirable. In modern democratic societies the term "egalitarian" is often used to refer to a position that favors, for any of a wide array of reasons, a greater degree of equality of income and wealth

across persons than currently exists. (Richard J. Arneson, s.v. "Egalitarianism," introduction, in Zalta, *Stanford Encyclopedia of Philosophy*)
The difficulty of specifying a distinctive content for egalitarianism may be appreciated from the fact that natural rights libertarianism would plausibly merit inclusion since it demands equal treatment—side constraints—for all rational agents.

4 Locke, *Two Treatises of Government*, chapter V, sec. 34, 291.

5 Ibid., chapter V, sec. 27, 287.

6 Ibid., sec. 27, 288.

7 Ibid., sec. 31, 290.

8 Ibid., sec. 28, 288–9.

9 On the same page, Nozick goes on to say that, "the crucial point is whether appropriation of an unowned object worsens the situation of others" (*ASU*, 175). I do not regard this statement as inconsistent with the improvement requirement described in the text. This "no worse off" condition is "crucial" because if privatization disadvantaged innocent others it would be difficult if not impossible to justify. As explored in greater depth below, it has been asserted that the first generation of appropriators did worsen the situation of latecomers by depriving them of the opportunity to appropriate. However, as Locke argued, by *cultivating* (i.e. improving) raw land the owner indirectly benefits non-appropriators by increasing the supply of food available for purchase and thus driving down the price. See note 15 below. Thus, satisfaction of the improvement condition will ordinarily ensure that the "no worse off" requirement is met.

10 For an extended argument in support of this position, see Narveson, *Libertarian Idea*, 87–93.

11 See Schmidtz, "The Institution of Property," in Paul et al., *Property Rights*, 46–50, and n.20. See also Steven N. S. Cheung, "Common Property Rights," in Eatwell et al., *The World of Economics*, 83–6.

12 Schmidtz, "When is Original Appropriation Required?" *The Monist* 73 (October 1990): 515.

13 See ibid., 511–12.

14 In fact, the opposite may be true, for as Schmidtz has observed, appropriation is not a zero-sum, but a positive-sum game:

> Consider the Jamestown colony of 1607. Exactly what was it, we should ask, that made their situation so much better than ours? They never had to worry about being overcharged for car repairs.... Many philosophers say, in effect, that original appropriators got the good stuff. We got ugly leftovers. But in truth, original appropriation benefits latecomers far more than it benefits original appropriators. Original appropriation is a cornucopia of wealth, but mainly for latecomers rather than for the appropriators themselves. The original appropriators never dreamt of things latecomers take for granted. The poorest among us have life expectancies exceeding theirs by several decades. (Schmidtz, "Institution of Property," 45–6)

15 Locke actually anticipates Nozick's point and the views of free market economists with his observation that land cultivated privately is much more productive than land farmed collectively:

> [H]e who appropriates land to himself by his labour, does not lessen but increase the common stock of mankind. For the provisions serving to the

support of humane life, produced by one acre of inclosed and cultivated land are...ten times more than those which are yielded by an acre of Land, of an equal richnesse, lyeing wast in common. (Locke, *Two Treatises of Government*, chapter V, sec. 37, 294)

The tragic loss of many millions of lives to starvation as a result of Stalin's forced collectivization of the Soviet Union's agricultural sector in the late 1920s confirms the soundness of Locke's reasoning.

[16] The two considerations identified in this paragraph cause me to reject Loren Lomasky's suggestion that Nozick's principle of rectification might leave him with no alternative but to accept a radical redistribution of holdings to effect strict equality before entitlement principles could legitimately operate. See Loren Lomasky, "Liberalism at Twin Harvard," in Paul et al., *Natural Rights Liberalism*, 197–8.

[17] This possibility is not fanciful. Even such an unimpeachably (pardon the pun) "progressive" politician as former President Clinton acknowledged that "the current welfare system undermines the basic value of work, responsibility, and family, trapping generation after generation in dependency and hurting the very people it was designed to help" (Bill Clinton, "Welfare Reform Must Protect Children and Legal Immigrants," in Charles P. Cozic, ed. *Welfare Reform* [San Diego: Greenhaven Press, 1997], 41).

[18] As Nozick recognizes, the derivation of a comprehensive and coherent theory of rectification is an extraordinarily complex task. For a good synthesis of the competing considerations that must be reconciled, see Tyler Cowen, "How Far Back Should We Go? Why Restitution Should be Small," in Jon Elster, ed. *Retribution and Reparation in the Transition to Democracy since 1945* (Cambridge: Cambridge University Press, 2006), 17–32.

[19] See ibid, 24–26.

[20] I do not discuss in the text a further argument Nozick makes against egalitarian theories of political justice, namely the analogy he draws between the right to emigrate from a society and the right to opt out of participating in the social insurance programs that characterize the welfare state (see *ASU*, 172–3). If, as most people concede, emigration is a moral right, why, asks Nozick, aren't persons also entitled to elect not to participate in these insurance programs? I ignore this argument because I believe it is less compelling than the two I discuss in the text, and because in any case it largely revolves around the same issues discussed there.

[21] Nagel, "Libertarianism without Foundations," 201–2. For an argument very similar to Nagel's, see Onara O'Neill, "Nozick's Entitlements," in Paul, *Reading Nozick*, 305–22.

[22] See Schmidtz, *The Limits of Government: An Essay on the Public Goods Argument* (Boulder, CO: Westview Press, 1991), 27–8.

[23] Wolff, *Robert Nozick*, 87 (referencing an argument by G. A. Cohen).

[24] It may be objected that this argument does not count against the compatibility of positive rights because it rests on the purely contingent fact that in my example A's "excess" wealth cannot satisfy the needs of both B and C. In a sufficiently affluent society there will be enough resources to satisfy the needs of all, and in such circumstances it will be possible to satisfy all welfare rights, i.e. B and C can both be helped. My response is that in the eyes of the least fortunate "need" will be felt in relative and not absolute terms, i.e. in comparison to how the rich

live, triggering the same problem of the mutual consistency of positive rights. Of course, egalitarians could simply deny the existence of welfare rights beyond some fixed level of assistance, but this gives rise to the problem of articulating some principled basis for drawing such a line.

25 Hillel Steiner, *An Essay on Rights* (Oxford: Blackwell, 1994), 2.

26 Ibid., 3.

27 See Norman P. Barry, *An Introduction to Modern Political Theory*, 3rd edn (Houndmills, UK: Macmillan, 1995), 238–42 and Feser, *On Nozick*, 38.

28 Wolff, *Robert Nozick*, 91–2. See also Nagel, "Libertarianism without Foundations," 199.

29 See Matt Zwolinski, "Price Gouging, Non-Worseness, and Distributive Justice," *Business Ethics Quarterly* 19 (2009): 295–306.

30 See David Lyons, "The New Indian Claims and Original Rights to Land," in Paul, *Reading Nozick*, 365.

31 See Steiner, *Essay on Rights*, 249–61.

32 See Thomas Scanlon, "Nozick on Rights, Liberty and Property," in Paul, *Reading Nozick*, 110–11.

33 According to *Forbes*, of the 400 richest Americans (as of October, 2009), 274 were entirely self-made, 74 inherited their fortunes and 52 fell somewhere in the middle. *Forbes*, special edition "The Forbes 400," October 19, 2009, 36.

34 See Friedrich A. Hayek, *The Constitution of Liberty* (Chicago: University of Chicago Press, 1960), 125–7.

35 See Steiner, *Essay on Rights*, 253.

36 Ibid., 253–4.

37 See Peter Jones, "Two Conceptions of Liberalism, Two Conceptions of Justice," *British Journal of Political Science* 25, no. 4 (1995): 540–1.

38 See Steiner, *Essay on Rights*, 254, n.37.

39 Hayek, *Constitution of Liberty*, 99.

40 Rawls, *Theory of Justice*, 74.

41 On this point, see Matt Cavanagh, *Against Equality of Opportunity* (Oxford: Oxford University Press, 2002), 96–8. See also David Schmidtz, "History and Pattern," in Paul et al., *Natural Rights Liberalism*, 163–8.

42 Rawls, *Theory of Justice*, 104.

43 John Kekes, *The Illusions of Egalitarianism* (Ithaca, NY: Cornell University Press, 2003), 73. I assume that Kekes's reference to "legally owned property" refers to property acquired and held under the laws of a tolerably just society.

I have an old and close friend named David. When circumstances permit, he and I golf together. David is a near scratch golfer, with a fluid, virtually picture-perfect swing. In contrast, I have a swing no one would want to emulate. Inevitably during the round, one of the golfers in our foursome will complement David on his swing. I will then interject my "standard" joke, stating dismissively: "*Anyone* can shoot par with a swing like *that*; it takes real character to get around this course with a swing like mine." Usually this draws a good laugh, because golfers understand that swings like David's don't just happen, but are the product of literally thousands of hours of practice and instruction.

44 Schmidtz, "History and Pattern," 164.

45 For Nozick's critique see *ASU*, 183–230. Additionally, a convenient collection of critical essays is found in Norman Daniels, ed. *Reading Rawls: Critical Studies of "A Theory of Justice"* (New York: Basic Books, 1976). See also Kekes, *Illusions of Egalitarianism*, 46–63 and Kymlicka, *Contemporary Political Philosophy*, 60–74.

46 Bernard Williams, "The Ideal of Equality," in Joel Feinberg, ed. *Moral Concepts* (New York: Oxford University Press, 1969), 153–71.

47 Ibid., 163.

48 Ibid.

49 Ibid.

50 Nagel, "Libertarianism without Foundations," 203.

Chapter 3

1 John Emerich Edward Dalberg-Acton (Lord Acton), collected in *History of Freedom and Other Essays* (London: Macmillan and Co. Limited, 1907), 297 (published posthumously).

2 Hohfeld's seminal contribution was *Fundamental Legal Conceptions* (1917). My analysis of this subject is heavily indebted to Leif Wenar, "The Concept of Property and the Takings Clause," 97 *Columbia Law Review*, no. 6 (1997): 1923–46. See also Wenar, "Rights," sec. 2.1.

3 Wenar, "Concept of Property," 1925–28.

4 Wenar, "Rights," sec. 2.1.

5 Loren Lomasky, *Persons, Rights, and the Moral Community* (New York: Oxford University Press, 1987), 118–19 and Barbara H. Fried, "Left-Libertarianism: A Review Essay," *Philosophy and Public Affairs* 32, no. 1 (2004): 72–84.

6 Lomasky, *Persons, Rights, Moral Community*, 118.

7 Ibid., 118–19.

8 Ibid., 119.

9 Wenar, "Concept of Property," 1925–28.

10 Wenar quotes at length Richard Epstein's utilitarian arguments in favor of "just compensation" when the state destroys one or more of the discrete "sticks" that in their totality constitute the grand bundle. See ibid., 1935–38.

11 Ibid., 1933.

12 Arthur Ripstein, "The Division of Responsibility and the Law of Tort," 72 *Fordham Law Review*, no. 5 (2004): 123, n. 72.

13 Wenar, "Concept of Property," 1943–44.

14 Lomasky, *Persons, Rights, Moral Community*, 119.

15 Ibid.

16 Lomasky's objection to the idea of Lockean appropriation is motivated by his commitment to the idea that,

> moral and legal rights...are the product of social determination...Property rights are social creations...Although material objects may have been used by human beings and other species from time immemorial, property only begins to exist when social collectivities come to generate shared conceptions of properties. (Lomasky, *Persons, Rights, Moral Community* ("*PRMC*"), 119)

On the following page of *PRMC*, he writes:

> I shall grant that moral and legal rights to property must arise as the product of social decision rather than be read off the moral landscape. As was argued in Chapter 5, this is true of *all* moral and legal rights, property rights being no exception. It need not be conceded, however, that property is *purely* a social construct, that basic rights to property do not in any respect constrain social determinations.

Lomasky's political philosophy is generally libertarian in its respect for property rights and skepticism of state intervention in our personal spheres, but his derivation of rights is complicated and multidimensional; a full summary and critique is well beyond the scope of this work. A brief outline will have to do. As indicated above, Lomasky rejects the idea of rights as implied by fundamental objective (mind-independent) moral principles or as derivable from the operation of Kantian pure practical reason. Nor does he subscribe to the Randian view, discussed in Chapter 1, of rights as a requirement for the fulfillment of human "rationality."

Rather, rights have objective value (in Lomasky's sense) because they are linked to certain experiences, such as the satisfaction of desire, that have universal human value. See *PRMC*, 237–42. Just social arrangements are those that rational individuals would agree to in order to allow them to pursue their projects (a quintessential human characteristic) without undue interference from others. However, as Eric Mack notes, for individuals to have the *right* to pursue their plans, Lomasky must show that my neighbor's projects have moral value, what he calls "impersonal value," for me, so that I am obligated to respect them and even cooperate with my neighbor to some extent, for reasons other than my naked self-interest. In return, I can demand the same from him with respect to my projects. However, the existence of "impersonal value" or what is more often called "agent-neutral value" is greatly controversial, and Mack articulates a variety of objections to the existence of such a thing. See Eric Mack, "Against Agent-Neutral Value," *Reason Papers* 14 (1989): 76–85.

However, I believe that an even more serious objection to Lomasky's strategy is the one identified by Christopher Morris, who argues that even if Lomasky could persuade us of the existence of "impersonal value," he would not have established the respect for rights as a *moral* obligation. See Morris, "Loren Lomasky's Derivation of Basic Rights," *Reason Papers* 14 (1989): 86–97. As Morris notes, if I perceive value in my neighbor's projects because of empathy toward my fellow creatures, then if I cease to experience this generally or with respect to particular individuals or groups, my obligation to respect their rights also vanishes: "for such agents 'respect rights' only insofar as doing so is the most efficient means to their (non-egoistic) ends" (ibid., 91). For those interested in a more detailed analysis of *PRMC*, both the Mack and Morris essays, plus reviews of *PRMC* by Douglas Rasmussen and Tibor Machan, as well as Lomasky's "Response to Four Critics" are available at *Reason Papers* vol. 14 (Spring 1989).

17 See Cohen, *Self-Ownership, Freedom, and Equality*, chapters 3 and 4.

18 See ibid., 79–84.

19 Ibid., 79–80. The "hard" libertarian answer is that it is not unjust to enforce the venerable principle of "you snooze, you lose." If *B* did not wish to live in a world

in which *A* emerges as his landlord, he should have appropriated first or worked out a mutually acceptable division of property. After all, *B* did not have the *right* to be protected against *A*'s appropriation. Thus, "anarcho-capitalists" (a.k.a "individual anarchists") generally reject the necessity of any "proviso" to justify the first acquisition of private property. See, e.g., Israel M. Kirzner, "Entrepreneurship, Entitlement and Economic Justice," in Paul, *Reading Nozick*, 383–411, and Rothbard, *For a New Liberty*, 29–37.

However, the short answer to this view is that without something like the Lockean proviso, the morality of private property would be called into question. If, for example, someone did manage to appropriate "all the water in the desert" or otherwise achieve a chokehold on the economy, we would be powerless to condemn it without simultaneously conceding that the institution of private property is responsible for this sorry state of affairs. The Lockean proviso allows us to acknowledge the injustice of such scenarios, while exonerating private property, since appropriations can only justly occur subject to the condition that others not be made "worse off," thus ruling out such moral catastrophes.

[20] Cohen, *Self-Ownership, Freedom, and Equality*, 80.

[21] Delineating a theory of intellectual property rights that convincing balances the competing moral claims of its creators and consumers has proven problematic for philosophers across the ideological spectrum. Libertarians are as deeply divided on this issue as other theorists. See, e.g., N. Stephan Kinsella, "Against Intellectual Property," *Journal of Libertarian Studies* 15, no. 2 (2001): 1–53, and Richard A. Epstein, "Why Libertarians Shouldn't Be (Too) Skeptical About Intellectual Property," Progress and Freedom Foundation, Progress on Point Paper No. 13.4, February 13, 2006.

Nozick's view regarding patents seems to be that they are morally justified as another form of Lockean appropriation, i.e. the inventor is claiming unowned property. However, since other persons would sooner or later have come up with the invention, "[t]his suggests placing a time limit on patents, as a rough rule of thumb to approximate how long it would have taken, in the absence of knowledge of the invention, for independent discovery" (*ASU*, 181).

[22] Cohen, *Self-Ownership, Freedom, and Equality*, 84.

[23] David Conway, "Nozick's Entitlement Theory: Three Critics Answered," *Philosophical Notes* (Libertarian Alliance, London), no. 15 (1990): 4.

[24] Cohen, *Self-Ownership, Freedom, and Equality*, 99.

[25] Ibid., 98.

[26] Ibid., 99–100.

[27] Ibid., 100.

[28] Ibid.

[29] See Narveson, *Libertarian Idea*, 68–73 for a similar argument.

[30] Peter Vallentyne, Hillel Steiner, and Michael Otsuka, "Why Libertarianism Is Not Incoherent, Indeterminate or Irrelevant: A Reply to Fried," *Philosophy and Public Affairs* 33, no. 2 (2005): 202, 204.

[31] Ibid., 209. For an excellent summary of the underlying premises, main tenets and doctrinal flaws of left-libertarianism, see Fried, "Left-Libertarianism: Review Essay."

32 See Vallentyne, s.v. "Libertarianism," secs 1 and 2, in Zalta, *Stanford Encyclopedia of Philosophy.*

33 See Vallentyne et al., "Reply to Fried," 202–3 and n.3.

34 See Vallentyne, "Introduction: Left Libertarianism—A Primer," in Peter Vallentyne and Hillel Steiner eds. *Left-Libertarianism and Its Critics: The Contemporary Debate* (Houndmills, U.K.: Palgrave, 2000), 8.

35 Ibid., 9.

36 Vallentyne et al., "Reply to Fried," 209–10.

37 Ibid., 214. Accordingly, Vallentyne et al. note that:

> On one left-libertarian interpretation [Otsuka's] ... the Lockean "enough and good" proviso calls for members of each generation to ensure that, at their deaths, resources that are at least as valuable as those they acquired lapse back into a state of nonownership so that the next generation has opportunities to acquire unowned resources which are at least as valuable as theirs. (Ibid.)

On the other hand, Steiner holds that,

> persons who appropriate a greater than equal portion ('over-appropriators') are thereby engaging in a redistribution. They are imposing an unjust distribution on some or all who have appropriated a less than equal portion ('under-appropriators'). And they consequently owe them redress (footnote omitted). (Steiner, *Essay on Rights*, 268)

38 Vallentyne, "Introduction: Left-Libertarianism," 12.

39 Steiner actually does believe that parents own their children, or at least share ownership with everyone else. The parents' ownership interest arises from the labor expended in conceiving, feeding, and caring for the child until majority. However, the child is not entirely the product of its parents' labor because they are not responsible for the germ line genetic information contained in the sperm and egg that produced the child. This genetic material was received from their parents, who in turn received it from their parents and back into eternity. Such information is a natural resource, so the net effect of this division of labor is that the child "is at the disposal of two sets of persons: his parents on the one hand and everyone else on the other, inasmuch as everyone has an equal claim to natural resources" (Steiner, *Essay on Rights*, 237–48 and n.25 (quote)).

Because rights stem from self-ownership, and because minors are, according to Steiner, not self-owners, his argument implies (as he acknowledges) that minor children have no rights. He argues that the fact that children are generally presumed not to be criminally responsible for their actions demonstrates that they lack the mental characteristics we expect of rights holders. Accordingly, what are generally thought to be children's rights are actually rights held by their parents or the state to *speak for* them. But, apart from the obvious fact that we often do hold minors substantially below the age of majority criminally responsible for their acts, his logic would apply equally to otherwise competent adults who lack the mental characteristics we expect of rights-holders because they are temporarily in comas. While I am only able to speak to my own intuitions, I find Steiner's views here not just markedly counterintuitive, but morally repulsive.

40 See Mathias Risse, "Does Left-Libertarianism Have Coherent Foundations?" *Politics, Philosophy & Economics* 3, no. 3 (2004): 355–6.

[41] Vallentyne et al., "Reply to Fried," 213.

[42] As indicated above, the latter idea is Steiner's view. See Steiner, *Essay on Rights*, 266–8.

[43] Feser, "Unjust Initial Acquisition," 60.

[44] Ibid.

[45] Vallentyne, "Libertarianism," sec. 2. See also Kymlicka, *Contemporary Political Philosophy*, 235–6.

[46] However, this truism hardly qualifies as a theory of egalitarian ownership; thus as Mathias Risse notes, "The idea that natural resources are owned in an egalitarian manner, central to left-libertarianism, and more generally the subject of the original ownership status of the world, is under-explored" (Risse, "Coherent Foundations?" 339).

[47] See Risse, "Original Ownership," 6.

[48] I borrow this term from Matthew O'Keeffe. See O'Keeffe, "World Ownership is Not Compatible with Self-Ownership: A Defence of Robert Nozick Against G.A. Cohen," *Philosophical Notes* (Libertarian Alliance, London), no. 20 (1992): 5.

[49] See Vallentyne et al., "Reply to Fried," 202 ("The second core claim of left-libertarianism is that natural resources are owned by all in some egalitarian manner").

[50] Michael Otsuka, "*Libertarianism without Inequality* (Oxford: Oxford University Press, 2003), 24.

[51] Otsuka, *Libertarianism without Inequality*, 27.

[52] Vallentyne, "Introduction: Left-Libertarianism," 7.

[53] Otsuka, *Libertarianism without Inequality*, 23.

[54] See ibid., n. 32.

[55] See David D. Gordon, "Is Inequality Indefensible?" Review of *Libertarianism without Inequality* by Michael Otsuka, *Mises Review* 9, no. 3 (2003): 4.

[56] Otsuka, *Libertarianism without Inequality*, 23–4.

[57] See Risse, "Coherent Foundations?" 354–6 and Tom G. Palmer, "John Locke Lite," Review of *Libertarianism without Inequality* by Michael Otsuka, *Reason.com* (January 2005): 3–5.

[58] See Risse, "Coherent Foundations?" 347–50.

[59] Ibid.

[60] Ibid.

[61] Ibid., 346.

[62] See Risse, "Coherent Foundations?" 354–6.

[63] Otsuka, *Libertarianism without Inequality*, 15.

[64] Even if there is no formal contradiction between Otsuka's position on self-ownership and his adoption of a stringent egalitarian proviso, I agree with Risse's judgment that Otsuka's views are still incoherent in that they cannot *both be plausible*. As he notes, the moral intuitions that motivate a rejection of the Lockean model of appropriation stand in "deep tension with the reasons required for endorsing the second bit of his libertarian right to self-ownership [the stringent right to one's labor income]" (Risse, "Coherent Foundations?" 355). In other words, the same moral intuitions that would lead persons to deny the possibility of justly acquired full capitalist property rights would also lead them to reject a stringent right to income. Ibid.

65 Fried, "Left-Libertarianism: Review Essay," 88–91.
66 Ibid., 90.
67 Ibid., 85.

Chapter 4

1   Posted on Real Clear Politics, http://www.realclearpolitics.com/articles/2007/11/the_frenchamerican_alliance_is.html
2   Murray N. Rothbard, *The Ethics of Liberty*, with a new introduction (New York: New York University Press, 1998), 187.
3   For Rothbard's elaboration of his views regarding the inherent immorality of the state, see ibid., 161–74.
4   Probably the most thorough treatment is found in J. Wolff, *Robert Nozick*, 36–72. See also Jeffery Paul, "The Withering of the Minimal State," in Paul, *Reading Nozick*, 68–76; R. Wolff, "Robert Nozick's Derivation," 77–104; Roy A. Childs, Jr, "The Invisible Hand Strikes Back," *The Libertarian Forum* 9, no. 5 (1976): 2–6, 8; Randy E. Barnett, "Whither Anarchy? Has Robert Nozick Justified the State?" *Journal of Libertarian Studies* 1, no. 1 (1977): 15–21; and Murray N. Rothbard, "Robert Nozick and the Immaculate Conception of the State," *Journal of Libertarian Studies* 1, no. 1 (1977): 45–57.
5   Nozick quotes Smith's famous observation that "Every individual intends only his own gain, and he is…led by an invisible hand to promote an end which was no part of his intention" (*ASU*, 18).
6   Wolff, *Robert Nozick*, 56.
7   See note 4 above. Edward Feser appears to be the lone dissenter to this judgment. See Feser, *On Nozick*, 59–64. However, it must be said that he uncritically accepts Nozick's premise that the market for protective services is a form of natural monopoly, and therefore does not address the implications of the DPA reserving for itself the exclusive right to determine which criminal procedures are too "risky." Moreover, he does not in my opinion take seriously enough the arguments presented in the text against the principle of compensation, dismissing these issues as merely the typical "line-drawing" problems that arise whenever abstract principles are applied in real world situations.
8   David Friedman, "Law as a Private Good: A Response to Tyler Cowen on the Economics of Anarchy," *Economics and Philosophy* 10 (1994): 319; see also Rothbard, "Robert Nozick," 46.
9   See Friedman, "Response to Tyler Cowen," 319.
10 Wolff, *Robert Nozick*, 56.
11 See Childs, "Invisible Hand Strikes Back," 3 and Rothbard, "Robert Nozick," 46–7.
12 Nozick also introduces an alternative to "procedural rights" as a justification for the DPA's monopolistic practices, i.e. the "epistemic principle of border crossing" (*ASU*, 106–7). If I understand Nozick here, this doctrine requires that a person not punish others unless the agent knows (or is in the best possible position to know) the accused is guilty. This principle would impose a moral constraint on the right to punish that is independent of the procedural rights of the accused. However, whatever its merits in the abstract, if intended as a justification of the DPA's refusal

to cooperate with competing PAs and independents, the epistemic principle fails for the same reason as does the invocation of procedural rights. That is, if valid, the principle should constrain the DPA to the same extent as it would its competitors and independents, and thus could not justify the DPA policy of punishing independents while refusing to allow independents to punish DPA members.

13 Childs, "Invisible Hand Strikes Back," 5.

14 Walter Nicholson, *Intermediate Microeconomics and Its Applications*, 3rd edn (New York: Dryden Press, 1983), 377.

15 Of course, it is not certain that the state would implode as suggested by Childs, but I believe his point is that there is no certainty in Nozick's account either. Whatever empirical grounds Nozick gives us for regarding the state as inevitable, Childs can give equally good reasons for thinking the opposite. In other words, he is drawing attention to the fact that Nozick's argument is essentially an empirical one and not a moral defense of the minimal state.

16 Nozick concedes that his concept presents problems of classification, in that it will not always be clear which activities are "important [and] done by almost all" and what prohibitions are a "serious disadvantage" (*ASU*, 82–3).

17 Barnett, "Whither Anarchy?" 20. See also Childs, "Invisible Hand Strikes Back," 5.

18 Randall G. Holcombe, "Government: Unnecessary but Inevitable," in *The Independent Review* 8, no. 3 (2004): 329.

19 Ibid., 333.

20 Ibid.

21 Ibid., 338.

22 Rand, "The Nature of Government," in Rand, *The Virtue of Selfishness*, 334.

23 See Tyler Cowen, "Law as a Public Good: The Economics of Anarchy," *Economics and Philosophy* 8, no. 2 (1992): 249–67.

24 Ibid., 256. By refusing to cooperate with an "outlaw" agency, its competitors would damage it commercially since its customers would be unable to obtain justice from the members of the boycotting agencies on a cost-effective basis. Note that Cowen is not committed to the idea that a cohesive network of PAs would develop. Rather he is asserting that if it did develop, it would be collusive: "Orderly anarchy again implies collusive anarchy" (ibid., 261).

25 Tyler Cowen, "Rejoinder to David Friedman on the Economics of Anarchy," *Economics and Philosophy* 10, no. 2 (1994): 330.

26 Ibid.

27 Cowen, "Law as Public Good," 262.

28 See John Hasnas, "Reflections on the Minimal State," *Politics, Philosophy and Economics* 2, no. 1 (2003): 115–28.

29 See Friedman, "Law as Private Good," 319 and Aeon J. Skoble, "The Anarchism Controversy," in Machan and Rasmussen, *Liberty for the Twenty-First Century*, 87–8. Skoble's essay provides an excellent overview of the controversy between minimal state libertarians and anarcho-capitalists.

30 See Skoble, "Anarchism Controversy," 85–7.

31 See Friedman, "Law as Private Good," 326–7.

32 See David Friedman, *The Machinery of Freedom*, 2nd edn (LaSalle, IL: Open Court, 1989), 202–8 and transcript of panel discussion, "Does Freedom Mean Anarchy?" *Liberty*, December 2004.

³³ Rothbard, *For a New Liberty*, 363.
³⁴ In his later book, *The Ethics of Liberty*, Rothbard forcefully presses a second argu-
    ment against any role for the state with respect to self-defense. Since modern
    warfare inevitably involves innocent civilian casualties, *all* modern wars are unjust:
    "War, then, even a just defensive war, is only proper when the exercise of violence
    is rigorously limited to the individual criminals themselves. We may judge for our-
    selves how many wars or conflicts in history have met this criterion" (Rothbard,
    Ethics of Liberty, 190). Therefore, according to Rothbard, it would not even be legit-
    imate for an innocent state to fight to retake territory conquered by an aggressor
    state: "The libertarian objective, then, should be, *regardless of the specific causes of any
    conflict*, to pressure States not to launch wars against other States and, should a war
    break out, to pressure them to sue for peace and negotiate a cease-fire and a peace
    treaty as quickly as physically possible" (emphasis added) (ibid., 194)
        Clearly, Rothbard is correct that all modern warfare inevitably involves a certain
    degree of "collateral damage." However, there is a huge logical chasm between
    this truth and the conclusion that an innocent state may not justly resist and
    repel an aggressor. Rothbard appears to be saying literally that immediately after
    the Pearl Harbor attack, the United States should have sued the Japanese and the
    Nazis for peace, which seems quite absurd on its face. Rothbard's doctrine would
    be a formula for the triumph of evil in this world, because lawless states would
    have everything to gain and nothing to lose by aggressing against peaceful ones.
    For a defense of the more traditional "just war" doctrine, see Eric Mack, "Rights,
    Just War, and National Defense," in Machan and Rasmussen, *Liberty for the Twenty-
    First Century*, 101–20.
³⁵ See Rothbard, *For a New Liberty*, 384–7.
³⁶ Ibid., 357.
³⁷ In addition to Rothbard's writings, cited above, see, e.g., Ron Paul, *The Revolution:
    A Manifesto* (New York: Grand Central Publishing, 2008), 9–40 and Harry Browne
    (the 1996 Libertarian Party presidential nominee), *Why Government Doesn't Work*
    (New York: St. Martin's Press, 1995), 138–58.
³⁸ Randy E. Barnett, "Libertarians and the War," *Wall Street Journal*, July 17, 2007,
    sec. A.
³⁹ George Klosko, *Political Obligation* (Oxford: Oxford University Press, 2005), 17.
⁴⁰ For useful explanations of the idea of public goods, see N. Greg Mankiw, *Princi-
    ples of Economics*, 3rd edn (New York: Dryden Press, 1998), 225–31 and Nicholson,
    Intermediate Microeconomics, 611–22.
⁴¹ Mankiw, *Principles of Economics*, 226.
⁴² See Mankiw, *Principles of Economics*, 228 and Nicholson, *Intermediate Microeconomics*,
    614–15.
⁴³ Richard Dagger, s.v. "Political Obligation," introduction, in Zalta, *Stanford Encyclo-
    pedia of Philosophy*.
⁴⁴ Ibid., sec. 3.1
⁴⁵ See, e.g., A. John Simmons, "Philosophical Anarchism," in A. John Simmons,
    ed. *Justification and Legitimacy: Essays on Rights and Obligations* (Cambridge: Cam-
    bridge University Press, 2001), 110.
⁴⁶ George Klosko, one of the leading advocates of this view, asserts that, "In recent
    years, the principle of fairness has come to be recognized as perhaps the most

promising counter to widespread skepticism [regarding political obligation]" (Klosko, *The Principle of Fairness and Political Obligation*, 2nd edn [Lanham, MD: Rowman & Littlefield, 2004], xx).

47 See H. L. A. Hart, "Are There Any Natural Rights?" 1955, in Jeremy Waldron, ed. *Theories of Rights* (New York: Oxford University Press, 1984), 77–90.

48 Ibid., 85.

49 See A. John Simmons, "Principle of Fair Play," in Simmons, *Justification and Legitimacy*, 328–9.

50 See ibid.

51 See ibid.

52 Ibid., 330.

53 Ibid., 335.

54 Ibid., 336.

55 In addition to Klosko's contributions, discussed in the text, see Richard Arneson, "Principle of Fairness and Free-Rider Problems," *Ethics* 92, no. 4 (1982): 616–33

56 Klosko, *Principle of Fairness*, 39, 51.

57 Ibid., 51–2.

58 Klosko, *Political Obligation*, 61.

59 See ibid.

60 See Klosko, *Principle of Fairness*, 38–9.

61 See Simmons, "Fair Play," 33–6.

62 Ibid., 36.

63 See Richard J. Arneson, "Notes for Philosophy 167: The Hart-Rawls Principle of Fairness—Nozick Chapter 5 Discussion, Spring 2008," http://philosophy.ucsd. edu/faculty/rarneson/Courses/167PrinofFair.pdf, 167

64 See Mack, "National Defense," 103. Here, Mack describes the theoretical problem facing minimal state libertarians, i.e. how to explain "why, contrary to appearances, coercive taking to finance the good of defending rights does not truly contravene libertarian strictures." This section is my attempt to answer this challenge.

65 This is not a completely new idea in libertarian circles. Leonard E. Read, a prominent figure in the movement from the late 1940s through the 1960s, wrote that:

> For one not to support that which he has inherited as an obligation is to put the burden on others. Others have a moral right to protect themselves against anyone who would burden their energy, or energy exchanges, against anyone who would siphon off their livelihood. A person who by failure to attend to his own obligation, thereby loading it onto others, engages in an inhibitive action against the society of which he is a member... Thus the agency of society must, in justice, collect from him. This collection does not, therefore, classify as aggressive force, but rather as repellent or defensive force (footnote omitted). (Leonard E. Read, *Government—An Ideal Concept* [Irvington-on-Hudson, NY: Foundation for Economic Freedom, 1954], 59)

66 See Klosko, *Principle of Fairness*, ix, 36.

67 Hayek, *Constitution of Liberty*, 206.

68 Ibid., 20–1, 206. One cannot overemphasize the importance for Hayek of the idea that the rule of law is a function of a community's shared norms:

> [I]t is the acceptance of such common principles that makes a collection of people a community. And this common acceptance is the indispensable

condition for a free society. A group of men normally become a society not by giving themselves laws but by obeying the same rules of conduct. This means that the power of the majority is limited by those commonly held principles and there is no legitimate power behind them. (Hayek, *Constitution of Liberty*, 106–7)

[69] See Hayek, *Constitution of Liberty*, 148–56, 207–10. Hayek was also deeply concerned about the abuse of administrative discretion in democratic societies, but this may be considered part of the requirement that the law be known and certain, rather than as a separate principle. See ibid., 212–14.

[70] See Hayek, *Constitution of Liberty*, 148–56, 207–8. In his earlier and more famous book, *The Road to Serfdom*, Hayek had described this concept in terms of the "formality" of legitimate legislation, but to achieve greater clarity he subsequently changed this terminology to refer to the "abstract" and "general" quality of the rule of law. See Hayek, *Constitution of Liberty*, 453 n.8.

[71] See Hayek, *Road to Serfdom*, 82–3.

[72] Ibid.; see also Hayek, *Constitution of Liberty*, 153–4.

[73] See Hayek, *Constitution of Liberty*, 209–10.

[74] Ibid., 210. For example, if physical strength is not a legitimate requirement for a particular job, a regulation specifying that all applicants must be able to carry 150 pounds for 50 yards would have the impact of excluding most women from consideration, and would thus run afoul of the "equality" principle.

[75] See ibid., 209–10.

[76] Ibid., 231.

[77] Ibid.

[78] Ibid., 106.

[79] See Klosko, *Principle of Fairness*, 127–30.

[80] See, e.g., Richard A. Epstein, *Takings: Private Property and the Power of Eminent Domain* (Cambridge, MA: Harvard University Press, 1985), 334–8 and Richard Posner, *Economic Analysis of the Law*, 2nd edn (Boston, MA: Little Brown, 1977), 40–1.

[81] See, e.g., Bruce L. Benson, "The Mythology of Holdout as a Justification for Eminent Domain and Public Provision of Roads," *The Independent Review* 10, no. 2 (2005): 165–94.

Chapter 5

[1] Ronald Reagan, "A Time for Choosing," Televised Address, October 27, 1964, from CNN online, http://www.cnn.com/SPECIALS/2004/reagan/stories/speech.archive/time.html

[2] Richard Pipes, *Property and Freedom* (New York: Alfred A. Knopf, 1999), xiii.

[3] Hayek, *Constitution of Liberty*, 207–8.

[4] Ibid., 106.

[5] Ibid., 107.

[6] See, e.g., James Madison:

It is of great importance in a republic not only to guard the society against the oppression of its rulers, but to guard one part of the society against the injustice of the other part.... If a majority be united by a common interest, the rights of the minority will be insecure. (Madison, "Federalist No. 51," in *The Federalist Papers*. 1778 [New York: New American Library, 1961], 323)

Lord Acton describes what may be the first recorded instance of a tyranny of the majority, i.e. the one arising in classical Athens following the death of Pericles:

> They [the Athenians] venerated the Constitution which had given them prosperity, and equality, and freedom, and never questioned the fundamental laws which regulated the enormous power of the Assembly...Thus they became the only people of antiquity that grew great by democratic institutions. But the possession of unlimited power, which corrodes the conscience, hardens the heart, and confounds the understanding of monarchs, exercised its demoralising (sic) influence on the illustrious democracy of Athens. It is bad to be oppressed by a minority, but it is worse to be oppressed by a majority. For there is a reserve of latent power in the masses which, if it is called into play, the minority can seldom resist. But from the absolute will of an entire people there is no appeal, no redemption, no refuge but treason. The humblest and most numerous class of the Athenians united the legislative, the judicial, and, in part, the executive power. The philosophy that was then in the ascendant taught them that there is no law superior to that of the State—the lawgiver is above the law. (Dalberg-Acton, "The History of Freedom in Antiquity," 11–12)

[7] Among the important political structures that come immediately to mind in this regard are the bicameral legislature (the nature of which makes it much more improbable that the same party could simultaneously establish a durable majority in both), the requirement that constitutional amendments be approved by three-quarters of the states, the appointment of Supreme Court justices for life terms, and the division of political authority between the federal government and the various states.

[8] Thomas Sowell, *The Quest for Cosmic Justice* (New York: The Free Press, 1999), 151.

[9] For a sobering description of the slow-motion political train-wreck now underway in Venezuela, see Simon Romero, "Criticism of Chavez Stifled by Arrests," *New York Times*, April 4, 2010, A6 (New York edn), http://www.nytimes.com/2010/04/04/world/americas/04venez.html and Fabiola Sanchez, "Chavez Gains Free Reign in Venezuela," Associated Press, January 31, 2007, http://news.yahoo.com/s/ap/20070201/ap_on_re_la_am_ca/venezuela_chavez_17

[10] Putin's critics and Russian investigative reporters have a nasty habit of being murdered under mysterious circumstances. See, e.g., Artemy Troitsky, "The Russia I Lost," *New Statesman*, November 27, 2006, http://www.newstatesman.com/200611270027. For a penetrating (and alarming) analysis of the current state of Russian politics, see Leon Aron, "What Does Putin Want?" *Commentary*, December 2006.

[11] According to Winston Churchill, immediately prior to the 1832 Reform, about 450,000 Britons had the vote. The 1832 Reform expanded the franchise to roughly 700,000 men, constituting approximately one adult male in six. See Churchill, *A History of the English Speaking Peoples*, vol. 4, *The Great Democracies* (New York: Dorset Press, 1990), 52, 97. See also George M. Trevelyan, *A*

Shortened History of England (Harmondsworth, UK: Penguin Books, 1982), 473–4, 489–90.

12 Emblematic are the famous words of William Pitt, Earl of Chatham, in 1777:

> The poorest man may in his cottage bid defiance to all the forces of the Crown. It may be frail—its roof may shake—the wind may blow through it—the storm may enter—the rain may enter—but the King of England cannot enter—all his force dares not cross the threshold of the ruined tenement! (Quoted in Beck, *Bartlett's Familiar Quotations*, 350)

See also Hayek, *Constitution of Liberty*, 169–74.

13 See John A. Garraty and Peter Gay, eds. *The Columbia History of the World* (New York: Harper & Row, 1972), 583.

14 See G. O. Sayles, *The Medieval Foundations of England*, 1st American edn (Philadelphia, PA: University of Pennsylvania Press, 1950), 224–8.

15 See ibid., 225–6.

16 See ibid., 393 (quote), 400–2.

17 See ibid., 395–400. It would be incorrect to view the struggle to impose the Magna Carta as a simple "face-off" between the king and his great barons. The clergy, freemen and the English people generally sided with the barons. See Trevelyan, *Shortened History of England*, 147–8.

18 Sayles, *Medieval Foundations of England*, 401.

19 Trevelyan, *Shortened History of England*, 148.

20 See ibid., 148–9.

21 See Pipes, *Property and Freedom*, 133–6.

22 See Trevelyan, *Shortened History of England*, 276–7, 286.

23 See ibid., 283–6.

24 Pipes, *Property and Freedom*, 138. Pipes make this illuminating observation regarding the absence of a tradition of property rights in feudal Russia:

> [T]he critical factor in the failure of Russia to develop rights and liberties was the liquidation of landed property in the Grand Duchy of Moscow, the principality which in time conquered all Russia and imposed on her a regime under which the monarch not only ruled the realm and its inhabitants but literally owned them. The fusion of sovereignty and ownership...vested all titles to the land in the hands of the monarch and allowed him to claim unlimited services from his subjects, nobles and commoners alike....The absence of property in land deprived Russians of all those levers by means of which the English succeeded in limiting the power of their kings. Since they required no taxes because all the land paid them rents and rendered them services, the tsars had no need to convene parliaments. (Ibid., 160)

Thus, Russia and England may be viewed as opposite "archetypes" with respect to the structure of land ownership in the early modern era.

25 Trevelyan, *Shortened History of England*, 286. On the emergence in England of the doctrine of natural rights, see Pipes, *Property and Freedom*, 139–40 and the sources cited therein.

26 Not, I think, coincidentally, less than a decade later the Jews, who had been expelled by Edward I in 1290, were allowed to return and granted the right to openly and freely practice their religion, subject only to the relatively minor discriminatory measures also enforced against Catholics and Nonconformists. From

the early eighteenth century onward they would play an increasingly important role in Britain's financial affairs and intellectual life, and their leaders moved in the highest circles of society. Full equality before the law was achieved in 1871 when Jews were for the first time authorized by Parliament to receive degrees from Oxford and Cambridge. I will not pursue this idea further here, but our abbreviated historical analysis tends to confirm Milton Friedman's claim that it "is a striking historical fact that the development of capitalism has been accompanied by a major reduction in the extent to which particular religious, racial or social groups have operated under special handicaps in respect of their economic activities" (Milton Friedman, *Capitalism and Freedom*, with the assistance of Rose D. Friedman [Chicago: University of Chicago Press, 1982], 108).

[27] See Garraty and Gay, *Columbia History of World*, 582–3 and Michael Zuckert, "Natural Rights and Imperial Constitutionalism: The American Revolution and the Development of the American Amalgam," in Paul et al., *Natural Rights Liberalism*, 35.

[28] See Trevelyan, *Shortened History of England*, 243–53.

[29] See ibid. and Robert Gibson-Jarvie, *The City of London: A Financial and Commercial History* (Cambridge: Woodhead-Faulkner, 1979), 17–18, 28, 36–7, 58–61.

[30] Many small farmers were forced off the "commons" by the "enclosure laws" of the eighteenth and nineteenth centuries, which formalized a trend that had begun centuries before. See Trevelyan, *Shortened History of England*, 134–5, 454–5. Locke, in his *Two Treatises*, published in the late seventeenth century, expressly defends the morality of the enclosure of the commons.

[31] See Linda Colley, s.v. "United Kingdom: History of England and Great Britain, British Society by the Mid-18th Century," in *Encyclopedia Britannica*, 1998 Multimedia edn. CD-ROM.

[32] David S. Landes, *The Wealth and Poverty of Nations: Why Some Are So Rich and Some So Poor* (New York: W. W. Norton, 1999), 217–18.

[33] See Trevelyan, *Shortened History of England*, 459.

[34] See Colley, "United Kingdom: British Society" and Trevelyan, *Shortened History of England*, 367–8.

[35] According to one expert:

> Most historians believe that the middle-income groups were increasing in number by the mid-18th century. Professional opportunities in law, medicine, schoolteaching, banking and government service certainly expanded at that time. In the town of Preston in Lancashire, for example, there was only one attorney in 1702; by 1728 there were 17. Growing prosperity also increased job opportunities in the leisure and luxury industries. Urban directories show that there were more musicians and music teachers and more dancing masters, booksellers, caterers, and landscape gardeners than in the 17th century. And there were more shops. Shops had expanded even into rural areas by the 1680s, but in the 18th century they proliferated at a much faster rate. By 1770 the new town of Birmingham in Warwickshire had 129 shops dealing in buttons and 56 selling toys, as well as 35 jewelers. (Colley, "United Kingdom: British Society")

See also Trevelyan, *Shortened History of England*, 367.

[36] Robert L. Heilbroner, s.v. "Economic Systems: The Evolution of Capitalism," in *Encyclopedia Britannica*. Milton Friedman makes the same point: "The kind of economic organization that provides economic freedom directly, namely

competitive capitalism, also promotes political freedom because it separates economic power from political power and in this way enables the one to offset the other" (Friedman, *Capitalism and Freedom*, 9). Friedman goes on to observe that he knows of no example in history of a society that enjoys political freedom whose economy was not organized along largely capitalist lines (ibid.).

[37] Hayek, *Road to Serfdom*, 235. Hayek reasons that capitalism imposes responsibility on the individual, and that such responsibility produces a distinct "moral sense" that atrophies under collectivism:

> Freedom to order our own conduct in the sphere where material circumstances force a choice upon us, and responsibility for the arrangement to our own conscience, is the air in which alone moral sense grows and in which moral values are daily re-created in the free decision of the individual. Responsibility, not to a superior, but to one's conscience, the awareness of a duty not exacted by compulsion, the necessity to decide which of the things one values are to be sacrificed to others, and to bear the consequences of one's own decision, are the very essence of any morals which deserve the name. (Ibid., 231–2)

[38] See Robert Middlekauff, *The Glorious Cause: The American Revolution, 1763–1789* (Oxford: Oxford University Press, 1982), 118–19 and Zuckert, "Natural Rights," 27–55.

[39] See Strauss, "Germany 1493 to c. 1769," in *Encyclopedia Britannica.*

[40] Hajo Holborn, *A History of Modern Germany, 1648–1840* (New York: Alfred A. Knopf, 1969), 198.

[41] See ibid., 65.

[42] See ibid., 262.

[43] Ibid., 266.

[44] See Holborn, *A History of Modern Germany, 1840–1945* (New York: Alfred A. Knopf, 1964), 94.

[45] See Angus Maddison, *Monitoring the World Economy, 1820–1992* (Paris: OECD Development Centre, 1995), tables chapter 1 (table 1–3). Maddison's data shows that German GDP per capita income (calculated in 1990 international dollars) was $1,112 and $1,913 in the years 1820 and 1870 respectively, versus figures of $1,756 and $3,263 for the United Kingdom in these two years.

[46] See Holborn, *History Modern Germany, 1840–1945*, 201–2.

[47] See ibid., 200–2.

[48] See ibid., 223–4.

[49] See ibid., 226–9.

[50] A. J. P. Taylor, *The Course of German History: A Survey of the Development of Germany since 1815* (New York: Capricorn Books, 1962), 125–6. See also Schleunes, "German Empire, 1871–1918," in *Encyclopedia Britannica.*

[51] According to Maddison's data, the German GDP per capita in 1913 in 1990 international dollars was $3,833, compared to $5,032 in the United Kingdom. See Maddison, *World Economy, 1820–1992*, chapter 1 tables (table 1–3). There is reason to believe that Maddison's figures actually understate the difference in the standard of living enjoyed by the *typical* German and Briton immediately prior to the Great War. One economist has posited the global diffusion of household sewing machine sales (the first mass produced and mass marketed consumer durable) as a reasonable proxy for global living standards. According to this

study, for which, according to the author reliable data is available, the number of machines per thousand population in 1913 was 104.55 in Britain, versus 66.88 in Germany. See Andrew Godley, "The Convergence in Global Living Standards from 1870 to 1914," Henley School of Management, University of Reading (UK), Discussion Paper No. 423, vol. 13 (2000/2001) 28 (table A1, appendix).

[52] See Holborn, *History Modern Germany, 1840–1945*, 287.

[53] For this paragraph, see ibid., 291–3.

[54] Taylor, *Course of German History*, 130.

[55] See Holborn, *History Modern Germany, 1840–1945*, 349.

[56] See ibid., 701.

[57] See William L. Shirer, *The Rise and Fall of the Third Reich* (New York: Ballantine Books, 1983), 67–8 and Pipes, *Property and Freedom*, 220–1.

[58] See Hayek, *Road to Serfdom*, 194–7.

[59] It appears that at the time Hitler entered government he was playing a double game, telling the industrialists one thing in order to induce financial contributions to the party while at the same time courting the masses with socialist rhetoric. See Shirer, *Rise and Fall*, 201–2, 283–4, 287.

Holborn describes the political appeal of the Nazis in the late 1920s through Hitler's assumption of power as follows:

> The party's participation, together with Hugenberg, in the referendum and plebiscite on the Young Plan and in the election of 1930 established it as a national party of the first order. The lower middle classes of town and countryside swelled its ranks. These classes, however, combined very heterogeneous groups whose economic demands were often at cross purposes...On the other hand, the anticapitalistic and at the same time antiproletarian note in the Nazi program particularly appealed to the lower middle classes which were threatened by the economic crisis with the loss of their identity. In a vague sense they made free capitalism responsible for the economic cataclysm, while they looked for the appearance of a power that would save them from being swallowed by the proletariat. To be sure, the Nazis offered every social group some advantages, but the strength of the party rested on the transformation of these materialistic interests into political faith. (Holborn, *History Modern Germany, 1840–1945*, 722)

[60] Taylor, *Course of German History*, 216.

[61] Ibid., 116.

[62] See *Holborn, History Modern Germany, 1840–1945*, 546–57.

[63] This is not to say that the Weimar constitution was of flawless design or the optimal political arrangement. Holborn notes that Article 48 allowed the president to issue (subject to *Reichstag* veto) emergency decrees in times of serious disturbances of public order and to dismiss the *Reichstag* and order new parliamentary elections if political deadlock arose. This structure allowed the major political parties to shirk their responsibility to make the difficult decisions required in a time of economic crisis. Such irresponsibility fostered the emergence of a charismatic leader who offered hope of cutting through the institutional deadlock that had emerged. See Holborn, *History Modern Germany, 1840–1945*, 547, 668. Nevertheless, given the complete breakdown in the rule of law prior to Hitler's power-grab and his utter ruthlessness, it is doubtful that any other institutional arrangement would have frustrated his seizure of power.

[64] I reference Marx's famous observation that:
> In the social production of their life, men enter into definite relations that are indispensable and independent of their will, relations of production which correspond to a definite stage of development of their material productive forces. The sum total of these relations of production constitute the economic structure of society, the real foundation on which rises a legal and political superstructure and to which correspond definite forms of social consciousness. (Karl Marx, "Preface to 'A Contribution to the Critique of Political Economy.'" 1859, in Robert C. Tucker, ed. *The Marx-Engels Reader* [New York: W. W. Norton & Company, 1972], 4)

[65] According to the CIA's "World Factbook," in 2009 Mexico exported (an estimated) 1.225 million barrels of oil per day. *The World Factbook*. Washington, DC: Central Intelligence Agency, https://www.cia.gov/library/publications/the-world-factbook/index.html

[66] The failure of this political ideal to take root in Mexico is (as discussed below in the text) reflected in the limited political and economic opportunities available to those not favored by the central authorities. It also manifests itself in the widespread, indeed endemic, graft and corruption that infect that nation's political and judicial institutions, which indicates that the legal system lacks such basic characteristics of the rule of law as "due process" and "equal protection." A survey of statistics and articles cataloging such corruption may be found in Robert Kossick, "The Rule of Law and Development in Mexico," 21 *Arizona Journal of International & Comparative Law*, no. 3 (2004): 715–834. For example, the author notes a "reliable" 1995 poll of Mexican citizens that revealed that 75 percent of those surveyed "felt that the justice system was riddled with corruption" (ibid., 715, n.2). See also, Dudley Althaus, "The Plague of Graft: Corruption Eats at the Heart of Mexico's Society," *Houston Chronicle*, November 20, 2000 (noting endemic level of corruption and identifying several spectacular examples of bribery and embezzlement at all levels of government), http://www.chron.com/cs/CDA/printstory.mpl/special//mexnewsun/752147

For the relative per capita income figures, see the CIA's "World Factbook."

[67] Lesley Byrd Simpson, "Santa Anna's Leg," in Raat, *Mexico: From Independence to Revolution, 1810–1910* (Lincoln: University of Nebraska Press, 1982), 60–1.

[68] Victor Alba, "Reforms," in Raat, *Mexico: Independence to Revolution*, 142.

[69] See W. Dirk Raat, "Agustin Aragon and Mexico's Religion of Humanity," in Raat, *Mexico: From Independence to Revolution*, 243, 253.

[70] Hayek, *Road to Serfdom*, 20.

[71] Howard F. Cline and Michael C. Meyer, s.v. "Mexico: History, the Mexican Revolution and Its Aftermath," in *Encyclopedia Britannica*.

[72] Stephen Haber, "The Commitment Problem and Mexican Economic History," in Jeffery L. Bortz and Stephen Haber, eds. *The Mexican Economy, 1870–1930: Essays on the Economic History of Institutions, Revolution and Growth* (Stanford, CA: Stanford University Press, 2002), 326.

[73] Ibid.

[74] Ibid., 331.

[75] William H. Beezley, "Chihuahua in the Diaz Era," in Raat, *Mexico: Independence to Revolution*, 225–6.

76 See ibid. and Haber, "Commitment Problem," in Bortz and Haber, *Mexican Economy*, 331.

77 See Cline and Meyer, "Mexico: History, Mexican Revolution," in *Encyclopedia Britannica*.

78 See Jeffery L. Bortz, "The Legal and Contractual Limits to Private Property Rights in Mexican Industry during the Revolution," in Bortz and Haber, *Mexican Economy*, 255–88.

79 Ibid., 282.

80 See Aurora Gomez-Galvarriato, "Measuring the Impact of Institutional Change in Capital-Labor Relations in the Mexican Textile Industry, 1900–1930," in Bortz and Haber, *Mexican Economy*, 324.

81 See ibid., 309–11.

82 See Cline and Meyer, "Mexico: History, Mexican Revolution," in *Encyclopedia Britannica*.

83 This paragraph is based on and quotes from Tim Weiner, "Mexico's Corrupt Oil Lifeline," *New York Times*, January 21, 2003, http://www.globalpolicy.org/nations/launder/regions/2003/0121mexico.htm

84 See Robert Samuelson, "Mexico's Missing Prosperity," June 28, 2006, *RealClearPolitics.com*, http://www.realclearpolitics.com/articles/2006/06/mexicos_missing_prosperity.html

85 See Weiner, "Mexico's Corrupt Oil Lifeline."

86 See Alberto Chong and Florencio Lopez-de-Silanes, "Privatization in Mexico," Inter-American Development Bank, Research Department. Working Paper No. 513 (August 2004), 6–10 and Kokila Doshi, "Privatization of State-Owned Enterprises in Mexico," *International Journal of Public Administration* 23, no. 5 (2000): 667–76.

87 See Chong and Lopez-de-Silanes, "Privatization in Mexico," 9.

88 Ibid., 9–10.

89 See ibid., 50–2 and Samuelson, "Mexico's Missing Prosperity."

90 For an in-depth analysis of Mexico's fragile grip on the rule of law, see Enrique Krauze, "Furthering Democracy in Mexico," *Foreign Affairs*, January/February 2006: 54–65.

91 Pipes, *Property and Freedom*, 281.

92 Most of what follows on this subject is based on Daniel Little, s.v. "Philosophy of History," in Zalta, *Stanford Encyclopedia of Philosophy*.

93 Ibid., sec. 3.2.

94 Ibid., sec. 5.

95 See Jonathan P. Macey, "Property Rights, Innovation, and Constitutional Structure," in Paul et al., *Property Rights*, 115–26.

96 Sowell, *Quest for Cosmic Justice*, 46.

97 Hayek, *Road to Serfdom*, 141.

98 See Friedman, *Capitalism and Freedom*, 183.

99 See Teresa T. King and H. Wayne Cecil. "The History of Major Changes to the Social Security System," *The CPA Journal.* May 2006.

100 See Samuelson, "Welfare Junkies," *Washington Post*, March 24, 2005, A19, http://www.washingtonpost.com/ac2/wp-dyn/A61696–2005Mar23. According to the data cited by the author, the difference between the value of all employee

contributions, plus the interest that would have been earned thereon, and what the system has actually paid out, stands at $16 trillion.

[101] Social Security also redistributes from single to married participants (due to survivors' benefits) and from two-earner couples to one-earner couples. See King and Cecil, "History of Major Changes."

[102] Hayek, *Constitution of Liberty*, 296.

[103] Our misguided policy of subsidizing domestic agriculture provides an egregious example of this common practice. Each year U.S. taxpayers are forced by law to pay billions of their hard earned dollars to farmers in the form of subsidies to produce crops, payments for *not* growing crops, and (indirectly) through tariffs on importing crops. The bulk of these payments go to large-scale farmers that generally earn incomes higher than the taxpayers compelled by their government to participate in this "Robin Hood in reverse" scheme. Political resistance to this perverse program is blunted by its being coupled with the "food stamp" program favored by urban legislators.

Chapter 6

[1] Quoted in Terry Teachout, "Satchmo and the Jews," *Commentary*, vol. 128, no. 4 (November 2009), 65.

[2] See, e.g., Kagan, *Normative Ethics*; Alexander and Moore, "Deontological Ethics;" J. J. C. Smart and Bernard Williams, *Utilitarianism: For and Against* (Cambridge: Cambridge University Press, 1973); and Gaus, "What is Deontology?"

[3] See James Buchanan, *The Limits of Liberty* (Chicago: University of Chicago Press, 1975), 10.

[4] See Friedrich A. Hayek, *New Studies in Philosophy, Politics, Economics and the History of Ideas* (London: Routledge & Kegan Paul, 1978), 149.

[5] See Kagan, *Normative Ethics*, 292 (quote), 280–92, 320.

[6] Eric Mack, "Moral Individualism and Libertarian Theory," in Machan and Rasmussen, *Liberty for the Twenty-First Century*, 56.

[7] See Joel Feinberg, "Voluntary Euthanasia and the Inalienable Right to Life," in Sterling McMurrin, ed. Vol 1, *The Tanner Lectures on Human Value* (Salt Lake City: University of Utah Press, 1980), 233. See also Richard J. Arneson, "The Shape of Lockean Rights: Fairness, Pareto Moderation, and Consent," in Paul et al., *Natural Rights Liberalism*, 263.

[8] Friedman, *Machinery of Freedom*, 175.

[9] After noting that he is uncertain as to how we should select the relevant baseline, Nozick refers to "differing theories of appropriation" (*ASU*, 177). This suggests that the baseline should be selected from a range of other (non-capitalist) ownership arrangements. On the other hand, in his discussion and tentative endorsement of Fourier's proposal for a guaranteed minimum, he appears to understand this guaranty as representing compensation for the foregone opportunity to engage in communal activities only possible in the pre-property world. As explained in the text, this latter understanding of our obligations to the disadvantaged does not require the selection of any *particular* non-capitalist welfare baseline (*ASU*, 178–9n).

[10] Richard Arneson was kind enough to point this out to me in a private communication.

[11] Kekes, *Illusions of Egalitarianism*, 113–14.

[12] Cavanagh, *Against Equality of Opportunity*, 214.

[13] See Nils Holtug and Kasper Lippert-Rasmussen, "An Introduction to Contemporary Egalitarianism," in Nils Holtug and Kasper Lippert-Rasmussen, eds. *Egalitarianism: New Essays in the Nature and Value of Equality* (Oxford: Oxford University Press, 2007), 22–6.

[14] Stefan Gosepath, s.v. "Equality," sec. 3.6, in Zalta, *Encyclopedia of Philosophy*. See also Holtug and Lippert-Rasmussen, "Introduction to Contemporary Egalitarianism," 18 ("In the past egalitarians held inequality to be bad per se. However, most of today's egalitarians hesitate to say this because they recognize the moral significance of choice and responsibility").

[15] Walter Sinnott-Armstrong, "Consequentialism," sec. 3, in Zalta, *Stanford Encyclopedia of Philosophy*.

[16] See Philip Stratton-Lake, "Can Hooker's Rule-Consequentialist Principle Justify Ross's Prima Facie Duties?" *Mind* New Series 106, no. 424 (1997): 531–2.

[17] Kagan, *Normative Ethics*, 81. See also Elinor Mason, "Value Pluralism," introduction, in Zalta, *Stanford Encyclopedia of Philosophy*.

[18] See Gosepath, "Equality," sec. 3.6.

[19] The Court held that New London could constitutionally exercise this authority to acquire 15 residential properties for purposes of facilitating a privately owned commercial development within the township. It was the private ownership of the project that the town sought to promote that made this case both so highly controversial and worthy of review by the Supreme Court. Had New London condemned this land for purposes of building a road or a sewage treatment facility, there would have been no constitutional challenge or general outcry, although many libertarians would still object that roads and other infrastructure can more efficiently be built by the private sector without the need to invoke eminent domain.

[20] See Wenar, "Rights," sec. 5.2.

[21] For two excellent elucidations of this view, see Russ Shafer-Landau, "Specifying Absolute Rights," 37 *Arizona Law Review* (1995): 209–24, and Christopher Heath Wellman, "On Conflicts Between Rights," *Law and Philosophy* 14 (1995): 271–95.

[22] See Feinberg, "Voluntary Euthanasia," 228–30.

[23] See Phillip Montague, "When Rights Conflict," *Legal Theory* 7, no. 3 (2001): 257–77.

[24] See Thomson, *Realm of Rights*, 118–22. She justifies the "infringement" theory by noting that,

> [T]he concept of a right is only one among many moral concepts, and understanding what it is to have a right requires us to get a sense of how that concept is related to the others...We might think of morality as a continent and of rights as a territory or realm somewhere in it; understanding what is within the realm of rights requires getting a sense of where the continent lies. (Ibid., 3)

[25] Shafer-Landau, "Specifying Absolute Rights," 215.

[26] See Waldron, "Nozick and Locke," 102 ("when the book [*ASU*] appeared, left liberals were so shocked that many of them complained that the book was written simply

to promote a political agenda"). Waldron then quotes Brian Barry's intemperate review of *ASU* that accused Nozick of "proposing to starve or humiliate ten percent of his fellow citizens by eliminating all transfer payments..." Along these same lines see also Kymlicka, *Contemporary Political Philosophy*, 105 ("Due to these undeserved differences in natural talents, some people will flourish while others starve").

27 It is necessary to focus our moral judgment here on a particular group or class of people, since the selection of any particular individual as the test case would be completely arbitrary, i.e. why is it that we care about Sam's welfare and not Sally's?

28 The argument presented below has received little if any attention in the literature. However, Loren Lomasky, at least, appears to be aware of the possibility that Nozick's interpretation of the Lockean proviso might yield a justification for a social safety net. In a relatively recent essay, Lomasky first describes Nozick as "the most conspicuous holdout" from the position taken by such classical liberals as Locke, Kant and Hayek in favor of "publicly provided subventions for those who are unable through their own voluntary undertakings or the assistance of willing others to elevate themselves above the floor of exigency." However, he caveats this statement in a footnote: "Assuming that his invocation of the Lockean proviso does not indeed join him with these predecessors" (Lomasky, "Libertarianism at Twin Harvard," 195–6). Lomasky may have in mind something like my argument. Although he does not go into detail, Jeremy Waldron also seems to have in mind something like the strategy I adopt here. See Waldron, "Nozick and Locke," 97–101. See also Wolff, *Robert Nozick*, discussed in the text.

29 See John Arthur, "Resource Acquisition and Harm," *Canadian Journal of Philosophy* 17, no. 2 (1987): 339–41.

30 See Allan Gibbard, "Natural Property Rights," *Nous* 10, no. 1 (1976): 77–86.

31 See Wolff, *Robert Nozick*, 111.

32 Ibid.

33 See Gosepath, "Equality," sec. 3.6; Holtug and Lippert-Rasmussen, "Introduction to Contemporary Egalitarianism," 18; and Barry, *Modern Political Theory*, 258–9.

34 Wolff, *Robert Nozick*, 111–12.

35 My discussion of Kantian ethics in this section in taken from Sullivan, *Immanuel Kant's Moral Theory*, 50–4, 204–8.

36 See, e.g., Hooker, *Ideal Code, Real World*, 27–8.

37 See Williams, "A Critique of Utilitarianism," in Smart and Williams, *Utilitarianism*, 114–17, and Sinnott-Armstrong, "Consequentialism," sec. 5.

38 See Barry, *Modern Political Theory*, 257–8.

39 See ibid., 257.

40 Starting with the same premise that I adopt in the text, i.e. that rights are not absolute, Eric Mack has proposed an alternative justification of state taxation for purposes of providing a minimal social safety net. See Mack, "Non-Absolute Rights and Libertarian Taxation," *Social Philosophy and Policy* 23 (2006): 109–41.

41 Kymlicka, *Contemporary Political Philosophy*, 123.

42 Ibid.

43 Ibid.

44 Ibid., 124.

45 Ibid., 122.

46 See ibid., 124.

47 Ibid., 125.

48 This is attributable to the Industrial Revolution occurring in England first. See Landes, *Wealth and Poverty*, 231–2 and Maddison, *World Economy, 1820–1992*, tables chapter 1 (table 1–3). Perhaps, to paraphrase Churchill, capitalism's sole virtue is that it is superior to all the alternatives.

49 Kymlicka, *Contemporary Political Philosophy*, 123.

50 Ibid.

51 Nicholson, *Intermediate Microeconomics*, 580.

52 Peter Railton, "Locke, Stock and Peril: Natural Property Rights, Pollution and Risk," in Mary Gibson, ed. *To Breathe Freely* (Tolowa, NJ: Rowman & Littlefield, 1985), 89–123.

53 It is clear from Railton's repeated citation to *ASU*, that he has Nozick specifically in mind for these criticisms. See, for example, his note 4 ("Perhaps the most explicit use of this boundary-based image of moral space is in Robert Nozick, *Anarchy, State and Utopia*.")

54 Railton, "Locke Stock and Peril," 90.

55 Ibid., 110.

56 See ibid., 92–3, 101.

57 Ibid., 95 (quote), see 101–3.

58 See Rothbard, *For a New Liberty*, 39–44.

59 David Gordon has written that in conversation with him, Nozick specifically denied that he held the "all rights are property rights" thesis. See Gordon, "Review of *On Nozick*."

60 See David McCarthy, "Rights, Explanation and Risks," *Ethics* 107 (January 1997): 208–10. McCarthy accepts that rights are not absolute, but argues that under deontological principles persons nevertheless have rights against the imposition of nonconsensual risk. Because such rights are not absolute, they may, on this account, be permissibly infringed under various conditions. One such condition is the payment of appropriate compensation. My analysis is intended to reach the conclusion (following Charles Fried) that agents may, as a matter of right, impose certain levels of non-consensual risk without the compensation requirement.

61 For a useful introduction to this procedure, see Raymond J. Kopp, Alan J. Krupnick, and Michael Toman, "Cost-Benefit Analysis and Regulatory Reform: An Assessment of the Science and the Art," Resources for the Future (Washington, DC), Discussion Paper 97–19 (January 1997).

62 Ike Brannon, "What Is a Life Worth?" *Regulation*, Winter 2004–5: 60.

63 See Thomas J. Kniesner, W. Kip Viscusi, Christopher Woock, and James P. Ziliak, "Pinning Down the Value of Statistical Life," Institute for the Study of Labor (Bonn, Germany), Discussion Paper No. 3107 (2007): 20. A prominent economist claims that the use of the most reliable method produces a U.S. VSL of about $10 million. See Mankiw, *Principles of Economics*, 232. Of course, nothing in my argument hangs on the exact amount of the VSL.

64 Fried, *An Anatomy of Value*, chapters 10 and 11. Nozick actually considers, but rejects, Fried's "risk pool" approach because, in his words, "the world is so constructed that in pursuing their ends people often must impose risks on others that they cannot take directly on themselves" (*ASU*, 76). In other words, the notional risk pool was fundamentally unfair because some would borrow from

this "pool" and never pay back, i.e. over their lifetimes they would impose far more risk than they would be exposed to. However, Nozick apparently failed to consider the idea, adopted in the text, that CBA might be employed as the standard for determining the moral status of everyday social *practices*, like driving, thus eliminating the need to concern ourselves with the extent of an individual's lifetime participation in such practices. In other words, the "typical" motorist is entitled to drive as many miles as he/she wishes because this *activity* satisfies the CBA test of utility relative to cost. On the other hand, the drunk driver fails the CBA test, and is not morally entitled to drive a single mile.

[65] Charles Fried, *An Anatomy of Values*, 189.

[66] Ibid., 185.

[67] See ibid.

[68] Railton, "Locke, Stock, and Peril," 109.

[69] Ibid.

[70] Ibid.

[71] Ibid.

[72] Ibid., 110.

[73] Ibid.

[74] Ibid.

[75] Ibid., 110–11.

[76] Ibid., 111.

[77] For an excellent review of the legitimate uses and unfair abuses of CBA, see David Schmidtz, "A Place for Cost-Benefit Analysis," *Philosophical Issues*, no. 11 (2001): 148–71.

[78] See, e.g., Steven Kelman, "Cost-Benefit Analysis: An Ethical Critique," *AEI Journal on Government and Society Regulation*, January/February 1981: 33–40.

[79] See, e.g., John C. Harsanyi, "Interpersonal Utility Comparisons," in Eatwell et al., *World of Economics*, 361–70.

[80] See Richard N. Langlois, "Cost-Benefit Analysis, Environmentalism, and Rights," *Cato Journal* 2, no. 1 (1982): 279–300.

[81] Ibid., 296, n. 44.

[82] Ibid., 296, n. 45.

Bibliography

Alba, Victor. "Reforms." In Raat, *Mexico: From Independence to Revolution,* 139–52.

Alexander, Larry and Michael Moore. S.v. "Deontological Ethics." In Zalta, *Stanford Encyclopedia of Philosophy.*

Althaus, Dudley. "The Plague of Graft: Corruption Eats at the Heart of Mexico's Society." *Houston Chronicle,* November 20, 2000, http://www.chron.com/cs/CDA/ printstory.mpl/special//mexnewsun/752147 (last accessed on October 17, 2010).

Arneson, Richard J. S.v. "Egalitarianism." In Zalta, *Stanford Encyclopedia of Philosophy.*

—. "Notes for Philosophy 167: The Hart-Rawls Principle of Fairness—Nozick Chapter 5 Discussion, Spring 2008," http://philosophy.ucsd.edu/faculty/ rarneson/Courses/167PrinofFair.pdf (last accessed on October 17, 2010).

—. "The Principle of Fairness and Free-Rider Problems." *Ethics* 92, no. 4 (1982): 616–33.

—. "The Shape of Lockean Rights: Fairness, Pareto Moderation, and Consent." In Paul et al., *Natural Rights Liberalism,* 255–85.

Aron, Leon. "What Does Putin Want?" *Commentary,* December 2006.

Arthur, John. "Resource Acquisition and Harm." *Canadian Journal of Philosophy* 17, no. 2 (1987): 337–47.

Barnett, Randy E. "Libertarians and the War." *Wall Street Journal,* July 17, 2007, sec. A.

—. "Whither Anarchy? Has Robert Nozick Justified the State?" *Journal of Libertarian Studies* 1, no. 1 (1977): 15–21, http://www.mises.org/journals/jls/1_1/1_1_3. pdf (last accessed on October 17, 2010).

Barry, Norman P. *An Introduction to Modern Political Theory.* 3rd edn. Houndmills, UK: Macmillan, 1995.

Beauchamp, Tom L. *Philosophical Ethics: An Introduction to Moral Philosophy.* 3rd edn. Boston, MA: McGraw-Hill, 2001.

Beck, Emily Morrison, ed., *Bartlett's Familiar Quotations.* 15th edn. Boston, MA: Little, Brown, 1980.

Beezley, William H. "Chihuahua in the Diaz Era." In Raat, *Mexico: From Independence to Revolution,* 219–31.

Begley, Sharon. "What Your Pet is Thinking." *Wall Street Journal,* October 27, 2006, sec. W.

Benson, Bruce L. "The Mythology of Holdout as a Justification for Eminent Domain and Public Provision of Roads." *The Independent Review* 10, no. 2 (2005): 165–94.

Bergstrom, Lars. "Reflections on Consequentialism." *Theoria* 62, no. 1–2 (1996): 74–94.

Bortz, Jeffrey L. "The Legal and Contractual Limits to Private Property Rights in Mexican Industry during the Revolution." In Bortz and Haber, *Mexican Economy*, 255–88.

Bortz, Jeffrey L. and Stephen Haber, eds. *The Mexican Economy, 1870–1930: Essays on the Economic History of Institutions, Revolution and Growth.* Stanford, CA: Stanford University Press, 2002.

Brannon, Ike. "What Is a Life Worth?" *Regulation*, Winter 2004–5.

Browne, Harry. *Why Government Doesn't Work.* New York: St. Martin's Press, 1995.

Buchanan, James. *The Limits of Liberty.* Chicago: University of Chicago Press, 1975.

Cavanagh, Matt. *Against Equality of Opportunity.* Oxford: Oxford University Press, 2002.

Cheung, Steven N. S. "Common Property Rights." In Eatwell et al., *The World of Economics*, 83–6.

Childs, Jr., Roy A. "The Invisible Hand Strikes Back." *The Libertarian Forum* 9, no. 5 (1976), http://www.mises.org/journals/jls/1_1/1_1_4.pdf (last accessed on October 17, 2010).

Chong, Alberto and Florencio Lopez-de-Silanes. "Privatization in Mexico." Inter-American Development Bank, Research Department. Working Paper No. 513 (August 2004), http://www.iadb.org/res/publications/pubfiles/pubwp-513.pdf (last accessed on October 17, 2010).

Churchill, Winston. *A History of the English Speaking Peoples.* Vol. 4, *The Great Democracies.* New York: Dorset Press, 1990.

Clapp, James G. S.v. "John Locke." In Edwards, *Encyclopedia of Philosophy*, vol. 4, 487–503.

Cline, Howard F. and Michael C. Meyer. S.v. "Mexico: History, the Mexican Revolution and Its Aftermath." In *Encyclopaedia Britannica.*

Clinton, Bill. "Welfare Reform Must Protect Children and Legal Immigrants." In Charles P. Cozic, ed. *Welfare Reform.* San Diego: Greenhaven Press, 1997, 40–4.

Cohen, Abraham. *Everyman's Talmud: The Major Teachings of the Rabbinic Sages.* New York: Schocken, 1975.

Cohen, G. A. *Self-Ownership, Freedom, and Equality.* Cambridge: Cambridge University Press, 1995.

Colley, Linda. S.v. "United Kingdom: History of England and Great Britain, British Society by the Mid-18th Century." In *Encyclopaedia Britannica.*

Conway, David. "Nozick's Entitlement Theory: Three Critics Answered." *Philosophical Notes* (Libertarian Alliance, London), no. 15 (1990), http://www.libertarian.co.uk/lapubs/philn/philn015.pdf (last accessed on October 17, 2010).

Cowen, Tyler. "How Far Back Should We Go? Why Restitution Should be Small." In Jon Elster, ed. *Retribution and Reparation in the Transition to Democracy Since 1945.* Cambridge: Cambridge University Press, 2006, 17–32.

—. "Law as a Public Good: The Economics of Anarchy." *Economics and Philosophy* 8, no. 2 (1992): 249–67.

—. "Rejoinder to David Friedman on the Economics of Anarchy." *Economics and Philosophy* 10, no. 2 (1994): 329–32.

Dagger, Richard. S.v. "Political Obligation." In Zalta, *Stanford Encyclopedia of Philosophy.*

Dalberg-Acton, John Emerich Edward. "The History of Freedom in Antiquity." 1877. In *The History of Freedom and Other Essays.* London: Macmillan, 1907, http://oll.libertyfund.org/Texts/Acton0003/HistoryOfFreedom/0030_Bk.html#hd_lf030.head.005 (last accessed on October 17, 2010).

Daniels, Norman. S.v. "Reflective Equilibrium." In Zalta, *Stanford Encyclopedia of Philosophy.*

—, ed. *Reading Rawls: Critical Studies of "A Theory of Justice."* New York: Basic Books, 1976.

Doherty, Brian. *Radicals for Capitalism: A Freewheeling History of the Modern American Libertarian Movement.* New York: PublicAffairs, 2007.

Doshi, Kokila. "Privatization of State-Owned Enterprises in Mexico." *International Journal of Public Administration* 23, no. 5 (2000): 667–76.

Eatwell, John, Murray Milgate and Peter Newman, eds. *The New Palgrave: The World of Economics.* 1st American edn. New York: W. W. Norton & Company, 1991.

Edwards, Paul, general ed. *The Encylopedia of Philosophy.* Reprint edn. 8 vols. New York: Macmillan, 1972.

Eliot, T. S. *Murder in the Cathedral.* In *The Complete Poems and Plays, 1909–1950.* New York: Harcourt Brace, 1971.

Engelhardt Jr., H. Tristram. *The Foundations of Bioethics.* New York: Oxford University Press, 1986.

Encyclopaedia Britannica. 1998 Multimedia edn. CD-ROM.

Epstein, Richard A. *Takings: Private Property and the Power of Eminent Domain.* Cambridge, MA: Harvard University Press, 1985.

—. "Why Libertarians Shouldn't Be (Too) Skeptical About Intellectual Property." Progress and Freedom Foundation, Progress on Point Paper No. 13.4, February 13, 2006, http://ssrn.com/abstract=981779 (last accessed on October 17, 2010).

Feinberg, Joel. "Voluntary Euthanasia and the Inalienable Right to Life." In Sterling McMurrin, ed. Vol. 1, *The Tanner Lectures on Human Value.* Salt Lake City: University of Utah Press, 1980, 221–51.

Feser, Edward. *On Nozick.* Toronto: Wadsworth, 2004.

—. "There is No Such Thing as an Unjust Initial Acquisition." In Paul et al., *Natural Rights Liberalism,* 56–80.

Forbes. Special edition "The Forbes 400," October 19, 2009.

Fried, Barbara H. "*Anarchy, State and Utopia* at Thirty Years." In Paul et al., *Natural Rights Liberalism,* 221–54.

—. "Left-Libertarianism: A Review Essay." *Philosophy and Public Affairs* 32, no. 1 (2004): 66–93.

Fried, Charles. *An Anatomy of Values: Problems of Personal and Social Choice.* Cambridge, MA: Harvard University Press, 1977.

Friedman, David. "Law as a Private Good: A Response to Tyler Cowen on the Economics of Anarchy." *Economics and Philosophy* 10 (1994): 319–27.

—. *The Machinery of Freedom.* 2nd edn. LaSalle, IL: Open Court, 1989.

—. Transcript of Panel Discussion, "Does Freedom Mean Anarchy?" *Liberty,* December 2004, http://www.libertyunbound.com/archive/2004_12/editors-anarchy.html (last accessed on October 17, 2010).

Friedman, Milton. *Capitalism and Freedom.* With the assistance of Rose D. Friedman. Chicago: University of Chicago Press, 1982.

Garraty, John A. and Peter Gay, eds. *The Columbia History of the World.* New York: Harper & Row, 1972.

Gaus, Gerald F. "Property, Rights, and Freedom." In Paul et al., *Property Rights,* 209–40.

——. "What is Deontology? Part One: Orthodox Views" and "What is Deontology? Part Two: Reasons to Act." *Journal of Value Inquiry* 35 (2001): 27–42 and 179–99.

Gibbard, Allan. "Natural Property Rights." *Nous* 10, no. 1 (1976): 77–86.

Gibson-Jarvie, Robert. *The City of London: A Financial and Commercial History.* Cambridge: Woodhead-Faulkner, 1979.

Godley, Andrew. "The Convergence in Global Living Standards from 1870 to 1914." Henley School of Management, University of Reading (UK), Discussion Paper No. 423, vol. 13 (2000/2001), http://www.henley.reading.ac.uk/management/research/mgmt-discussionpapers.aspx (last accessed on October 17, 2010).

Gomez-Galvarriato, Aurora. "Measuring the Impact of Institutional Change in Capital-Labor Relations in the Mexican Textile Industry, 1900–1930." In Bortz and Harber, *Mexican Economy,* 289–323.

Gordon, David D. "Bibliographic Essay: Contemporary Currents in Libertarian Political Philosophy." *Literature of Liberty: A Review of Contemporary Liberal Thought* 4, no. 1 (1981), http//app.libraryofliberty.org/?option=com_staticxt&staticfile=show.php%3Ftitle=1298&chapter=101075&layout=html&Itemid=27 (last accessed on October 17, 2010).

——. "Freedom or Slavery." Review of *On Nozick,* by Edward Feser. *Mises Review* 9, no. 2 (2003), http://mises.org/misesreview_detail.aspx?control=2328sortorder=issue (last accessed on October 17, 2010).

——. "Is Inequality Indefensible?" Review of *Libertarianism without Inequality* by Michael Otsuka. *Mises Review* 9, no. 3 (2003), http://mises.org/misesreview_detail.aspx?control=257 (last accessed on October 17, 2010).

——. Review of *Robert Nozick: Property, Justice and the Minimal State,* by Jonathan Wolff. *Review of Austrian Economics* 5, no. 2 (1991): 129–33.

Gosepath, Stefan. S.v. "Equality." In Zalta, *Encyclopedia of Philosophy.*

Haber, Stephen. "The Commitment Problem and Mexican Economic History." In Bortz and Haber, *Mexican Economy,* 324–36.

Habib, M. A. R. "The Prayers of Childhood: T. S. Eliot's Manuscripts on Kant." *The Journal of the History of Ideas* 51, no. 1 (1990): 93–114.

Harman, Gilbert H. "The Inference to the Best Explanation." *The Philosophical Review* 74, no. 1 (1965): 88–95.

Harrison, Jonathan. S.v. "Ethics, Naturalism." In Edwards, vol. 3, *Encyclopedia of Philosophy,* 69–71.

Harsanyi, John C. "Interpersonal Utility Comparisons." In Eatwell et al., *World of Economics,* 361–70.

——. "Value Judgments." In Eatwell et al., *World of Economics,* 702–5.

Hart, H. L. A. "Are There Any Natural Rights?" 1955. In Jeremy Waldron, ed. *Theories of Rights.* New York: Oxford University Press, 1984, 77–90.

Hasnas, John. "Reflections on the Minimal State." *Politics, Philosophy and Economics* 2, no. 1 (2003): 115–28.

——. "Toward a Theory of Empirical Natural Rights." In Paul et al., *Natural Rights Liberalism,* 118–22.

Hayek, Friedrich A. *The Constitution of Liberty.* Chicago: University of Chicago Press, 1960.

—. *New Studies in Philosophy, Politics, Economics and the History of Ideas.* London: Routledge & Kegan Paul, 1978.

—. *The Road to Serfdom.* Anniversary edition, with a new introduction by Milton Friedman. Chicago: University of Chicago Press, 1994.

Heilbroner, Robert L. S.v. "Economic Systems: The Evolution of Capitalism." In *Encyclopaedia Britannica.*

Hohfeld, Wesley. "Fundamental Legal Conceptions as Applied in Judicial Reasoning." 26 *Yale Law Journal,* 16–59 (1917).

Holborn, Hajo. *A History of Modern Germany, 1840–1945.* New York: Alfred A. Knopf, 1964.

—. *A History of Modern Germany, 1648–1840.* New York: Alfred A. Knopf, 1969.

Holcombe, Randall G. "Government: Unnecessary but Inevitable." *The Independent Review* 8, no. 3 (2004): 325–42.

Holtug, Nils and Kasper Lippert-Rasmussen. "An Introduction to Contemporary Egalitarianism." In Nils Holtug and Kasper Lippert-Rasmussen, eds. *Egalitarianism: New Essays in the Nature and Value of Equality.* Oxford: Oxford University Press, 2007, 1–37.

Hooker, Brad. *Ideal Code, Real World: A Rule-Consequentialist Theory of Morality.* Oxford: Oxford University Press, 2003.

Hospers, John. *An Introduction to Philosophical Analysis.* 2nd edn. Englewood Cliffs, NJ: Prentice-Hall, 1967.

—."What Libertarianism Is." In Machan and Rasmussen, *Liberty for the Twenty-First Century,* 5–17.

Huemer, Michael. *Ethical Intuitionism.* New York: Palgrave Macmillan, 2005.

Hume, David. *A Treatise of Human Nature.* 1739. In *The Philosophy of David Hume,* edited by V. C. Chappell. New York: Random House, 1963, 11–311.

Johnson, Robert. S.v. "Kant's Moral Philosophy." In Zalta, *Stanford Encyclopedia of Philosophy.*

Jollimore, Troy. S.v. "Impartiality." In Zalta, *Stanford Encyclopedia of Philosophy.*

Jones, Peter. "Two Conceptions of Liberalism, Two Conceptions of Justice." *British Journal of Political Science* 25, no. 4 (1995): 515–50.

Jones, W. T. *A History of Western Philosophy: Vol. 3 Hobbes to Hume.* 2nd edn. New York: Harcourt, Brace & World, 1969.

Kagan, Shelly. *Normative Ethics.* Boulder, CO: Westview Press, 1998.

Kamm, Frances. "In Search of the Deep Structure of Morality: An Interview with Frances Kamm by Alex Voorhoeve." *Imprints* 9 (2006): 93–117.

—. "Non-consequentialism, the Person as an End-in-Itself, and the Significance of Status." *Philosophy and Public Affairs* 21, no. 4 (1992): 354–89.

Kant, Immanuel. *Groundwork of the Metaphysic of Morals.* 1785. Translated and edited by H. J. Paton. New York: Harper & Row, 1964.

Kekes, John. *The Illusions of Egalitarianism.* Ithaca, NY: Cornell University Press, 2003.

Kelman, Steven. "Cost-Benefit Analysis: An Ethical Critique." *AEI Journal on Government and Society Regulation,* January/February 1981: 33–40.

King, Teresa T. and H. Wayne Cecil. "The History of Major Changes to the Social Security System." *The CPA Journal.* May 2006, http://www.nysscpa

org/cpajournal/2006/506/infocus/p15.htm (last accessed on October 17, 2010).

Kinsella, N. Stephan. "Against Intellectual Property." *Journal of Libertarian Studies* 15, no. 2 (2001): 1–53.

Kirzner, Israel M. "Entrepreneurship, Entitlement and Economic Justice." In Paul, *Reading Nozick*, 383–411.

Klosko, George. *Political Obligation.* Oxford: Oxford University Press, 2005.

—. *The Principle of Fairness and Political Obligation.* 2nd edn. Lanham, MD: Rowman & Littlefield, 2004.

Kniesner, Thomas J., W. Kip Viscusi, Christopher Woock, and James P. Ziliak. "Pinning Down the Value of Statistical Life." Institute for the Study of Labor (Bonn, Germany), Discussion Paper No. 3107 (2007), http://papers.ssrn.com/sol3/papers.cfm?abstract_id=1029912 (last accessed on October 17, 2010).

Kopp, Raymond J., Alan J. Krupnick, and Michael Toman. "Cost-Benefit Analysis and Regulatory Reform: An Assessment of the Science and the Art." Resources for the Future (Washington, DC), Discussion Paper 97–19 (January 1997), http://www.rff.org/document/rff-dp-97-19.pdf (last accessed on October 17, 2010).

Kossick, Robert. "The Rule of Law and Development in Mexico." 21 *Arizona Journal of International & Comparative Law,* no. 3 (2004): 715–834.

Krauze, Enrique. "Furthering Democracy in Mexico." *Foreign Affairs,* January/February 2006: 54–65.

Kymlicka, Will. *Contemporary Political Philosophy: An Introduction.* 2nd edn. New York: Oxford University Press, 2001.

Landes, David S. *The Wealth and Poverty of Nations: Why Some Are So Rich and Some So Poor.* New York: W. W. Norton, 1999.

Langlois, Richard N. "Cost-Benefit Analysis, Environmentalism, and Rights." *Cato Journal* 2, no. 1 (1982): 279–300.

Laslett, Peter. Introduction to *John Locke, Two Treatises of Government.* Cambridge: Cambridge University Press, 1988.

Lenman, James. S.v. "Moral Naturalism." In Zalta, *Stanford Encyclopedia of Philosophy.*

Lippert-Rasmussen, Kasper. "Against Self-Ownership: There Are No Fact-Insensitive Ownership Rights Over One's Body." *Philosophy and Public Affairs* 36 (2008): 86–118.

—. *Deontology, Responsibility, and Equality.* Copenhagen: University of Copenhagen, 2005.

Little, Daniel. S.v. "Philosophy of History" In Zalta, *Stanford Encyclopedia of Philosophy.*

Locke, John. *Two Treatises of Government.* Student edition. Edited with an introduction by Peter Laslett. Cambridge: Cambridge University Press, 1988.

Lomasky, Loren. "Liberalism at Twin Harvard." In Paul et al., *Natural Rights Liberalism,* 178–99.

—. *Persons, Rights, and the Moral Community.* New York: Oxford University Press, 1987.

—. "Response to Four Critics." *Reason Papers* 14 (1989): 110–29.

Lyons, David. "The New Indian Claims and Original Rights to Land." In Paul, *Reading Nozick,* 355–79.

Macey, Jonathan P. "Property Rights, Innovation, and Constitutional Structure." In Paul et al., *Property Rights,* 181–208.

Machan, Tibor R. *Generosity: Virtue in Civil Society.* Washington, DC: Cato Institute, 1998.

—. *Individuals and Their Rights.* LaSalle, IL: Open Court, 1989.

Machan, Tibor and Douglass Rasmussen eds. *Liberty for the Twenty-First Century: Contemporary Libertarian Thought.* Lanham, MD: Rowman & Littlefield, 1995.

MacIntyre, Alasdair. "Pluralistic Philosophy." Review of *Philosophical Explanations* by Robert Nozick. *New York Times*, Late City Final Edition. September 20, 1981: sec. 7, p. 7.

Mack, Eric. "Against Agent-Neutral Value." *Reason Papers* 14 (1989): 76–85.

—. "Moral Individualism and Libertarian Theory." In Machan and Rasmussen, *Liberty for the Twenty-First Century,* 41–58.

— . "Non-Absolute Rights and Libertarian Taxation." *Social Philosophy and Policy* 23 (2006): 109–41.

—. "Rights, Just War, and National Defense." In Machan and Rasmussen, *Liberty for the Twenty-First Century,* 101–20.

Maddison, Angus. *Monitoring the World Economy, 1820–1992.* Paris: OECD Development Centre, 1995, http://www.ggdc.net/MADDISON/oriindex.htm (last accessed on October 17, 2010).

Madison, James. "Federalist No. 51." In *The Federalist Papers.* 1778. New York: New American Library, 1961, 320–5.

Mankiw, N. Greg. *Principles of Economics.* 3rd edn. New York: Dryden Press, 1998.

Marx, Karl. "Preface to 'A Contribution to the Critique of Political Economy.'" 1859. In Robert C. Tucker, ed. *The Marx-Engels Reader.* New York: W. W. Norton & Company, 1972, 3–6.

Mason, Elinor. S.v. "Value Pluralism." In Zalta, *Stanford Encyclopedia of Philosophy.*

McCarthy, David. "Rights, Explanation and Risks." *Ethics* 107 (January 1997): 208–10.

Mexican Constitution of 1917, http://www.intute.ac.uk/cgi-bin/fullrecord pl?handle=sosig1028190922–3799 (last accessed on October 17, 2010).

Middlekauff, Robert. *The Glorious Cause: The American Revolution, 1763–1789.* Oxford: Oxford University Press, 1982.

Montague, Phillip. "When Rights Conflict." *Legal Theory* 7, no. 3 (2001): 257–77.

Morris, Christopher. "Loren Lomasky's Derivation of Basic Rights." *Reason Papers* 14 (1989): 86–97.

Murphy, Mark. S.v. "The Natural Law Tradition in Ethics." In Zalta, *Stanford Encyclopedia of Philosophy.*

Nagel, Thomas. "Libertarianism without Foundations." In Paul, *Reading Nozick,* 191–205.

—. "Personal Rights and Public Space." *Philosophy and Public Affairs* 24, no. 2 (1995): 83–107.

Narveson, Jan. *The Libertarian Idea.* Philadelphia, PA: Temple University Press, 1988.

Nicholson, Walter. *Intermediate Microeconomics and Its Applications.* 3rd edn. New York: Dryden Press, 1983.

Nielsen, Kai. "Why Should I Be Moral?" In Sellars and Hospers, *Readings in Ethical Theory,* 747–68.

Nozick, Robert. *Anarchy, State, and Utopia.* New York: Basic Books, 1974.

—. *Philosophical Explanations.* Cambridge, MA: Harvard University Press, 1981.

—. "On the Randian Argument." In Paul, *Reading Nozick,* 206–31.

O'Keeffe, Matthew. "World Ownership is Not Compatible with Self-Ownership: A Defence of Robert Nozick against G.A. Cohen." *Philosophical Notes* (Libertarian Alliance, London), no. 20 (1992), http://www.libertarian.co.uk/lapubs/philn/philn020.pdf (last accessed on October 17, 2010).

O'Neill, Onora. "Nozick's Entitlements." In Paul, *Reading Nozick,* 305–22.

Otsuka, Michael. *Libertarianism without Inequality.* Oxford: Oxford University Press, 2003.

—. "Reponses" [English version]. *Raisons Politiques,* no. 23 (2006): 163–74, http://www.ucl.ac.uk/~uctymio/Replies_Raisons_Politiques.pdf (last accessed on October 17, 2010).

Palmer, Tom G. "John Locke Lite." Review of *Libertarianism without Inequality* by Michael Otsuka. *Reason.com* (January 2005), http://reason.com/archives/2005/01/01/john-locke-lite (last accessed on October 17, 2010).

Paul, Ellen Frankel, Fred D. Miller, Jr., and Jeffry Paul, eds. *Natural Rights Liberalism from Locke to Nozick.* Cambridge: Cambridge University Press, 2005.

—. *Property Rights.* Cambridge: Cambridge University Press, 1994.

Paul, Jeffrey. "The Withering of the Minimal State." In Paul, *Reading Nozick,* 68–76.

Paul, Jeffrey, ed. *Reading Nozick: Essays on "Anarchy, State, and Utopia."* Oxford: Basil Blackwell, 1982.

Paul, Ron. *The Revolution: A Manifesto.* New York: Grand Central Publishing, 2008.

Pettit, Philip. "Non-Consequentialism and Political Philosophy." In David Schmidtz, ed. *Robert Nozick.* Cambridge: Cambridge University Press, 2002, 83–104.

Pipes, Richard. *Property and Freedom.* New York: Alfred A. Knopf, 1999.

Posner, Richard. *Economic Analysis of the Law.* 2nd edn. Boston, MA: Little Brown, 1977.

Raat, W. Dirk. "Agustin Aragon and Mexico's Religion of Humanity." In Raat, *Mexico: From Independence to Revolution,* 241–59.

—, ed. *Mexico: From Independence to Revolution, 1810–1910.* Lincoln, NE: University of Nebraska Press, 1982.

Railton, Peter. "Alienation, Consequentialism, and the Demands of Morality." *Philosophy and Public Affairs* 13, no. 2 (1984): 134–71.

—. "Locke, Stock and Peril: Natural Property Rights, Pollution and Risk." In Mary Gibson, ed. *To Breathe Freely.* Tolowa, NJ: Rowman & Littlefield, 1985, 89–123.

Rand, Ayn. "The 'Conflicts' of Man's Interests." In Ayn Rand, *The Virtue of Selfishness,* with additional articles by Nathan Brandon. New York: Signet Books, 1970, 50–6.

—. "The Ethics of Emergencies." In Rand, *The Virtue of Selfishness,* 43–9.

—. "Man's Rights." In Rand, *The Virtue of Selfishness,* 92–100.

—. "The Nature of Government." In Rand, *The Virtue of Selfishness,* 107–15.

—. "The Objectivist Ethics." In Rand, *The Virtue of Selfishness,* 13–35.

Rawls, John. *A Theory of Justice.* London: Oxford University Press, 1971.

Read, Leonard E. *Government—An Ideal Concept.* Irvington-on-Hudson, NY: Foundation for Economic Freedom, 1954.

Reagan, Ronald. "A Time for Choosing." Televised Address, October 27, 1964, from CNN online, http://www.cnn.com/SPECIALS/2004/reagan/stories/speech.archive/time.html (last accessed on October 17, 2010).

Ripstein, Arthur. "The Division of Responsibility and the Law of Tort." 72 *Fordham Law Review*, no. 5 (2004): 101–32.

Risse, Mathias. "Does Left-Libertarianism Have Coherent Foundations?" *Politics, Philosophy & Economics* 3, no. 3 (2004): 337–64.

—. "Original Ownership of the Earth: A Contemporary Approach." John F. Kennedy School of Government, Faculty Research Working Papers, RWP08–073, December 2008, http://web.hks.harvard.edu/publications/getFile.aspx?Id=325 (last accessed on October 17, 2010).

Romero, Simon. "Criticism of Chavez Stifled by Arrests." *New York Times*, April 4, 2010, A6 (New York edn), http://www.nytimes.com/2010/04/04/world/americas/04venez.html (last accessed on October 17, 2010).

Rothbard, Murray N. *The Ethics of Liberty*. With a new introduction. New York: New York University Press, 1998. First published in 1982 by Humanities Press, http://www.mises.org/rothbard/ethics.pdf (last accessed on October 17, 2010).

—. *For a New Liberty: The Libertarian Manifesto*. Rev. edn. New York: Macmillan, 1978, http://mises.org/rothbard/foranewlb.pdf (last accessed on October 17, 2010).

—. "Robert Nozick and the Immaculate Conception of the State." *Journal of Libertarian Studies* 1, no. 1 (1977): 45–57, http://www.mises.org/journals/jls/1_1/1_1_6.pdf (last accessed on October 17, 2010).

Royle, Trevor, ed. *A Dictionary of Military Quotations*. 1st American edn. New York: Simon & Schuster, 1989.

Russell, Bertrand. "The Elements of Ethics." In Sellars and Hospers, *Readings in Ethical Theory*, 3–28.

Samuelson, Robert. "Mexico's Missing Prosperity." June 28, 2006, *RealClearPolitics.com*, http://www.realclearpolitics.com/articles/2006/06/mexicos_missing_prosperity.html (last accessed on October 17, 2010).

—. "Welfare Junkies." *Washington Post*, March 24, 2005, A19, http://www.washingtonpost.com/ac2/wp-dyn/A61696-2005Mar23 (last accessed on October 17, 2010).

Sanchez, Fabiola. "Chavez Gains Free Reign in Venezuela." Associated Press, January 31, 2007, http://news.yahoo.com/s/ap/20070201/ap_on_re_la_am_ca/venezuela_chavez_17

Sayles, G. O. *The Medieval Foundations of England*. 1st American edn. Philadelphia, PA: University of Pennsylvania Press, 1950.

Scanlon, Thomas. "Nozick on Rights, Liberty and Property." In Paul, *Reading Nozick*, 107–29.

Scherman, Rabbi Nasson, ed. *The Chumash: The Torah, Haftors and Five Megillos with Commentary Anthologized from the Rabbinic Writings*. 11th edn. Brooklyn, NY: Mesorah Publications, 2000.

Schmidtz, David. "History and Pattern." In Paul et al., *Natural Rights Liberalism*, 148–77.

—. "The Institution of Property." In Paul et al., *Property Rights*, 42–62.

—. *The Limits of Government: An Essay on the Public Goods Argument*. Boulder, CO: Westview Press, 1991.

—. "A Place for Cost-Benefit Analysis." *Philosophical Issues*, no. 11 (2001): 148–71.

—. "When is Original Appropriation Required?" *The Monist* 73 (October 1990): 504–18.

Searle, John R. "How to Derive 'Ought' From 'Is.'" In Sellars and Hospers, *Readings in Ethical Theory*, 63–72.

Sellars, Wilfrid and John Hospers, eds. *Readings in Ethical Theory*. 2nd edn. New York: Appleton-Century-Crofts, 1970, 3–28.

Shafer-Landau, Russ. "Specifying Absolute Rights." 37 *Arizona Law Review* (1995): 209–24.

Shaver, Robert. S.v. "Egoism." In Zalta, *Stanford Encyclopedia of Philosophy*.

Shirer, William L. *The Rise and Fall of the Third Reich*. New York: Ballantine Books, 1983.

Simmons, A. John. "Fair Play and Political Obligation: Twenty Years Later." In A. John Simmons, ed. *Justification and Legitimacy: Essays on Rights and Obligations*. Cambridge: Cambridge University Press, 2001, 27–42.

—. "Philosophical Anarchism." In Simmons, *Justification and Legitimacy*, 102–21.

—. "The Principle of Fair Play." *Philosophy & Public Affairs* 8, no. 4 (1979): 307–37.

Simpson, Lesley Byrd. "Santa Anna's Leg." In Raat, *Mexico: From Independence to Revolution*, 60–83.

Singer, Peter. "The Right to be Rich or Poor." In Paul, *Reading Nozick*, 37–53.

Sinnott-Armstrong, Walter. S.v. "Consequentialism." In Zalta, *Stanford Encyclopedia of Philosophy*.

Skoble, Aeon J. "The Anarchism Controversy." In Machan and Rasmussen, *Liberty for the Twenty-First Century*, 77–96.

Smart, J. J. C. and Bernard Williams. *Utilitarianism: For and Against*. Cambridge: Cambridge University Press, 1973.

Sowell, Thomas. *The Quest for Cosmic Justice*. New York: The Free Press, 1999.

Steiner, Hillel. *An Essay on Rights*. Oxford: Blackwell, 1994.

—. "Justice and Entitlement." In Paul, *Reading Nozick*, 380–2.

Stratton-Lake, Philip. "Can Hooker's Rule-Consequentialist Principle Justify Ross's Prima Facie Duties?" *Mind* New Series 106, no. 424 (1997): 751–8.

—. "Introduction" to Philip Stratton-Lake, ed. *Ethical Intuitionism: Re-evaluations*. Oxford: Oxford University Press, 2002, 1–28.

Sullivan, Roger. *Immanuel Kant's Moral Theory*. Cambridge: Cambridge University Press, 1989.

Taylor, A. J. P. *The Course of German History: A Survey of the Development of Germany since 1815*. New York: Capricorn Books, 1962.

Teachout, Terry. "Satchmo and the Jews." *Commentary* 128, no. 4 (November 2009): 65.

Thomson, Judith. *The Realm of Rights*. Cambridge, MA: Harvard University Press, 1990.

Trevelyan, George M. *A Shortened History of England*. Harmondsworth, UK: Penguin Books, 1982.

Troitsky, Artemy. "The Russia I Lost." In the *New Statesman*, November 27, 2006, http://www.newstatesman.com/200611270027 (last accessed on October 17, 2010).

Tuckness, Alex. S.v. "Locke's Political Philosophy." In Zalta, *Stanford Encyclopedia of Philosophy*.

Uyl, Douglas Den and Douglas Rasmussen. "Nozick on the Randian Argument." In Paul, *Reading Nozick*, 232–69.

Vallentyne, Peter. "Introduction: Left Libertarianism—A Primer." In Vallentyne and Steiner, *Left-Libertarianism and Its Critics*, 1–22.

—. S.v. "Libertarianism." In Zalta, *Stanford Encyclopedia of Philosophy.*

Vallentyne, Peter and Hillel Steiner eds. *Left-Libertarianism and Its Critics: The Contemporary Debate.* Houndmills, U.K.: Palgrave, 2000.

Vallentyne, Peter, Hillel Steiner, and Michael Otsuka. "Why Left-Libertarianism Is Not Incoherent, Indeterminate or Irrelevant: A Reply to Fried." *Philosophy and Public Affairs* 33, no. 2 (2005): 201–15.

van Inwagen, Peter. "The Mystery of Metaphysical Freedom." In Peter van Inwagen and David Zimmerman, eds. *Metaphysics: the Big Questions.* Oxford: Blackwell, 1998.

Waldron, Jeremy. "Nozick and Locke, Filling the Space of Rights." In Paul et al., *Natural Rights Liberalism,* 88–97.

Walsh, W. H. "Immanuel Kant." In Edwards, *Encyclopedia of Philosophy,* vol. 4, 305–24.

Weiner, Tim. "Mexico's Corrupt Oil Lifeline." *New York Times,* January 21, 2003, http://www.globalpolicy.org/nations/launder/regions/2003/0121mexico.htm (last accessed on October 17, 2010).

Wellman, Christopher Heath. "On Conflicts Between Rights." *Law and Philosophy* 14 (1995): 271–95.

Wenar, Leif. "The Concept of Property and the Takings Clause." 97 *Columbia Law Review,* no. 6 (1997): 1923–46.

—. S.v. "Rights." In Zalta, *Stanford Encyclopedia of Philosophy.*

Williams, Bernard. "The Ideal of Equality." In Joel Feinberg, ed. *Moral Concepts.* New York: Oxford University Press, 1969, 153–71.

—. "The Minimal State." In Paul, *Reading Nozick,* 27–36.

Wolff, Robert Paul. "Robert Nozick's Derivation of the Minimal State." In Paul, *Reading Nozick,* 77–104.

Wollheim, Richard. S.v. "Natural Law." In Edwards, *Encyclopedia of Philosophy,* vol. 5, 450–4.

The World Factbook. Washington, DC: Central Intelligence Agency, 2009, https://www.cia.gov/library/publications/the-world-factbook/index.html (last accessed on October 17, 2010).

Zalta, Edward N., principal ed. *The Stanford Encyclopedia of Philosophy.* Stanford, CA: Centre for the Study of Language and Information, Stanford University, available online at http://plato.stanford.edu

Zuckert, Michael. "Natural Rights and Imperial Constitutionalism: The American Revolution and the Development of the American Amalgam." In Paul et al., *Natural Rights Liberalism,* 27–55.

Zwolinski, Matt. "Price Gouging, Non-Worseness, and Distributive Justice." *Business Ethics Quarterly* 19 (2009): 295–306.

—. "The Separateness of Persons and Liberal Theory." *Journal of Value Inquiry* 42 (2008): 147–65.

Index